A Primer in S

**LSE Perspectives in Economic Analysis**

*Series editors*

Timothy Besley and Frank Cowell

The LSE Perspectives in Economic Analysis series provides concise and original insight into a wide range of topics in economics. Each book is accessibly written but scholarly to appeal to advanced students of economics, and academics and professionals wishing to expand their knowledge outside their own particular field.

*Books in the series*

A Primer in Social Choice Theory by Wulf Gaertner

Forthcoming books

Econometric Analysis of Panel Data by Vassilis Hajivassiliou

# A Primer in
# Social Choice Theory

Wulf Gaertner

OXFORD
UNIVERSITY PRESS

# OXFORD

**UNIVERSITY PRESS**

Great Clarendon Street, Oxford OX2 6DP

Oxford University Press is a department of the University of Oxford.
It furthers the University's objective of excellence in research, scholarship,
and education by publishing worldwide in

Oxford New York

Auckland Cape Town Dar es Salaam Hong Kong Karachi
Kuala Lumpur Madrid Melbourne Mexico City Nairobi
New Delhi Shanghai Taipei Toronto

With offices in

Argentina Austria Brazil Chile Czech Republic France Greece
Guatemala Hungary Italy Japan Poland Portugal
Singapore South Korea Switzerland Thailand Turkey Ukraine Vietnam

Oxford is a registered trade mark of Oxford University Press
in the UK and in certain other countries

Published in the United States
by Oxford University Press Inc., New York

© Wulf Gaertner, 2006

British Library Cataloguing in Publication Data

Data available

Library of Congress Cataloging in Publication Data

Data available

Typeset by Newgen Imaging Systems (P) Ltd., Chennai, India
Printed in Great Britain
on acid-free paper by
Biddles Ltd., King's Lynn, Norfolk     1005 3400 41

ISBN 0–19–929750–9   978–0–19–929750–4
ISBN 0–19–929751–7   978–0–19–929751–1(Pbk.)

10 9 8 7 6 5 4 3 2 1

*To the memory of my parents*
*and*
*to my family*

# ☐ PREFACE AND ACKNOWLEDGEMENTS

This book is meant to be an introductory text into the theory of social choice. It is not a book for readers who have already acquired a basic knowledge of social choice theory and now wish to tackle more specialized issues. There do exist some very fine advanced textbooks on collective choice and related questions. This primer is written for undergraduates and first year graduates. Prerequisites are very small: some knowledge of elementary set theory and some basic knowledge of mappings in $\mathbb{R}^n$. The main aim is to attract readers to an area which revolves around the problem of aggregating individual preferences. These questions are interesting and highly relevant both for small communities and large societies. It would be nice if, while going through the various chapters of this primer, the reader were to develop an interest and curiosity for more. There is so much more which is not covered in this book. As said above, there are very good books that will guide the reader beyond what is being discussed in the present text.

This primer in social choice theory is based on various courses that the author has taught at different places over the years. Long and very fruitful discussions with Nick Baigent, Prasanta Pattanaik, Maurice Salles, Amartya Sen, Kotaro Suzumura, John Weymark, and Yongsheng Xu are gratefully acknowledged. Without the gentle advice and guidance of these and other eminent scholars, this book would never have been written. I am deeply indebted to all of them.

I am very grateful to Constanze Binder at Groningen University who took pains to read most parts of the text. I received a lot of interesting and very helpful comments from her. I also wish to thank two referees for their constructive criticism. I am grateful to Brigitte Arnold who helped me tremendously to turn the various versions of my manuscript into a readable text. I also wish to thank Christian Aumann who did a fine job in producing the figures for this primer. We hope that these graphs will enhance the understanding on the part of the reader.

Tim Besley and Frank Cowell from STICERD at the London School of Economics were kind enough to accept this primer as one of the first books in a new series. Special thanks to them. Last but not least I wish to thank Sarah Caro and her collaborators at Oxford University Press for the production of this book.

# ☐ CONTENTS

# ☐ **ABOUT THE AUTHOR**

Wulf Gaertner is Professor of Economics at the University of Osnabrück, Germany. He is one of the managing editors of the journal *'Social Choice and Welfare'*. In the past, he has been visiting scholar at Harvard University and the London School of Economics. He was recently awarded a Ludwig Lachmann Research Fellowship given by the London School of Economics.

# 1 Introduction

## 1.1. Basic questions

Social choice theory is an analysis of collective decision making. The theory of social choice starts out from the articulated opinions or values of the members of a given community or the citizens of a given society and attempts to derive a collective verdict or statement. Such a situation can be called direct democracy, where public actions are determined directly by the members of society. Another form of democratic government is also possible and, actually, more frequent in modern societies, viz. representative government where public actions lie in the hands of public officials who are elected by citizens. We shall largely abstract from these two forms and say a bit later on in this book, and this sounds, admittedly, somewhat 'technical', that the preferences of the individual members of a given society are 'aggregated' into a social preference that reflects the general opinion or will of this society.

Isn't such a procedure superfluous in an era where the market is the predominant mechanism? Not necessarily. There are quite a few issues on which decision making is done collectively. Think, for example, of defence outlays, investments within health care or in the educational sector. Other examples are the election of candidates for a political party or a committee, or, somewhat more mundanely, the choice of candidates to run a tennis club. Such decisions are an integral part of modern societies. Also, there is the possibility of 'market failure'. The existence of externalities such as air pollution or noise may lead to serious inefficiencies so that policy measures are necessary in order to internalize these (or at least some of these) external effects. Such measures will normally be decided collectively, within a committee or by the members of a government. Very often, these decisions are complicated in the sense that a particular measure favours one group in society but is simultaneously detrimental to another group. Should free trade be promoted even if some branches within domestic industry have a high chance of going out of business? The majority of consumers will most likely favour free trade since prices may fall, thus increasing consumer surplus. But how about those who will lose their job because of massive competition coming from foreign firms that enter the market?

How can such a decision be made in a transparent and rational way? Is there a handy criterion or are there several criteria available? Is there, perhaps, a construct that one might call a social welfare function which says that the welfare of society is a function of the individual welfare levels of all members of this society? If so, one could, perhaps, write, with $W$ being an index for the welfare or well-being of society,

$$W = f(w_1, w_2, \ldots, w_n).$$

We then have to ask what the meaning of the individual $w_i$, $i \in \{1, \ldots, n\}$, is. Does $w_i$ stand for individual $i$'s general well-being or is it individual $i$'s personal utility, a concept that we know from a course in introductory microeconomics? In the latter case, we could write

$$W = g(u_1, u_2, \ldots, u_n).$$

Can one perhaps argue that $w_i$ is a broader concept of individual well-being and $u_i$ is a more narrow notion?

A difficult question that we shall discuss throughout this book is: how do we obtain societal $W$? The answer clearly lies in the properties and the 'functioning' of mappings $f$ and $g$. These mappings can, in principle, have 'all kinds' of properties. Of the ones one might think of, one is rather uncontroversial, at least in many cases. Given that mappings $f$ and $g$ are differentiable, we can require that

$$\frac{\partial f}{\partial w_i} > 0 \quad \text{for all } i \in \{1, \ldots, n\};$$

$$\frac{\partial g}{\partial u_i} > 0 \quad \text{for all } i \in \{1, \ldots, n\}.$$

To demand that the first derivative of functions $f$ and $g$ be strictly positive means that welfare is to increase whenever the well-being or personal utility of any individual $i$ goes up. Such a property has been called a Paretian property. Most economists find it highly desirable, at least in a world without externalities. This Paretian property obviously does not lead us very far in cases where a particular policy improves the situation of person $i$, let's say, in terms of either $w_i$ or $u_i$ but makes worse the situation of at least one other person $j$. The reader will recall our free trade example given above. This problem would be relatively easy to solve if we could write our mappings $f$ and $g$ as

$$W = w_1 + w_2 + \cdots + w_n \quad \text{and}$$

$$W = u_1 + u_2 + \cdots + u_n, \quad \text{respectively.}$$

However, both specifications presuppose that the individual values $w_i$ and $u_i$ are cardinally measurable (like temperature) and comparable across persons.

This is more easily said than done. Economic history has witnessed a long and intense debate on this question. Is there some common utility scale for all individuals? Those who have been following this debate (or have actively participated in this controversy) will certainly remember the fierce and fiery discussions on this issue. There are various answers to this question, and we shall certainly come back to them in the course of this book.

There are many other issues which we want to discuss and share with the reader of this primer:

- Should social choices be based on binary or pairwise decision procedures – the well-known simple majority rule is a typical candidate in this class – or rather on non-binary mechanisms such as positional ranking procedures? The Borda rule is the best-known example in this category.

- Is it possible to generate social decisions via aggregating the preferences of many and still grant some autonomy to the individual persons? In other words, can the latter be sure to determine or shape certain aspects within their private sphere without fearing the dictum of a majority of others in the society?

- Can we safely assume that people always truthfully report their preferences? What can be done if they don't?

- Is it possible to introduce distributional aspects into the procedure of aggregating individual preferences? Can one express the fact that some persons in society are worse off than others and then attach special emphasis to the situation of the worst-off?

- Are there situations where vote counting is not an adequate way to reach social decisions and what would these situations be like?

- Is there any hope that some empirically oriented analysis can be done in social choice theory? If so, how could this be achieved?

We hope that the reader's curiosity has been aroused by at least some of the questions posed above.

## 1.2. **Catching a glimpse of the past**

For McLean and London (1990), the roots of the theory of social choice can be traced back to the end of the thirteenth century when Ramon Lull who was a native of Palma de Mallorca designed two voting procedures that have a striking resemblance to what, 500 years later, has become known as the Borda method and the Condorcet principle. However, McLean and London also refer to the *Letters of Pliny the Younger* (around AD 90) who described secret ballots in the Roman senate. In Chapter 5, we shall return to Pliny since in one of his letters (see, e.g. the text in Farquharson (1969), pp. 57–60), he discussed a case of manipulation of preferences in a voting situation. Coming back to Ramon Lull, in his novel *Blanquerna* (around 1283) the author proposed a method consisting of exhaustive pairwise comparisons; each candidate is compared to every other candidate under consideration. Lull advocated the choice of the candidate who receives the highest number of votes in the aggregate of the pairwise comparisons. This procedure is identical to a method suggested by Borda in 1770 which, as was demonstrated by Borda (1781) himself, must generate the same result as his well-known rank-order method that we shall discuss in Chapter 6.

Lull devised a second procedure in 1299. He published it in his treatise *De Arte Eleccionis*. A successive voting rule is proposed that ends up with a so-called Condorcet winner, if there exists one. However, this method does not necessarily detect possible cycles, since not every logically possible pairwise comparison is made in determining the winner.

There is evidence that Nicolaus Cusanus (1434) had studied *De Arte Eleccionis* so that he knew about Lull's Condorcet procedure of pairwise comparisons. However, Cusanus rejected it and proposed a Borda rank-order method with secret voting instead; secret voting because otherwise, there would be too many opportunities and incentives for strategic voting. McLean and London indicate that Cusanus rejected Lull's Condorcet method 'on principle and not out of misunderstanding' (1990, p. 106).

In 1672 Pufendorf published his magnum opus *De Jure Naturae et Gentium* (The Law of Nature and of Nations) where he discussed, among other things, weighted voting, qualified majorities and, very surprisingly, a preference structure that in the middle of the twentieth century has become known as single-peaked preferences (see Lagerspetz (1986) and Gaertner (2005)). The reader will learn more about this preference structure in Chapters 3 and 5. Pufendorf was also very much aware of manipulative voting strategies. He mentioned an instance of manipulation of agendas, reported by the Greek historian Polybios, which was similar to the one discussed by Pliny, but considerably earlier in time.

Much better known than the writings of Lull, Cusanus and Pufendorf is the scientific work by de Borda (1781) and the Marquis de Condorcet (1785). Condorcet strongly advocated a binary notion, i.e. pairwise comparisons of candidates, whereas Borda focused on a positional approach where the positions of candidates in the individual preference orderings matter. Condorcet extensively discussed the election of candidates under the majority rule, and he was probably the first to demonstrate the existence of cyclical majorities for particular profiles of individual preferences. We shall spend considerable time on this and related problems in Chapters 3 and 6.

Almost 100 years later, Dodgson (1876), better known as Lewis Carroll from his *Alice in Wonderland*, explicitly dealt with cyclical majorities. Dodgson proposed a rule, based on pairwise comparisons, which avoids such cycles. It will be described in Chapter 6. According to McLean and London, Dodgson, a mathematician at Christ Church College, Oxford, worked in ignorance of his predecessors.

We now take a big leap and briefly mention a construct proposed by Scitovsky (1942), viz. the community or social indifference curves which have their basis in the much-used Edgeworth-box situation of mutual exchange. Starting from a set of smooth and strictly convex indifference curves for each individual in society, a set of smooth and strictly convex social indifference curves was derived. Two alternative commodity bundles belong to the same community indifference curve if and only if every individual in society is indifferent between the two bundles for some a priori distribution of commodities over the individuals. Scitovsky's method of construction which was highly original is based on the requirement that the marginal rates of substitution between any two commodities be equalized among all individuals. The derivation of social indifference curves becomes much more difficult in cases where the individual indifference curves no longer have a 'nice' curvature. On the other hand, if the elementary textbook indifference curves are given for the individual agents, a set of smooth social indifference curves is obtained for each a priori distribution of commodities among the members of society (for more details, see e.g. Mishan (1960) and Ng (1979)).

Finally, we wish to describe Bergson's (1938) concept of a social welfare function, a real-valued mapping $W$, the value of which depends on all the elements that affect the welfare of a community during any given period of time, e.g. the amounts of the various commodities consumed, the amounts of the different kinds of work done, the amounts of non-labour factors in each of the production units, etc. Such a social welfare function $W$ may naturally subsume the Paretian condition to which we referred earlier, but not necessarily. Bergson speaks of specific decisions on ends which have to be taken in order to specify the properties of the function (1938 (1966), pp. 8–26, and 1948 (1966), pp. 213–216). So if value propositions are introduced that require that in a maximum position it should be impossible to improve the situation of any one individual without rendering another person worse off, the Pareto principle is one of the guiding judgments. Suzumura (1999, p. 205) states that a social welfare function à la Bergson 'is rooted in the belief that the analysis of the logical consequences of any value judgements, irrespective of whose ethical beliefs they represent, whether or not they are widely shared in the society, or how they are generated in the first place, is a legitimate task of welfare economics'. Suzumura goes on to say that 'the social welfare function is nothing other than the formal way of characterizing such an ethical belief which is *rational* in the sense of being complete as well as transitive over the alternative states of affairs' (p. 205). A Paretian welfare function in the sense of Bergson establishes an ordering over social states while the Pareto condition alone only provides a quasi-ordering. The latter implies that this principle cannot distinguish among Pareto optimal alternatives.

## 1.3. **Basic formalism**

It is high time to introduce some notation and various definitions as well as structural concepts that will be used at various stages of this book.

Let $X = \{x, y, z, \ldots\}$ denote the set of all conceivable social states and let $N = \{1, \ldots, n\}$ denote a finite set of individuals or voters ($n \geq 2$). Let $R$ stand for a binary relation on $X$; $R$ is a subset of ordered pairs in the product $X \times X$. We interpret $R$ as a preference relation on $X$. Without any index, $R$ refers to the social preference relation. When we speak of individual $i$'s preference relation we simply write $R_i$. The fact that a pair $(x, y)$ is an element of $R$ will be denoted $xRy$; the negation of this fact will be denoted by $\neg xRy$. $R$ is reflexive if for all $x \in X : xRx$. $R$ is complete if for all $x, y \in X, x \neq y : xRy$ or $yRx$. Note that 'or' is the inclusive 'or'. $R$ is said to be transitive if for all $x, y, z \in X :$ $(xRy \wedge yRz) \rightarrow xRz$. The strict preference relation (the asymmetric part of $R$) will be denoted by $P : xPy \leftrightarrow [xRy \wedge \neg yRx]$. The indifference relation (the symmetric part of $R$) will be denoted by $I : xIy \leftrightarrow [xRy \wedge yRx]$. We shall call $R$ a preference ordering (or an ordering or a complete preordering) on $X$ if $R$ is reflexive, complete and transitive. In this case, one obviously obtains for all $x, y \in X : xPy \leftrightarrow \neg yRx$ (reflexivity and completeness of $R$ are sufficient for this result to hold), $P$ is transitive and $I$ is an equivalence relation; furthermore for all $x, y, z \in X : (xPy \wedge yRz) \rightarrow xPz$. $R$ is said to be quasi-transitive if $P$ is transitive. $R$ is said to be acyclical if for all finite sequences $\{x_1, \ldots, x_k\}$ from $X$ it is not the case that $x_1 P x_2 \wedge x_2 P x_3 \wedge \ldots \wedge x_{k-1} P x_k$ and $x_k P x_1$. The following implications clearly hold: $R$ transitive $\rightarrow$ $R$ quasi-transitive $\rightarrow$ $R$ acyclical.

In the context of social choice theory, the following interpretations can be attached to the relations $R$, $P$ and $I$. $xRy$ means that '$x$ is at least as good as $y$'; $xPy$ means that '$x$ is strictly better than $y$', and $xIy$ means that there is an indifference between $x$ and $y$. We use the term 'weak ordering' when the binary relation $R$ stands for 'at least as good as'. In a strict or strong ordering, the binary relation is interpreted as 'strictly better than'.

We now introduce the notions of a maximal element of a set $S \subseteq X$, let's say, and of a best element of set $S$.

**Definition 1.1 (Maximal set).**  An element $x \in S$ is a maximal element of $S$ with respect to a binary relation $R$ if and only if there does not exist an element $y$ such that $y \in S$ and $yPx$. The maximal elements of a set $S$ with respect to a binary relation $R$ obviously are those elements which are not dominated via the strict relation $P$ by any other elements in $S$. The set of maximal elements in $S$ will be called its maximal set, denoted by $M(S, R)$.

**Definition 1.2 (Choice set).**   An element $x \in S$ is a best element of $S$ with respect to a binary relation $R$ if and only if for all $y \in S$, $xRy$ holds. Best elements of a set $S$ have the property that they are at least as good as every other element of $S$ with respect to the given relation $R$. The set of best elements in $S$ will be called its choice set, denoted by $C(S, R)$.

Note that a best element is always a maximal element. Why? Because if some element $x \in S$ is a best element of $S$, there does not exist any other element of $S$ that is strictly preferred to $x$. The opposite direction does not hold. Consider a set $S = \{x, y\}$ and neither $xRy$ nor $yRx$ holds (this is a case where the property of completeness is not satisfied). Then both $x$ and $y$ are maximal elements of the set $\{x, y\}$, but neither of them is a best element. Thus, for finite sets $S$, $C(S, R) \subset M(S, R)$.

In order to clarify the difference between choice sets and maximal sets, it may appear useful to introduce non-completeness explicitly. We define $x$ *nc* $y$ if and only if $[\neg xRy \wedge \neg yRx]$. We just discussed a situation where this relationship would apply. Non-completeness is also a characteristic of the Pareto relation to which we already referred briefly at the end of section 1.2.

Note also that it is possible that both $C(S, R)$ and $M(S, R)$ are empty sets. Consider the situation that $xPy$, $yPz$ and $zPx$. In this case, which will re-occur at various instances in this primer, there is neither a best element nor any element that is not dominated by some other element via the relation $P$. If $S$ is finite and $R$ is an ordering, it is always the case that $C(S, R) = M(S, R) \neq \emptyset$.

We now come to an important concept, the choice function.

**Definition 1.3 (Choice function).**   Let $X$ be a finite set of feasible alternatives and let $K$ be the set of all non-empty subsets of $X$. A choice function $C : K \rightarrow K$ assigns a non-empty subset $C(S)$ of $S$ to every $S \in K$.

To state that a choice function $C(S)$ exists for every $S \in K$ is tantamount to saying that there exists a best element for every non-empty subset of $X$. Sen (1970b, p. 14) emphasizes that 'the existence of a choice function is ... important for rational choice'. This will become clearer in a few moments.

First, we wish to state an important result by Sen (1970b) concerning the existence of a choice function (see also an earlier result by von Neumann and Morgenstern (1944, chapter XII)). We follow Sen's proof.

**Theorem 1.1.**   If $R$ is reflexive and complete, a necessary and sufficient condition for a choice function to be defined over a finite set $X$ of alternatives is that $R$ be acyclical over $X$.

*Proof. Necessity.* Suppose $R$ is not acyclical. Then there exists some subset of $k$ alternatives in $X$ such that $x_1 P x_2, \ldots, x_{k-1} P x_k, x_k P x_1$. Clearly, there is no best element in this subset of $k$ alternatives so that there does not exist a choice function over $X$ according to the definition above.

*Sufficiency.* We consider two cases. (a) All alternatives are indifferent to each other. Then they are all best elements, acyclicity is trivially satisfied and the choice set is non-empty for every $S \in K$. (b) If case (a) does not hold, there are two alternatives in $S$, say $x_1$ and $x_2$, such that $x_2 P x_1$. Then $x_2$ can fail to be a best element of $S$ only if there is some $x_3$ such that $x_3 P x_2$. If now $x_1 P x_3$, then, since $x_2 P x_1$, the property of acyclicity would be contradicted. Thus $x_3 R x_1$, and $x_3$ is a best element of $\{x_1, x_2, x_3\}$. If we continue this way, we can exhaust all elements of $S$, which is finite due to the assumption in the theorem, such that the choice set is always non-empty.

Given this result, we shall henceforth write $C(S, R)$ for a choice function generated by a binary relation $R$. Sen notes (1970b, p. 16) that acyclicity over triples only is not a sufficient condition for the existence of a choice function, for acyclicity over triples does not imply acyclicity over the whole set. Consider, for example, $S = \{x_1, x_2, x_3, x_4\}$ with $x_1 P x_2, x_2 P x_3, x_3 P x_4, x_4 P x_1, x_1 I x_3$ and $x_2 I x_4$. Acyclicity over triples means that for all $a, b, c \in \{x_1, x_2, x_3, x_4\}$, it is not the case that $aPb \wedge bPc \wedge cPa$. It is easily checked that acyclicity over triples holds. But acyclicity does not hold over the whole set $S$ so that there does not exist a best element for the whole set.

Later on in Chapter 4, we will encounter the notion of a social decision function. This is a social aggregation rule, the range of which is restricted to those preference relations $R$ each of which generates a choice function $C(S, R)$ over the whole set of alternatives $X$ (Sen, 1970b, p. 52). Note that in this book, we shall use the terms 'social aggregation rule' and 'collective choice rule' in a non-specific sense, whereas, for example, 'social decision function' and 'Arrovian social welfare function', two central concepts in this primer, have very specific meanings.

Next, we want to talk about consistency and rational choice. We consider a binary relation $R_c$ that can be obtained from any choice function $C(\cdot)$ such that for all $x, y \in X$ :

$$ x R_c y \quad \text{iff} \quad x \in C(\{x, y\}). \tag{*} $$

We now define the choice function generated by the binary relation $R_c$ for any non-empty set $S \subseteq X$ as

$$ \hat{C}(S, R_c) = \{x : x \in S \text{ and for all } y \in S : x R_c y\}. \tag{**} $$

We have learned above that given reflexivity and completeness, acyclicity of $R_c$ is necessary and sufficient for $\hat{C}(S, R_c)$ to be defined. Binary relation $R_c$ generates the set of best elements of any $S \subseteq X$. $R_c$ has sometimes been called the base relation of the choice function. It is by now standard terminology (see, e.g. Sen (1977a)) to say that a choice function is 'normal' or 'rationalizable' if and only if the binary relation $R_c$ generated by a choice function $C(\cdot)$ via $(*)$ regenerates that choice function through $(**)$, i.e. $C(S) = \hat{C}(S, R_c)$, for all $S \in K$.

We finally consider two consistency conditions of choice, viz. properties $\alpha$ and $\beta$.

Property $\alpha$ is a consistency condition for set contraction.

**Property $\alpha$ (Contraction consistency).** For all $x \in S \subseteq T$, if $x \in C(T)$, then $x \in C(S)$.

Property $\beta$ is a consistency condition for set expansion.

**Property $\beta$ (Expansion consistency).** For all $x, y$, if $x, y \in C(S)$ and $S \subseteq T$, then $x \in C(T)$ if and only if $y \in C(T)$.

Two examples from sports may illustrate the two conditions. Let $S$ be the group of girls in a class $T$ consisting of boys and girls. If Sabine is the fastest runner over 100 m in the whole class, then Sabine is also the fastest among the subgroup of girls in this class. This is the content of property $\alpha$. In terms of choices, we would say that if $x$ is one of the best elements in set $T$, then $x$ is also a best element in subset $S$, as long as $x$ is contained in $S$.

If Sabine and Katinka are the fastest girls in the 100 m dash, then Sabine and Katinka are among the fastest runners in the whole class, or neither of the two girls is among the fastest. This is the content of property $\beta$. In terms of choices, if $x$ and $y$ are considered to be best in subset $S$, then either both of them are best in superset $T$ or neither of them is best in $T$.

It turns out (see, e.g. Sen (1977a)) that a choice function $C(\cdot)$ is rationalizable by a weak ordering if and only if it satisfies properties $\alpha$ and $\beta$. This implies that the binary relation $R_c$ generated by $C(\cdot)$ and generating $\hat{C}(S, R_c)$ is complete and transitive on all $S \in K$ (see also Arrow (1959)).

## 1.4. Aggregation of preferences – how can this be done?

The purpose of this section is to show how social choices can be made in a very simple situation. Let us consider the division of a cake among three persons who all prefer more cake to less cake and only consider their own share. Therefore, altruism and malice are absent. Cake is the only commodity present in this example. We assume furthermore (this renders our example even simpler) that there are only four possibilities to divide the cake, viz.

$$x = \left(\tfrac{1}{2}, \tfrac{1}{2}, 0\right); \quad y = \left(\tfrac{1}{2}, 0, \tfrac{1}{2}\right); \quad z = \left(0, \tfrac{1}{2}, \tfrac{1}{2}\right); \quad w = \left(\tfrac{1}{3}, \tfrac{1}{3}, \tfrac{1}{3}\right).$$

We want to repeat that the three individuals only care about their own shares of the cake. Therefore, the following weak orderings appear rather plausible:

| 1 | 2 | 3 |
|---|---|---|
| $x, y$ | $x, z$ | $y, z$ |
| $w$ | $w$ | $w$ |
| $z$ | $y$ | $x$ |

These preferences have to be read from top to bottom. Alternatives which are arranged on the same level (or line) are considered to be equivalent for the individual concerned. We now wish to ask how social choice would (could) look like in this community of three persons. We know from our earlier discussion that in order to answer this question, we have to introduce collective decision mechanisms. Actually, in what follows we shall introduce various collective choice rules. All of them will be defined more precisely in the course of this book.

(a) Simple majority rule

The rule will be defined formally in chapter 3. We assume that the reader is familiar with this method of simply counting votes 'for' and 'against' even without seeing a proper definition at this point. On the basis of simple majority voting, alternative $w$ will be eliminated, while alternatives $x$, $y$ and $z$ prove to be socially equivalent. A random mechanism could then be used to determine the final choice among the three options. Using majority rule in this case by no means implies that we think that this rule is the 'right' mechanism in the given situation. Notice that two of the three persons can collude to take more and more cake away from the third. But this is not our point here. We just discuss possible aggregation rules in the given situation.

(b) Borda rank-order rule

The Borda rule briefly mentioned above and described in detail in Chapter 6, attaches ranks to all alternatives. In the given case with two elements on the same line, the best alternatives get a rank of 2.5 each, $w$ achieves a weight of 1, and the worst alternative gets in all three rankings a weight of zero. So according to Borda's method, the final choice again has to be made among $x$, $y$ and $z$.

(c) A utilitarian approach

The argument in this and the two following cases is based on the assumption that there is a simple linear utility function in terms of quantities of cake. In other words, $u\left(\frac{1}{2}\text{cake}\right) = \frac{1}{2}$, $u\left(\frac{1}{3}\text{cake}\right) = \frac{1}{3}$, $u\,(\text{no cake}) = 0$, and this applies to all individuals equally. We now use one of Harsanyi's models of 1955 (see Chapter 7) and make the following suppositions: there is a so-called ethical observer who determines that distribution of cake which is maximal for society in terms of aggregate utilities. In this procedure, it is assumed that each individual will have an equal probability of 1/3 to occupy each of the three positions. Let $Eu(x)$, $Eu(y)$, ... be the expected utilities with respect to alternatives $x, y, ...$ We then obtain

$$Eu(x) = 1/3 \cdot 1/2 + 1/3 \cdot 1/2 + 1/3 \cdot 0 = 1/3$$

$$Eu(y) = 1/3 \cdot 1/2 + 0 + 1/3 \cdot 1/2 = 1/3$$

$$Eu(z) = 0 + 1/3 \cdot 1/2 + 1/3 \cdot 1/2 = 1/3$$

$$Eu(w) = 1/3 \cdot 1/3 + 1/3 \cdot 1/3 + 1/3 \cdot 1/3 = 1/3$$

According to this procedure, all four alternatives are socially equivalent.

(d) Maximizing the situation of the worst-off

According to this maxim and given the assumptions on the common utility function from above, that alternative has to be picked which guarantees the highest possible utility level to the person who is worst off. In order to see which person is worst-off under each of the four alternatives, consider the following matrix representation:

|   | 1 | 2 | 3 |
|---|---|---|---|
| x | 1/2 | 1/2 | 0 |
| y | 1/2 | 0 | 1/2 |
| z | 0 | 1/2 | 1/2 |
| w | 1/3 | 1/3 | 1/3 |

Clearly, under alternative $w$ alone, the utility level of the worst-off person is highest (for more details, see Chapter 7).

(e) Maximizing the product of utilities

We now consider an approach which is somewhat different from the preceding schemes. It will be discussed at greater length in Chapter 8. Let us presuppose that the utility level of the three cake-eaters was zero before dividing up the cake. We now look for the maximal product of utility increases for the three persons, calculated from status quo zero. We obtain

$$N(x) = 1/2 \cdot 1/2 \cdot 0 = 0$$
$$N(y) = 1/2 \cdot 0 \cdot 1/2 = 0$$
$$N(z) = 0 \cdot 1/2 \cdot 1/2 = 0$$
$$N(w) = 1/3 \cdot 1/3 \cdot 1/3 = 1/27$$

According to this approach, there is a unique winner, viz. alternative $w$.

We could go on discussing other resolution schemes but we abstain from this, hoping that the examples above were sufficient to provide a first insight into the functioning of various forms of collective choice.

## 1.5. **The informational aspect**

The uninitiated reader (and most readers of a primer probably belong to this group) will wonder what we are now heading for. We wish to cover briefly the following aspects: (1) informational constraints that exclude information on 'other' alternatives; (2) the 'welfaristic' view; (3) informational constraints with respect to usable utility information.

(1) When a society decides collectively whether to implement tax policy $a$, let's say, or alternatively policy $b$, or $c$ or $d$, should a decision between $a$ and $b$, for example, depend on information concerning $c$ and/or $d$? Information of the latter kind will primarily be information on preferences. How does $a$ fare preference-wise with respect to $c$, with respect to $d$? How does $b$ fare in relation to $c$ and/or $d$? Would this be relevant information in a social decision between $a$ and $b$? There is no clear-cut and simple answer to this. The rule of simple majority decision does *not* take account of information relating to other alternatives when there is a social choice between, say, $a$ and $b$. The Borda rule (remember that we have applied both mechanisms in our previous example) uses such information quite extensively. The Borda rule considers ranks or positions of alternatives. The term 'position' becomes vacuous when the 'embedding' of an alternative in its environment (namely, the other feasible alternatives) is no longer taken into consideration. Positionalist rules take note of the fact that an alternative $x$, let's say, is 'close' to another alternative $y$ or 'far away' from $y$ with other options in between. In his justly celebrated work on social choice, Arrow, in the second edition of 1963, gave several reasons why ignoring information on other, i.e. 'irrelevant' alternatives

makes good sense. One is that '... social decision processes which are independent of irrelevant alternatives have a strong practical advantage. After all, every known electoral system satisfies this condition' (1951, 1963, p. 110). Bergson (1976) does not at all agree when, in connection with the independence condition, he speaks 'of the implied waste of ethically relevant information' (p. 184). The issue of irrelevant alternatives will occupy us quite a bit in the chapters to come.

(2) We shall see in the following chapter that a condition which cuts off information on irrelevant alternatives will yield, when combined with two other requirements, a situation where all non-utility information on alternatives is ignored. This consequence has been widely discussed under the heading of 'welfarism'. What kinds of information could be labelled non-utility information? These could stem from rights or entitlements (Nozick, 1974), historical information on past savings and inheritance, or other kinds of claims. A mentally retarded or physically handicapped person has (or at least should have) certain claims to the community she is living in. A denial of such claims is not necessarily manifested in lower utility values, particularly not in the case of a mentally retarded person. Being poor is not necessarily reflected in lower utility values either. Self-taught simple needs may blur the picture. With respect to individual rights, Sen (1987) writes that 'if it is asserted that a person should be free to do what he or she likes in certain purely personal matters, that assertion is based on the non-utility characteristics of the "personal nature" of these choices, and not primarily on utility considerations'. More shall be said in the chapters which follow.

(3) The reader will remember from his or her class in microeconomics that within the purely ordinal approach, any given utility function is, informationally speaking, as good as any other utility function which is a strictly increasing transform of the first one. The only thing which matters in terms of available information is whether, say, commodity bundle $a$ is preferred to or indifferent to or dispreferred to commodity bundle $b$ or, expressed in terms of utility indices, whether $a$ has a higher or equally high or lower utility index than $b$. Such an approach does not permit us to speak of *utility differences* between two commodity bundles $a$ and $b$ nor about absolute *levels of utility*. Since, as we just stated, any utility function can be changed (by a strictly monotone transformation) into another one which gives exactly the same amount of information as the original one, this implies that the class of informationally equivalent transformations is very large.

The class of informationally equivalent transformations becomes smaller in the case of cardinal utility values where only positive affine transformations, a strict subset of the class of strictly increasing transformations, is admissible. In this 'world', it is meaningful to consider utility differences, for example between bundle $a$ and bundle $b$. Furthermore, it makes sense to compare the utility difference between $a$ and $b$ to the difference between bundles $c$ and $d$. A nice analogy is the concept of temperature where it is reasonable to consider the temperature in New York and London, let's say, on a particular day in July and compare the difference in temperature between these two cities with the difference in temperature between Los Angeles and Rome. This can be done either in Celsius or Fahrenheit (or on the basis of some other scale). And if it turns out that the temperature in New York is higher than in London, the temperature in L.A. a little higher than in Rome so that the difference in temperature between New York and London is higher than the difference between L.A. and Rome, then this latter assertion holds independently of whether we measure temperature in Celsius or Fahrenheit (the absolute numbers of these temperature differences will, of course, be different). To go from Celsius to Fahrenheit (or vice versa) is nothing else but applying a positive affine transformation to the Celsius values (or another positive affine transformation to the Fahrenheit values). A positive affine transformation changes the origin and the scale unit.

What has all this to do with social choice theory? It is perfectly legitimate to pose this question. One way to distinguish between different approaches in the theory of collective choice is to consider the informational requirements within each set-up. Assumptions of measurability then specify which types of transformations may be applied to an individual's utility function without altering the individually usable information. In other words, different informational set-ups will be linked to different solution concepts. In Chapter 2, we will discuss at length Arrow's famous impossibility result. This result is established in a purely ordinal framework, i.e. utility differences cannot be formed and compared to each other and, what would have been a further step towards using more information, there is no comparability of utility values across persons. Several scholars have argued that a major reason for Arrow's negative result is the informational parsimony in his approach. In the third proof of Arrow's theorem in section 2.4, this 'fact' will be amply used to establish the result (while the first two proofs of his theorem show very clearly the strength and consequences of cutting off information that could come from irrelevant alternatives).

Utilitarianism considers gains and losses across individuals so that, since utility differences in this set-up can be formed and, in a further step, be compared interpersonally, summation becomes possible. The Rawlsian approach is ordinal but allows for a comparison of utility levels across persons. The bargaining solutions are conceived within the cardinal framework, but two of the best-known solution concepts avoid any trace of utility comparisons across persons.

After all this argumentation, we hope to have convinced the reader that the informational aspect proves to be a rather powerful tool to distinguish among major approaches in social choice theory. This information can be in terms of positional information about the various alternatives available for choice; it can come in terms of rich or parsimonious utility information both with respect to alternatives and across persons.

## 1.6. **A path through haze or how to read this book**

Let us briefly describe the contents of this primer. Chapter 2 discusses Arrow's famous impossibility theorem. We shall present three different proofs of this result. Each proof highlights a different aspect, viz. the contagion property of individual decisiveness, the role of the independence condition and, finally, the informational aspect within the Arrovian set-up. Chapter 3 examines various domain restrictions of individual preferences. The purpose of this exercise is to see what can be done under the method of majority decision to avoid 'irrational' social choice such as preference cycles. The most prominent restriction examined is the condition of single-peaked preferences. Chapter 4 discusses the exercise of individual rights. The starting point is Sen's very influential result of the 'impossibility of a Paretian liberal'. We ask under which conditions the consistent exercise of personal rights becomes possible. We also propose a game-form formulation of rights and contrast it with Sen's original social choice set-up.

Chapter 5 discusses another famous impossibility result, the Gibbard–Satterthwaite theorem on strategy-proof decision rules. We also present Moulin's generalized median voter scheme. Again the property of single-peaked preferences proves to be very successful in getting out of impossibilities. Chapter 6 looks at social choice rules that were designed to avoid various problems that simple majority voting has, particularly the occurrence of empty choice sets due to cycles of social preference. A prominent example is the Borda rank-order method. We shall also present an example from recent Parliamentary history which shows that different choice rules may engender quite different outcomes.

Alternative theories of distributive justice are the topic of Chapter 7. The two main 'contestants', viz. utilitarianism and the Rawlsian maximin/leximin principle, are contrasted with each other. In order to do this, the informational basis of utility information has to be widened. Interpersonal comparability of different kinds has to be rendered possible.

Chapter 8 discusses alternative approaches to bargaining. The underlying idea is that starting from a particular status quo point, people cooperate in order to achieve mutual benefits. The reader will see that there are quite a few substantial differences to the standard social-choice theoretical set-up. But there are also similarities, particularly in relation to the Nash bargaining solution. The latter can be interpreted as the societal outcome of an effort to maximize the product of the net utility gains of all participants. Chapter 9 explores two different but somewhat related ways to find out how people (students) evaluate particular situations that are shaped by aspects of needs or efficiency or simply are a matter of taste. 'Empirical social choice' is a fairly recent phenomenon, at least when compared with the vast body of literature in the field of experimental game theory which was started roughly 40 years ago. The final Chapter 10, admittedly, goes a little beyond what one would expect a primer to cover. Among other topics, we shall briefly describe aggregation rules in continuous space.

Having said all this, how should the reader proceed? Arrow's theorem in Chapter 2 is the starting point for everything else. It would, of course, be very nice if the reader read all chapters consecutively. However, should the reader be particularly interested in the informational aspects within social choice theory, he or she might like to go directly to Chapters 7 and 8, after having studied the various proofs of Arrow's theorem in Chapter 2. Those readers who are primarily interested in impossibility theorems, and these are ubiquitous in social choice theory, might like to proceed from Chapter 2 to Chapters 4 and 5. Those who are interested in ways to avoid cyclic social choice might like to read Chapters 2, 3 and 6, and then have a look at the rest of the book.

Once a few moments have been spent with the formal concepts in section 1.3, these different paths through the book should all be possible without greater difficulties. At the end of each of the chapters, there are a few recommendations for reading. References to more detailed descriptions of various issues discussed in this primer can be found throughout the text. Figure 1.1 graphically depicts the different paths we have just been talking about. These could also be alternative paths a lecturer might want to consider.

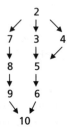

**Figure 1.1.**

# 2 Arrow's impossibility result

## 2.1. **The axiom system and the theorem**

When Arrow showed the general impossibility of the existence of a social welfare function in 1951, quite a few welfare economists were confused. Hadn't Bergson, in his seminal paper of 1938, developed the notion of a social welfare function and hadn't Samuelson (1947) successfully employed this concept in various welfare–economic analyses? What went wrong? Was Arrow right and were Bergson and Samuelson wrong or was it just the other way round?

First of all, Arrow's notion of a social welfare function is different from the Bergson–Samuelson concept in so far as Arrow considered an aggregation mechanism that specifies social orderings for any logically possible set of individual preferences (the multiple profile approach). Bergson claimed that for a given set of individual preferences there always exists the real-valued representation of an ordering for the society (single or fixed profile approach). Furthermore while Bergson emphasized that any set of value propositions may be introduced when the welfare of a community is being analysed (see section 1.2 above), Arrow was very specific on what basic properties a process should fulfil that maps any set of individual orderings into a social preference.

Let us consider a few examples. Imagine that there is a society with $n$ members one of whom is constantly expressing opinions that all the other members of this society view as unacceptable or at least very strange. Therefore, the aggregation scheme could be such that whenever this particular person prefers $a$ to $b$, society should prefer $b$ to $a$. Let us assume now that with respect to two particular alternatives $c$ and $d$, there happens to be complete unanimity, i.e. everybody strictly prefers $c$ to $d$. Should society now prefer $d$ to $c$? This outcome would violate one of the basic properties in the sense used above, viz. the weak Pareto principle to be defined below.

Another aggregation rule could declare that whenever a particular option $z$ is among those alternatives about which the members of the society should make up their mind, alternative $z$ should always be preferred to each of the other options. If one requires that this rule be applied to any given set of individual preferences, a clash with the Pareto principle will again occur.

Finally, a third example. Imagine that in a decision between two social alternatives $x$ and $y$, not only the individuals' preferences between these two alternatives but also the individuals' preferences between $x$ and some other options $z$ and $w$ and also the individuals' preferences between $y$ and the options $z$ and $w$ should be taken into consideration. Actually, there is a class of aggregation rules which does exactly this. Then again, one of Arrow's basic properties would be violated as we shall see in a moment.

We now wish to state and discuss Arrow's general result in greater detail. In order to do this, we will use the notation and definitions introduced in section 1.3.

Let $\mathcal{E}$ denote the set of preference orderings on $X$ and let $\mathcal{E}'$ stand for a subset of orderings that satisfies a particular restriction. $\mathcal{E}'^n$ will denote the cartesian product $\mathcal{E}' \times \cdots \times \mathcal{E}'$, $n$-times. An element of $\mathcal{E}'^n$ is an $n$-tuple of preference orderings $(R_1, \ldots, R_n)$ or the profile of an $n$-member society consisting of preference orderings.

A social welfare function in the sense of Arrow is a mapping from $\mathcal{E}'^n$ to $\mathcal{E}$. Arrow's fundamental result says that there does not exist a social welfare function if this mapping which we denote by $f(R_1, \ldots, R_n)$ is to satisfy the following four conditions:

**Condition $U$ (Unrestricted domain).** The domain of the mapping $f$ includes all logically possible $n$-tuples of individual orderings on $X (\mathcal{E}' = \mathcal{E})$.

**Condition $P$ (Weak Pareto principle).** For any $x, y$ in $X$, if everyone in society strictly prefers $x$ to $y$, then $xPy$.

**Condition $I$ (Independence of irrelevant alternatives).** If for two profiles of individual orderings $(R_1, \ldots, R_n)$ and $(R'_1, \ldots, R'_n)$, every individual in society has exactly the same preference with respect to any two alternatives $x$ and $y$, then the social preference with respect to $x$ and $y$ must be the same for the two profiles. In other words, if for any pair $x, y$ and for all $i$, $xR_iy$ iff $xR'_iy$, and $yR_ix$ iff $yR'_ix$, then $f(R_1, \ldots, R_n)$ and $f(R'_1, \ldots, R'_n)$ must order $x$ and $y$ in exactly the same way.

**Condition $D$ (Non-dictatorship).** There is no individual $i$ in society such that for all profiles in the domain of $f$ and for all pairs of alternatives $x$ and $y$ in $X$, if $xP_iy$, then $xPy$.

Condition $U$ requires that no individual preference ordering be excluded a priori. Even the 'most odd' ordering(s) should be taken into consideration. Condition $P$, the weak Pareto rule, prescribes that if all individuals unanimously strictly prefer $x$ to an alternative $y$, the same should hold for society's preference. Condition $I$, perhaps a bit more difficult to understand than the other conditions, demands that the social welfare function be parsimonious in informational requirements. More concretely, if society is to take a decision with respect to some pair of alternatives $(x, y)$, only the individuals' preferences with respect to this pair should be taken into consideration and not more. The individuals' preferences between $x$ and a third alternative $z$ and the preferences between $y$ and $z$ should not count, nor should the individuals' preferences between $z$ and a fourth alternative $w$ play any role in the social decision between $x$ and $y$. Finally, there should be no individual in society such that whenever this person strictly prefers $x$ over $y$, let's say, this preference must become society's preference; and this for all pairs of alternatives from $X$ and for all profiles in the domain of $f$. Such a person who always has his or her way in terms of strict preferences would have dictatorial power in the preference aggregation procedure, and this is to be excluded.

For Arrow, his four conditions on $f$ (or five conditions if the demand that the social preference relation be an ordering is counted as a separate requirement) were necessary requirements in the sense that 'taken together they express the doctrines of citizens' sovereignty and rationality in a very general form, with the citizens being allowed to have a wide range of values' (Arrow, 1951, 1963, p. 31). The aspect of sovereignty shows itself very clearly in conditions $U$, $P$ and $D$.

**Theorem 2.1 (Arrow's general possibility theorem (1951, 1963)).** For a finite number of individuals and at least three distinct social alternatives, there is no social welfare function $f$ satisfying conditions $U$, $P$, $I$ and $D$.

## 2.2. **The original proof**

On the following pages, we shall prove Arrow's result. Actually, we shall provide three different proofs of his theorem. These proofs highlight different aspects within his impossibility result and we hope that the three ways of proving his theorem provide sufficient insight into why, at the end, there is a *general* impossibility. The first proof follows very closely Arrow's own proof from the 1963 edition of his book as well as Sen's proof in chapter 3* of his book from 1970. Both proofs show in a transparent way that decisiveness over some pair of social alternatives spreads to decisiveness over all pairs of alternatives which belong to a finite set of alternatives. This phenomenon has sometimes been called a contagion property. Sen (1995) speaks of 'field-expansion' in this context. We start with two definitions which will prove to be very helpful in the sequel.

**Definition 2.1.** A set of individuals $V$ is almost decisive for some $x$ against some $y$ if, whenever $xP_iy$ for every $i$ in $V$ and $yP_ix$ for every $i$ outside of $V$, $x$ is socially preferred to $y$ ($xPy$).

**Definition 2.2.** A set of individuals $V$ is decisive for some $x$ against some $y$ if, whenever $xP_iy$ for every $i$ in $V$, $xPy$.

We now concentrate on a particular individual $J$ and denote the 'fact' that person $J$ is almost decisive for $x$ against $y$ by $D(x, y)$ and the 'fact' that $J$ is decisive for $x$ against $y$ by $\bar{D}(x, y)$. It is immediately clear that $\bar{D}(x, y)$ implies $D(x, y)$; so the former is stronger than the latter. If $J$ is decisive no matter how the preferences of all the other individuals look, $J$ is decisive a fortiori if all the other individuals' preferences are strictly opposed to $J$'s. Now comes a very important contagion result which contains the hardest part of the proof.

**Lemma 2.1.**   If there is some individual $J$ who is almost decisive for some ordered pair of alternatives $(x, y)$, an Arrovian social welfare function $f$ satisfying conditions $U, P$ and $I$ implies that $J$ must have dictatorial power.

*Proof.*   Let us assume that person $J$ is almost decisive for some $x$ against some alternative $y$, i.e. for some $x, y \in X, D(x, y)$. Let there be a third alternative $z$ and let index $i$ refer to all the other members of the society. According to condition $U$, we are absolutely free to choose any of the logically possible preference profiles for this society. Let us suppose that the following preferences hold:

$$xP_Jy, \quad yP_Jz \quad \text{and}$$
$$yP_ix, \quad yP_iz.$$

The reader should notice that for all persons other than $J$ the preference relation between $x$ and $z$ remains unspecified. Since $D(x, y)$, we obtain $xPy$. Then, because $yP_Jz$ and $yP_iz$ for all other persons, the weak Pareto principle yields $yPz$. But since $f$ *per definitionem* is to generate orderings, we obtain, by transitivity from $xPy$ and $yPz$, $xPz$.

The reader will realize that we started off by using condition $U$. In the next step, we applied condition $P$. Then, our argumentation used the ordering property of the social preference relation. What about the independence condition? We arrived at $xPz$ without any information about the preferences of individuals other than person $J$ on alternatives $x$ and $z$. We have, of course, assumed $yP_ix$ and $yP_iz$, but according to condition $I$, these preferences have no role to play in the social decision between $x$ and $z$. Therefore, $xPz$ must be the consequence of $xP_Jz$ alone, regardless of the other orderings (remember that individual preferences are assumed to be transitive). But this means that person $J$ is decisive for $x$ against $z$ and for the first step in our proof, we obtain: $D(x, y) \rightarrow \bar{D}(x, z)$.

Let us consider the second step. Again assume that $D(x, y)$ but the preferences of all members of the society now read

$$zP_Jx, \quad xP_Jy \quad \text{and}$$
$$zP_ix, \quad yP_ix.$$

Notice that this time $i$'s preferences between $z$ and $y$ remain unspecified. We obtain, of course, $xPy$ from $D(x, y)$ and $zPx$ from condition $P$. The transitivity requirement now yields $zPy$. An argument analogous to the one in the previous case, using the independence condition, shows that $zPy$ must be the consequence of $zP_Jy$ alone. Therefore, in the present situation we obtain: $D(x, y) \rightarrow \bar{D}(z, y)$.

In order to demonstrate the contagion phenomenon, we could continue along the lines of the first two steps. This, however, would be a bit boring for the reader. We could also argue via permutations of alternatives. For example, since we have already shown that $\bar{D}(x, z)$ and therefore $D(x, z)$, we could interchange $y$ and $z$ in $[D(x, y) \rightarrow \bar{D}(z, y)]$ and show that $D(x, z)$ implies $\bar{D}(y, z)$. Other interchanges would provide further steps in our proof of the lemma.

Given the verbal argumentation in steps 1 and 2, we want to prove the lemma in a rather schematic way. We shall reiterate steps 1 and 2. In the following scheme, $x \longrightarrow y$ stands for '$x$ is preferred to $y$' and $x \longleftarrow y$ stands for '$y$ is preferred to $x$'. The following six steps can be distinguished:

1. $J : x \longrightarrow y \longrightarrow z$

$$xPy, yPz \rightarrow xPz$$

$i : x \longleftarrow y \longrightarrow z$

$$D(x, y) \rightarrow \bar{D}(x, z) \rightarrow D(x, z)$$

2. $J : z \longrightarrow x \longrightarrow y$

$$zPx, xPy \rightarrow zPy$$

$i : z \longrightarrow x \longleftarrow y$

$$D(x, y) \rightarrow \bar{D}(z, y) \rightarrow D(z, y)$$

3. $J : y \longrightarrow x \longrightarrow z$

$$yPx, xPz \rightarrow yPz$$

$i : y \longrightarrow x \longleftarrow z$

$$D(x, z) \rightarrow \bar{D}(y, z) \rightarrow D(y, z)$$

4. $J : y \longrightarrow z \longrightarrow x$

$$yPz, zPx \rightarrow yPx$$

$i : y \longleftarrow z \longrightarrow x$

$$D(y, z) \rightarrow \bar{D}(y, x) \rightarrow D(y, x)$$

5. $J: z \longrightarrow y \longrightarrow x$

$$zPy, yPx \rightarrow zPx$$

$i: z \longrightarrow y \longleftarrow x$

$$D(y, x) \rightarrow \bar{D}(z, x) \rightarrow D(z, x)$$

6. $J: x \longrightarrow z \longrightarrow y$

$$xPz, zPy \rightarrow xPy$$

$i: x \longleftarrow z \longrightarrow y$

$$D(x, z) \rightarrow \bar{D}(x, y) \rightarrow D(x, y).$$

Our scheme shows that starting from $D(x, y)$, individual $J$ is decisive (and therefore almost decisive) for every ordered pair from the triple of alternatives $(x, y, z)$, given conditions $U$, $P$ and $I$. Therefore, individual $J$ is a dictator for any three alternatives that contain $x$ and $y$.

Can this contagion property be extended beyond three alternatives? The answer is 'yes'. We do not want to provide the full argument since the reader will easily see how the reasoning works. Let us consider four elements, viz. $x, y$, $u$ and $v$ where both $u$ and $v$ are different from $x$ and $y$. We start with the triple $(x, y, u)$. Due to the result above and due to condition $U$, we arrive at $\bar{D}(x, u)$ and $D(x, u)$. Next, we take the triple $(x, u, v)$. Since we have $D(x, u)$, the argumentation above shows that $\bar{D}(u, v)$ and $\bar{D}(v, u)$ follow. Therefore, $D(x, y)$ for some $x$ and $y$ implies $\bar{D}(u, v)$ for all possible ordered pairs $(u, v)$. Thus, the contagion result holds for any finite number of alternatives and the lemma is proved.

The remainder of the proof of Arrow's theorem is rather easy. The logical consequence of the lemma above is that we cannot allow an individual to be almost decisive over some ordered pair of alternatives since this would clash with the condition of non-dictatorship. Let us therefore assume that there is no almost decisive individual. As the reader will see shortly, this leads to a contradiction.

Remember that our frame of argumentation is given by conditions $U$, $P$ and $I$ together with the ordering property of $f$.

By condition $P$, there is at least one decisive set for any ordered pair $(x, y)$, viz. the set of all individuals. Therefore, there also exists at least one almost decisive set. Among all the sets of individuals that are almost decisive for some pair of alternatives, let us choose the smallest one (not necessarily unique). According to the result of the lemma, it must contain at least two individuals, for the case of one almost decisive person would yield dictatorship, and the proof were complete. Let us call this set $V$ and let $V$ be almost decisive for $(x, y)$. We now divide $V$ into two parts: $V_1$ contains only a single individual, $V_2$ contains all the others from $V$. Let $V_3$ be the individuals outside of $V$. Due to condition $U$, we postulate the following profile:

$$
\begin{array}{ll}
\text{For } i \text{ in } V_1: & xP_iy \text{ and } yP_iz \\
\text{For all } j \text{ in } V_2: & zP_jx \text{ and } xP_jy \\
\text{For all } k \text{ in } V_3: & yP_kz \text{ and } zP_kx.
\end{array}
$$

Since $V$ is almost decisive for $(x, y)$, we obtain $xPy$. Can $zPy$ hold? If this were the case, then $V_2$ would be almost decisive for $(z, y)$, since $zP_jy$ and all the other individuals (in $V_1$ and $V_3$) prefer $y$ to $z$. However, according to our assumption, $V$ is a smallest decisive set, and $V_2$ is a strict subset of $V$. Therefore, $zPy$ is impossible and thus $yRz$. Transitivity of the social relation now yields $xPz$. But then the single member of $V_1$ would be almost decisive, in contradiction to what we have assumed at the outset. The impossibility result now follows from the lemma.

The reader should note two points. The first refers to the profile that we have used above. It has the structure of the so-called paradox of voting to which we shall come back in the next chapter. The second refers to the fact that the preferences of the individuals in $V_3$ are not needed in our argumentation. In other words, we could have dispensed with a part of the profile of the voting paradox. It would, perhaps, be a good exercise for the reader to check that the last statement actually holds.

## 2.3. **A second proof**

The second proof can be found in Jehle and Reny (2001) and in Reny (2001). It is largely based on Geanakoplos (1996). While the first proof was particularly good in bringing out the contagion property of decisiveness, the second proof shows very clearly the function of Arrow's independence condition.

The proof starts by postulating a finite set of alternatives $X$ and $n$ individuals who have strict orderings over these alternatives. The social ordering is assumed to be a weak order. We pick any two distinct alternatives $a$ and $b$ from $X$. In step 1, alternative $a$ is ranked highest and alternative $b$ lowest by every person $i \in \{1, \ldots, n\}$. Condition $P$ then requires that $a$ is strictly at the top of the social ordering. Imagine now that alternative $b$ is raised, step by step or rank by rank, to the top of individual 1's ordering, while the ranking of all other alternatives is left unchanged. Due to the independence condition, $a$ either remains at the top of the social ordering or is replaced by $b$. If $a$ remains at the top, raise $b$ in individual 2's ranking until it reaches the top, then do the same in the third, fourth, ... individual's ranking. We know from the weak Pareto condition that 'in the end', when we have moved $b$ to the top of every individual's ranking, the social relation will rank $b$ above $a$. We now focus on individual $m$ where, after $b$ has risen to the top in his or her ordering, $b$ for the first time is socially preferred to $a$. Figures 2.1 and 2.2 show the situation just before and just after $b$ was raised to the top of individual $m$'s ordering.

| $R_1$ | ... | $R_{m-1}$ | $R_m$ | $R_{m+1}$ | ... | $R_n$ | social order $R$ |
|---|---|---|---|---|---|---|---|
| $b$ | ... | $b$ | $a$ | $a$ | ... | $a$ | $a$ |
| $a$ | | $a$ | $b$ | . | | | . |
| . | | . | . | . | | . | $b$ |
| . | | . | . | | | . | . |
| . | | . | $b$ | $b$ | | | . |

**Figure 2.1.**

| $R_1$ | ... | $R_{m-1}$ | $R_m$ | $R_{m+1}$ | ... | $R_n$ | social order $R$ |
|---|---|---|---|---|---|---|---|
| $b$ | ... | $b$ | $b$ | $a$ | ... | $a$ | $b$ |
| $a$ | | $a$ | $a$ | . | | . | $a$ |
| . | | . | . | . | | . | . |
| . | | . | . | | | . | . |
| . | | . | $b$ | $b$ | | | . |

**Figure 2.2.**

In step 2, we introduce the following changes into figures 2.1 and 2.2. We move alternative $a$ to the lowest position of individual $i$'s ordering for $i < m$ and move $a$ to the second lowest position in the orderings of $i > m$. With respect to figure 2.2, the reader will realize that moving $a$ downwards does not alter anything in the relationship between $b$ and any of the other alternatives. Therefore, due to condition $I$, $b$ must remain top-ranked in the social ordering. The only difference between the new constellations, let's call them 1′ and 2′, lies in $m$'s ranking of alternatives $a$ and $b$. Therefore, due to condition $I$, $b$ must in situation 1′ remain socially ordered above every alternative but possibly $a$. But if $b$ were socially ordered at least as high as $a$ in situation 1′, then, again due to condition $I$, $b$ would have to be socially ranked at least as high as $a$ in figure 2.1. But this would be in contradiction to what we had obtained in step 1. Therefore, in constellation 1′, $a$ is top-ranked socially.

In step 3, we focus on any third alternative $c$ which is distinct from $a$ and $b$. Remember that in situation 1′, $a$ was ranked lowest for $i < m$ and second lowest for $i > m$. Individual $m$ had $a$ at the top of the ordering. We now construct a profile in figure 2.3 which is such that the ranking of $a$ in relation to any other alternative in any individual's ordering remains the same as in situation $1'$. A preference profile is picked where every individual has $c$ ordered above $b$. The main insight within this step is that due to condition $I$, alternative $a$ must again be top-ranked socially.

| $R_1$ | $\ldots$ | $R_{m-1}$ | $R_m$ | $R_{m+1}$ | $\ldots$ | $R_n$ | social order $R$ |
|---|---|---|---|---|---|---|---|
| . | | . | $a$ | . | | . | $a$ |
| . | | . | $c$ | . | | . | . |
| $c$ | | $c$ | $b$ | $c$ | | $c$ | . |
| $b$ | | $b$ | . | $a$ | | $a$ | . |
| $a$ | | $a$ | . | $b$ | | $b$ | . |

**Figure 2.3.**

In step 4, the preference profile from figure 2.3 is modified in the following way, and this is the only change: for individuals $i > m$, the rankings of altern-atives $a$ and $b$ are reversed. What are the consequences of this alteration? Due to condition $I$, the social ranking of $a$ versus all the other alternatives except for $b$ remains the same. Can $b$ become top-ranked socially? The answer is 'no' since $c$ must be socially preferred to $b$ due to the Pareto condition. Therefore, $a$ is at the top of the social ordering and $c$ is socially ranked above $b$.

In the final step 5, we construct an arbitrary profile of orderings with $a$ above $b$ in the ordering of person $m$. For example, the profile could have, as depicted in figure 2.4, alternative $c$ between $a$ and $b$ in $m$'s ordering whereas all the other individuals order $c$ at the top. Condition $I$ disallows the ranking of $c$ to have any effect on the social ranking between $a$ and $b$. The ranking of $a$ versus $c$ is as in step 4. Due to our inferences in step 4, $a$ must be ranked above $c$ due to condition $I$, and $c$ is Pareto-preferred to $b$. Therefore, by transitivity of the social relation, $a$ is preferred to $b$, and this holds whenever person $m$ orders $a$ above $b$.

If we now permute alternatives $b$ and $c$ in the arguments above, we obtain the same qualitative result. The ranking of $a$ is above alternative $c$ when person $m$ orders $a$ above that alternative. And this holds for any alternative distinct from $a$. In other words, individual $m$ has dictatorial power over $a$ versus any other alternative. Since alternative $a$ was chosen arbitrarily in step 1, it is now evident that there is a dictator for every $a$ from $X$. But can there be different dictators for different alternatives? The reader will easily see that this would lead to contradictions in the construction of a social ranking whenever these 'potential dictators' have individual orderings that are not the same. Therefore, there can only be one dictator for all elements from $X$.

| $R_1$ | ... | $R_{m-1}$ | $R_m$ | $R_{m+1}$ | ... | $R_n$ | social order $R$ |
|---|---|---|---|---|---|---|---|
| c |  | c | a | c |  | c | a |
| . |  | . | c | . |  | . | . |
| . |  | . | b | . |  | . | c |
| . |  | . | . | . |  | . | . |
| b |  | b | . | b |  | b | . |
| a |  | a | . | a |  | a | b |

**Figure 2.4.**

## 2.4. **A third diagrammatic proof**

The third proof provides a diagrammatic representation of Arrow's theorem and was introduced by Blackorby, Donaldson and Weymark (1984). In order to keep the diagrams two-dimensional, the proof was given for only two individuals (though the authors briefly indicate how their proof can be extended to more than two persons). The reader certainly remembers our remark at the end of the first (original) proof that two individuals would suffice to show the Arrovian impossibility.

The diagrammatic proof unfolds in utility space. Strictly speaking, this would require us to redefine the whole Arrovian set-up in terms of utility functions that are defined in Euclidian space. This would be extremely cumbersome and very tiring for the reader. Therefore, in the process of redefining concepts, we shall try to be as parsimonious as possible.

The first thing for the reader is to remember from a basic course in microeconomics that a preference ordering can be transformed into a utility function if continuity is postulated in addition to the other properties that turn a binary preference relation into an ordering. In other words, the better-than-or-indifferent set and the worse-than-or-indifferent set with reference to any point in Euclidian space are assumed to be closed sets. The second point to remember is that given any preference ordering and its corresponding utility function, any other utility function which is generated by applying a strictly monotone transformation to the original utility function has the same informational content as the original. This property of ordinal utility will prove to be important in the sequel (remember that the Arrovian framework is purely ordinal). Different individuals can pick different strictly monotone transformations without changing or distorting the original information contained in the preference orderings of the $n$ members of the society. This being said, it is very clear that any 'degree' of comparability of utilities across individuals is excluded. When looking back to our reasoning in the first two proofs, the reader will immediately agree that comparability assumptions had nowhere been postulated.

The social welfare function $f$ à la Arrow is now turned into a social evaluation functional $F$. Its domain are sets of $n$-tuples of individual utility functions $u_1, u_2, \ldots, u_n$. Each individual $i \in \{1, \ldots, n\}$ evaluates social states $x \in X$ in terms of utility function $u_i(x)$. We postulate that all logically possible $n$-tuples of utility functions are admissible (unrestricted domain). The functional $F$ then is a mapping from the set of all logically possible $n$-tuples or profiles of utility functions into the set of all orderings of $X$, which we denoted by $\mathcal{E}$ earlier on. For $U = (u_1, u_2, \ldots, u_n)$ being a profile, $F(U) = R_U$ is the ordering generated by $F$, when the utility profile is $U$.

After unrestricted domain, the second condition on $F$ that we introduce is Arrow's independence of irrelevant alternatives, now defined for $n$-tuples of individual utility functions. The meaning of condition $I$ is precisely the same as before. If for any two social alternatives $x, y \in X$ and two utility profiles $U'$ and $U''$, both $x$ and $y$ obtain the same $n$-tuple of utilities in $U'$ and $U''$, then $R_{U'}$ and $R_{U''}$ must coincide on $\{x, y\}$. As promised above, we abstain from giving a redefinition of the independence condition (see, however, section 7.3). Nor do we want to redefine the weak Pareto condition which, of course, also has the same meaning as before. However, we now introduce a condition called Pareto indifference, which requires that if all members of the society are indifferent between a pair of alternatives, the same should hold for society's preference over this pair.

**Condition $PI$ (Pareto indifference).** For all $x, y \in X$ and for all $U$ from the (unrestricted) domain, if $U(x) = U(y)$, then $x I_U y$.

$x I_U y$ means that $x R_U y$ and $y R_U x$, and $U(x) = U(y)$ means that $u_i(x) = u_i(y)$ for all $i \in \{1, \ldots, n\}$.

Conditions $U$, $I$ and $PI$ have very strong implications for $F$. Sen (1977b) has shown that the three conditions together imposed on $F$ are equivalent to a property called strong neutrality. Strong neutrality requires that the social evaluation functional $F$ ignore all non-utility information with respect to the alternatives, such as names or rights or claims or procedural aspects. The only information that counts is the vector of individual utilities associated with any social alternative. This 'fact' has been termed 'welfarism' in the literature of social choice theory as well as bargaining theory (we briefly discussed this issue in our introduction) and has been sharply criticized from different angles. The total disregard of non-utility information not only holds within a single utility profile but also across profiles. All this is rather debatable and we shall return to the welfarism issue later on in this book.

For the present analysis, however, the welfaristic set-up has a great advantage. Instead of considering the orderings $R_U$ generated by $F$, we can focus on an ordering $R^*$ of $\mathbb{R}^n$, the space of utility $n$-tuples, that orders vectors of individual utilities which correspond to the social alternatives from the given set $X$. The formal result that Blackorby et al. state in this context (it is due to

D'Aspremont and Gevers (1977)) says that if the social evaluation functional $F$ satisfies the three axioms of welfarism (viz. conditions $U$, $I$, and $PI$), there exists an ordering $R^*$ of $\mathbb{R}^n$ such that for all $x, y \in X$ and all logically possible utility profiles $U$, $x R_U y \leftrightarrow \bar{u} R^* \bar{\bar{u}}$, where $\bar{u} = U(x)$ and $\bar{\bar{u}} = U(y)$.

D'Aspremont and Gevers show that when the functional $F$ fulfils the three axioms of welfarism, the ordering $R^*$ in utility space inherits these properties. Therefore, one can redefine these conditions together with other requirements and impose them directly on $R^*$. However, we shall refrain from doing this except for one case because, otherwise the reader would, perhaps, feel terribly bored. Let us just look at the formulation of dictatorship within the new framework. The ordering $R^*$ is a dictatorship if and only if there exists an individual $i \in \{1, \ldots, n\}$ such that for all $\bar{u}, \bar{\bar{u}} \in \mathbb{R}^n$, if $\bar{u}_i > \bar{\bar{u}}_i$, then $\bar{u} P^* \bar{\bar{u}}$. Whenever individual $i$ gets more utility under vector $\bar{u}$ than under vector $\bar{\bar{u}}$, $\bar{u}$ is socially ordered above $\bar{\bar{u}}$.

What is now shown diagrammatically is that if the social evaluation functional $F$ satisfies the three axioms of welfarism, the framework of ordinally measurable and non-comparable utilities together with the weak Pareto rule are necessary and sufficient for the social ordering $R^*$ to be a dictatorship.

The diagram in figure 2.5 will be widely used in the following proof for the two-person case. Let $\bar{u}$ in $\mathbb{R}^2$ be our point of reference. The plane has been divided into four regions. For the moment, we do not consider the boundaries between the regions but only the interior of the four regions. From the weak Pareto principle, it is clear that all utility vectors in region I are socially preferred to the reference point $\bar{u}$, and the latter is preferred to all vectors in region III.

What can be said about the points in region II in comparison with $\bar{u}$ and the points in region IV against $\bar{u}$? In the following, it will be shown in several steps that either all points in II are preferred to $\bar{u}$ and the latter is preferred to all points in IV or all points in IV are preferred to $\bar{u}$ and $\bar{u}$ again is preferred to all points in II.

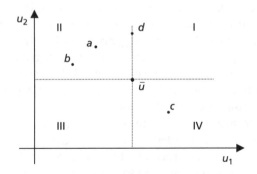

**Figure 2.5.**

Let us show first that all points in region II (region IV) must be ranked identically against $\bar{u}$. Notice that points in II are such that $u_1 < \bar{u}_1$ and $u_2 > \bar{u}_2$. Consider the points $a$ and $b$ in II and let us assume that $aP^*\bar{u}$. We will now argue that we then obtain $bP^*\bar{u}$ as well. Why? Remember that each of the two persons is totally free to map his or her utility scale into another one by a strictly increasing transformation. It is easy to find a transformation (there are infinitely many) that maps $a_1$ into $b_1$ and $\bar{u}_1$ into $\bar{u}_1$. Similarly, one can find another transformation that maps $a_2$ into $b_2$ and $\bar{u}_2$ into itself. Figures 2.6(a) and (b) depict two such transformations.

We know that since we are in the framework of ordinal and non-comparable utilities, these transformations do not change the rankings of the two persons. Therefore, if $aP^*\bar{u}$ as assumed, then $bP^*\bar{u}$. Notice that this result holds for any points $a$, $b$ in the interior of region II. Therefore, all points in the interior of region II are ranked identically with respect to reference point $\bar{u}$ (but not, of course, ranked identically with respect to each other). The reasoning above holds analogously for all points in region IV with respect to $\bar{u}$.

Since $R^*$ is an ordering, three ways of ranking points in region II against $\bar{u}$ are possible: the points in II could be preferred, indifferent or worse. In our argument above, we had postulated a strict preference against $\bar{u}$. We could also have started by assuming $\bar{u}$ to be preferable to all points in II. The inferences

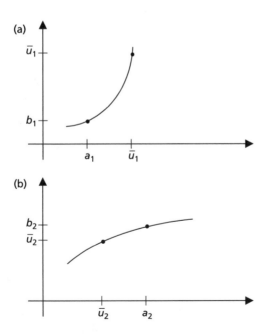

**Figure 2.6.**

would have been completely analogous. However, indifference between points in II and $\bar{u}$ would lead to a contradiction. We would, for example, have $aI^*\bar{u}$ and $bI^*\bar{u}$. But since $R^*$ is an ordering, we would also obtain $aI^*b$. Clearly, point $a$ in figure 2.5 must be Pareto-preferred to point $b$. Therefore, indifference cannot hold.

We now wish to show that the ranking of points in region II against $\bar{u}$ must be opposite to the ranking of points in region IV against $\bar{u}$. Again, we shall use the argument that strictly monotone transformations of individual utility scales do not change the informational content. Let us assume once more that points in region II are preferred to $\bar{u}$, more concretely that $(a_1, a_2)P^*(\bar{u}_1, \bar{u}_2)$. Consider the following transformations for individuals 1 and 2. Change person 1's utility scale such that each point is shifted to the right by $\bar{u}_1 - a_1$, a constant amount, and change person 2's scale such that each point is shifted downwards by $a_2 - \bar{u}_2$, another constant amount. This means that $(a_1, a_2)$ is moved to $(a_1 + (\bar{u}_1 - a_1), a_2 - (a_2 - \bar{u}_2)) = (\bar{u}_1, \bar{u}_2)$ and $(\bar{u}_1, \bar{u}_2)$ is shifted 'south-east' to $(2\bar{u}_1 - a_1, 2\bar{u}_2 - a_2) = (c_1, c_2)$. More briefly, the independent transformations map $a$ into $\bar{u}$ and $\bar{u}$ into $c$. Since $a$, by assumption, is preferred to $\bar{u}$, this relationship continues to hold after the transformations, viz. $\bar{u}$ is preferred to $c$. And from our earlier steps in this proof we infer that $\bar{u}$ is preferred to all points in region IV. Remember that assuming region II to be preferred to $\bar{u}$ was arbitrary. If region II had been assumed to be worse than $\bar{u}$, all points in region IV would turn out to be better than $\bar{u}$.

The proof is almost complete. We still have to deal with points on the boundaries. Consider, for example, point $d$ in Figure 2.5. Suppose region II is preferred to $\bar{u}$. For $d$, there always exists a point in II (such as $a$) that is Pareto-inferior to $d$. Therefore, $dP^*a$ and $aP^*\bar{u}$. Transitivity of $R^*$ yields $dP^*\bar{u}$. This result holds for any choice of $d$. In other words, if two adjacent regions have the same preference relationship to $\bar{u}$, the same ranking holds for any point on their common boundary.

Let us lean back for a moment and see what we have shown. There are two cases possible that are depicted in Figures 2.7(a) and (b). If we assume that region II is preferred to $\bar{u}$, then regions I and II and their common boundary are preferred to $\bar{u}$. In this case, the direction of social preference is vertical, and person 2 is a dictator in the sense defined. If region IV is preferred to $\bar{u}$, then regions I and IV and their common boundary are preferred to $\bar{u}$. In this case, the direction of social preference is horizontal, and person 1 is a dictator.

Let us add two more remarks. The first refers to the chosen reference point $\bar{u}$. The position of this point is totally arbitrary for the arguments above. Any other point $\bar{\bar{u}}$ can be reached by transforming the utility scales of person 1 and 2 by adding $\bar{\bar{u}}_1 - \bar{u}_1$ and $\bar{\bar{u}}_2 - \bar{u}_2$ to person 1's scale and person 2's scale, respectively. The proof would then proceed in the same way as before.

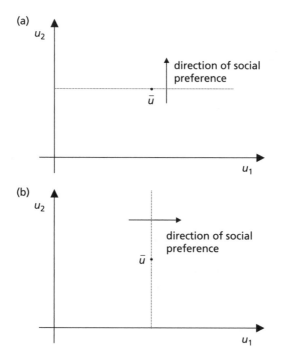

**Figure 2.7.**

The second remark refers to the fact that we have said nothing about points lying on the dotted lines. As a matter of fact, without introducing a further assumption, nothing precise can be said about the relationship among points on the dotted lines. What we can say is the following. Consider, for example, figure 2.7(a). Because of the informational set-up, any two points on the horizontal dotted line can be ranked either that one of the two points is better than the other, or that it is worse than the other, or that the two points are indifferent. Take a point to the right of $\bar{u}$. If this point is, for example, better than $\bar{u}$, then whenever one moves to the right on any horizontal line, this is an improvement socially. Two things could be done to 'remedy' this situation. One would be to introduce a continuity requirement with respect to $R^*$. Then all points on the dotted line through $\bar{u}$ would become indifferent to each other. The second thing would be to introduce a strong version of the Pareto principle. A consequence of this assumption would be that whenever the dictator (either person 1 or person 2) is indifferent between two utility allocations, the second person becomes decisive, i.e. determines the social preference. In other words, we obtain a serial or lexicographic dictatorship. Finally, the reader should note how important and far-reaching the assumption of informational invariance with respect to strictly monotone transformations of the individuals' utility scales has been in the proof above.

## 2.5. **A short summary**

When Arrow had published his by now famous impossibility theorem, it came as a surprise to various welfare economists. Arrow's negative result was met with disbelief by some. Others, such as Samuelson (1967), claimed that this result might have importance for politics but not so much for economics proper. Others again tried to construct counterexamples to the theorem. Actually, Blau (1957) had a good point which forced Arrow to reformulate the original statement of his theorem to some, though minor degree.

We presented three different proofs to make the logical implications within the Arrovian set-up more transparent and to show the generality of his result. The spread of decisiveness from a single 'cell' (strict preference over one pair) to all other 'cells' in the first proof may be quite stunning for the beginner. The second proof reveals how restrictive (in terms of barring profile information) Arrow's condition of independence of irrelevant alternatives is. The third proof demonstrates the far-reaching consequences of the purely ordinal approach where utilities are determined up to arbitrary strictly monotone transformations, a property that remains largely in the dark in the first two proofs. All the different properties interact, of course, but each proof seems to highlight one of these in particular.

## ☐ RECOMMENDED READING

Blackorby, Ch., Donaldson, D. and Weymark J. A. (1984). 'Social Choice with Interpersonal Utility Comparisons: A Diagrammatic Introduction'. *International Economic Review*, 25: 327–56.

Reny, Ph. J. (2001). 'Arrow's Theorem and the Gibbard–Satterthwaite Theorem: A Unified Approach'. *Economics Letters*, 70: 99–105.

Sen, A. K. (1970b). *Collective Choice and Social Welfare*, chapter 3. San Francisco, Cambridge: Holden-Day.

## ☐ HISTORICAL SOURCE

Arrow, K. J. (1951, 1963). *Social Choice and Individual Values* (2nd edn.), chapter 5. New York: John Wiley.

## ☐ MORE ADVANCED

Sen, A. K. (1995). 'Rationality and Social Choice'. *American Economic Review*, 85: 1–24.

# 3 Majority decision under restricted domains

## 3.1. The simple majority rule

We have seen in Chapter 2 that *any* social welfare function satisfying unrestricted domain and the weak Pareto condition as well as Arrow's independence condition and the requirement that the generated social relation be an ordering is doomed to be dictatorial. As already mentioned in Chapter 2, Arrow considered these conditions as necessary requirements in the sense that they express both rationality and the doctrines of citizens' sovereignty in a very general way.

Is this then the end of the story? Before answering this question with a clear 'no' (and honestly speaking, this book as well as several others that already exist would not have been written if the answer were 'yes'), it does, perhaps, make sense to follow Arrow's remark and ask which basic properties a social aggregation rule that is used and applied in real life should reasonably satisfy.

A very basic feature of democratic voting procedures is the property of anonymity. It requires that in social decision making all individuals should count the same. More concretely, let us postulate a voting procedure with only two answers, viz. 'yes' and 'no'. Anonymity now demands that it does not matter whether Mr $i$ and Mrs $j$ say 'yes' and Mrs $k$ says 'no' or whether Mrs $j$ and Mrs $k$ say 'yes' and Mr $i$ says 'no'. Only the number of answers 'yes' and answers 'no' count. Renumbering the individuals or changing their name-tags should not matter or, more technically, permutations among the set of voters should play no role in the social decision procedure. So we can formulate

**Condition $A$ (Anonymity).** If $(R_1, \ldots, R_n)$ and $(R'_1, \ldots, R'_n)$ are two profiles of preferences that are permutations of one another via some one-to-one correspondence, then for any $x, y \in X$, $xRy \leftrightarrow xR'y$, where $R$ and $R'$ are the social relations corresponding to the two profiles.

Note that anonymity is a stronger requirement than Arrow's non-dictatorship condition. In other words, if anonymity is postulated, there cannot be a dictator in the Arrovian sense.

Another condition which is often demanded is that a social decision mechanism should treat alternatives equally or, expressed differently, if the name-tags of alternatives were permuted on the level of individual preferences, the same permutation would have to occur on the level of social preference. More technically,

**Condition $N$ (Neutrality).** For any $x, y, z, w \in X$, if for all $i$, $xR_iy$ iff $zR_i'w$, and $yR_ix$ iff $wR_i'z$, then $xRy$ iff $zR'w$, and $yRx$ iff $wR'z$, where for all $i$, $R_i$ and $R_i'$ belong to two profiles of individual preferences and $R$ and $R'$ are the corresponding social relationships.

Note that this condition is stronger than Arrow's independence axiom (just equate $x$ with alternative $z$ and $y$ with $w$ and you arrive at the formulation of Arrow's independence requirement). The present condition is closely related to the axiom of strong neutrality that was discussed in the context of the third proof of Arrow's impossibility result in the preceding chapter. Remember that individual utility functions and utility profiles formed the basis of analysis in the third proof.

As a matter of fact, neutrality, the equal treatment of issues or alternatives, is satisfied by quite a few decision rules, for instance by the simple majority rule and the absolute majority rule which will be defined in this chapter. A violation of neutrality would mean that the social decision between two tax programmes, for example, would be made in a different way than, say, the decision whether to legalize a market for organs or preserve the status quo (i.e. disallowing such a market), or the decision whether to re-introduce the death penalty. Sen (1970, p. 78) mentions that purely procedural matters may be decided by simple majority voting in the United Nations' General Assembly, while more important issues require a two-thirds majority. In the next chapter, we will see that under certain circumstances and for certain issues it may appear plausible to give up neutrality.

Social preferences should be based on the expressed preferences of the individuals. The social preference should also be responsive to changes in the individuals' preferences. This can be reached in different ways. The so-called constant rule which says that for any pair $x, y \in X$, the social relation always declares indifference between $x$ and $y$, no matter what the individual preferences are, is totally unresponsive to the individuals' orderings (note, however, that the constant rule fulfils the conditions of anonymity and neutrality just defined). An aggregation rule that is based on the Pareto principle, asserting that given some status quo $y \in X$, for any $x \in X$, $xPy$ socially if and only if all individuals strictly prefer $x$ to $y$, otherwise the status quo is socially preferred to $x$, is responsive to changes in the preference profile of the members of society, but in a minimal way, so to speak. A four-fifths majority rule apparently is a bit more responsive than the rule just given but less responsive than a two-thirds majority rule which, again, is less responsive than the absolute majority rule. We use more respectively less responsive here in the sense of inducing a change of social preference 'away from' the status quo $y$. More (less) responsive then means to induce a change to $x$, let's say, with the support of a smaller (larger) fraction of the voters who strictly prefer $x$ to $y$. For the present purposes, we wish to consider the following definition of responsiveness.

**Condition *PR* (Positive responsiveness).** For any two profiles $(R_1, \ldots, R_n)$ and $(R'_1, \ldots, R'_n)$ and any $x, y \in X$, if individual preferences are such that for all $i \in N$, $xP'_i y$ whenever $xP_i y$ and $xR'_i y$ whenever $xI_i y$ and there exists some $k \in N$ such that either $xP'_k y$ whenever $xI_k y$ or $xR'_k y$ whenever $yP_k x$, then $xRy$ under $(R_1, \ldots, R_n)$ implies $xP'y$ under $(R'_1, \ldots, R'_n)$.

Positive responsiveness considers the effect on the social preference relation when some person $k$ expresses a change in favour of $x$. Either a strict preference for $y$ over $x$ turns into at least an indifference between the two, or an indifference turns into a strict preference in favour of $x$, with everyone else's preference between $x$ and $y$ remaining the same. Positive responsiveness requires for such a case that social preference move in the direction of $x$. In particular, if before the change society was indifferent between $x$ and $y$, it now strictly prefers $x$ to $y$.

Consider the following two rules which are widely applied in the real world. Let $N(xP_i y)$ stand for the number of voters with $xP_i y$, let $N(xR_i y)$ represent the number of persons with $xR_i y$ and let $|N|$ denote the total number of voters.

**Definition 3.1 (Simple majority rule).** For all $(R_1, \ldots, R_n)$ and for any $x, y \in X : xRy \leftrightarrow [N(xP_i y) \geq N(yP_i x)]$.

Note that an equivalent formulation is that for all $(R_1, \ldots, R_n)$ and for any $x, y \in X : xRy \leftrightarrow [N(xR_i y) \geq N(yR_i x)]$.

**Definition 3.2 (Absolute majority rule).** For all $(R_1, \ldots, R_n)$ and for any $x, y \in X : xPy \leftrightarrow [N(xP_i y) > \frac{1}{2} \cdot |N|], yPx \leftrightarrow [N(yP_i x) > \frac{1}{2} \cdot |N|]$, and $xIy$ otherwise.

In the following example, it is argued that positive responsiveness is satisfied by the simple majority rule but not by the absolute majority rule. Consider a small society of seven voters where two individuals prefer $x$ to $y$, two individuals prefer $y$ to $x$ and the rest is indifferent between $x$ and $y$. Then both the simple majority rule and the absolute majority rule yield social indifference, i.e. $xIy$. Now assume that one of the hitherto indifferent voters declares a strict preference for $x$ over $y$, with everyone else's preference between $x$ and $y$ remaining the same. Positive responsiveness requires that $xPy$ socially which is what the simple majority rule but not the absolute majority rule brings about. Thus simple majority voting is more sensitive to changes in the preference profile of society. But this argument can be turned around. If in the example above $y$ again represents the status quo, absolute majority voting requires a stronger backing in order to move away from $y$. This may be desirable when much is at stake.

The following result was first proved by May.

**Theorem 3.1 (May's characterization of simple majority voting (1952)).** The conditions of unrestricted domain, anonymity, neutrality and positive responsiveness are necessary and sufficient for a social aggregation rule to be the simple majority rule.

In the sequel, we wish to give a sketch of May's original proof. In order to do this, we can introduce a somewhat different yet simpler notation which is made to fit the simple majority rule. For each individual $i$, we associate a variable $d_i$ that takes the values $+1, -1, 0$, respectively, when $xP_iy$, $yP_ix$, $xI_iy$. Similarly, for society, we write $D = g(d_1, \ldots, d_n)$, taking the values $+1, -1, 0$ according as $xPy$, $yPx$, $xIy$ socially where $g$ is the social aggregation rule that maps lists of individual $d_i$ into either $+1$, or $-1$, or 0 (note that $g$ is single valued). The condition of unrestricted domain has the same meaning as before, yet expressed somewhat differently.

**Condition $U'$.** The domain of the mapping $g$ comprises all logically possible lists of $n$ entries of $+1, -1$, or 0.

**Condition $A'$.** If $(d_1, \ldots, d_n)$ and $(d'_1, \ldots, d'_n)$ in the domain of $g$ are two lists of entries of $+1, -1$, or 0 that are permutations of one another via some one-to-one correspondence, then $g(d_1, \ldots, d_n) = g(d'_1, \ldots, d'_n)$.

**Condition $N'$.** Whenever $(d_1, \ldots, d_n)$ and $(-d_1, \ldots, -d_n)$ are both in the domain of $g$, then $g(-d_1, \ldots, -d_n) = -g(d_1, \ldots, d_n)$.

Note that if $d_i$, for example, takes the value $-1$, thus representing $yP_ix$, $-d_i$ takes the value $+1$, thus standing for $xP_iy$. Therefore, $d_i$ and $-d_i$ stand for a permutation of alternatives $x$ and $y$.

**Condition $PR$.** Whenever $(d_1, \ldots, d_n)$ and $(d'_1, \ldots, d'_n)$ are such that $d'_i = d_i$ for all $i \neq k$ and $d'_k > d_k$, then $g(d_1, \ldots, d_n) \geq 0$ implies $g(d'_1, \ldots, d'_n) = +1$.

**Proof of theorem 3.1.** It is easy to see that the simple majority rule fulfils all four conditions above. Under the new notation, simple majority voting represents a social aggregation rule $g$ that gives $D = +1, -1, 0$ according as the number of $+1$'s, denoted as $N(1)$, minus the number of $-1$'s, denoted as $N(-1)$, is positive, negative, or zero. Let us turn to the sufficiency part of the proof.

The first thing to notice is that since $g$ satisfies condition $A'$, the value of $g(d_1, \ldots, d_n)$ only depends on the number of $+1$'s, $-1$'s and the number of 0's in the list and not on the positions of the $+1$'s, $-1$'s, and 0's in the list. The number of 0's, however, is determined by $|N| - N(1) - N(-1)$. Therefore, condition $A'$ implies that the value of $g(d_1, \ldots, d_n)$ entirely depends on $N(1)$ and $N(-1)$.

Secondly, if $N(1) = N(-1)$, then $D = 0$. Suppose that $D = g(d_1,\ldots,d_n) = +1$. Let us now examine the list $(-d_1,\ldots,-d_n)$ which is admissible due to condition $U'$. Because of the neutrality axiom, $g(-d_1,\ldots,-d_n) = -g(d_1,\ldots,d_n) = -1$. On the other hand, from step 1 and the assumption that $N(1) = N(-1)$, we must have $g(d_1,\ldots,d_n) = g(-d_1,\ldots,-d_n)$. Since $g$ is a function, the hypothesis that $D = +1$ therefore leads to a contradiction. The same argumentation can be used to show that $D = -1$ is not possible either. Thus, the only possibility in the case of $N(1) = N(-1)$ is $D = 0$.

Thirdly, assume that $N(1) > N(-1)$. We want to show that $D = g(d_1,\ldots,d_n) = +1$. Let us suppose that $N(1) = N(-1) + m$, where $m$ is a positive integer with $m \le |N| - N(-1)$. Let us first assume that $m = 1$ so that $N(1) = N(-1)+1$. Because of the latter, there exists at least one $d_k = +1$. We now consider another constellation, $(d'_1,\ldots,d'_n)$, with $d'_i = d_i$ for $i \ne k$ and $d'_k = 0$, while $d_k = 1$. Then $N(1) = N(-1)$ for profile $(d'_1,\ldots,d'_n)$ which belongs to the domain of $g$ due to condition $U'$, and from the second step we know that $g(d'_1,\ldots,d'_n) = 0$. Positive responsiveness now requires that $g(d_1,\ldots,d_n) = +1$.

The last step is by mathematical induction. Suppose that $N(1) = N(-1)+m$ implies $g(d_1,\ldots,d_n) = +1$. We have to prove that $N(1) = N(-1) + (m+1)$ implies $g(d_1,\ldots,d_n) = +1$. Therefore, suppose that $N(1) = N(-1) + (m+1)$. Again, there is at least one $d_i = +1$ in the profile $(d_1,\ldots,d_n)$. We consider another profile $(d'_1,\ldots,d'_n)$ with $d'_i = d_i$ for $i \ne k$ and $d'_k = 0$. For the latter profile, we have $N(1) = N(-1) + m$ and from induction $g(d'_1,\ldots,d'_n) = +1$. Using positive responsiveness, we obtain $g(d_1,\ldots,d_n) = +1$.

To summarize, in this third step we have shown that if $N(1) > N(-1)$, then $D = g(d_1,\ldots,d_n) = +1$. From this and the neutrality condition, we can infer that if $N(1) < N(-1)$, then $D = -1$. All three steps together define the simple majority rule, and sufficiency is proved.

In his paper from 1952, May showed that the four conditions that define the simple majority rule are logically independent. May wrote that in order to show independence of the conditions, 'it is sufficient to exhibit functions that violate each one while satisfying all the others' (1952, p. 683). We do not want to discuss the issue of independence at length. We only wish to refer to the absolute majority rule defined above (for more details on this rule, see Fishburn (1973), chapter 6) that violates positive responsiveness but satisfies unrestricted domain, anonymity and neutrality. Other cases can be constructed similarly.

Is the simple majority rule a social welfare function in the Arrovian sense? Clearly not. But we have to ask *why* simple majority voting is not a counterexample to Arrow's impossibility result. The simple majority rule is clearly non-dictatorial, from May's theorem we know that this rule satisfies unrestricted domain and the independence condition (remember that the latter is weaker than neutrality), and one can easily see that the method of majority rule fulfils the weak Pareto principle (actually, neutrality and positive responsiveness together imply the Pareto rule). Where lies the problem? The problem comes from the fact that simple majority voting can yield a social relation that is not transitive. And transitivity of the social preference relation is an important feature within the Arrovian concept of a welfare function.

Consider the following profile of individual preferences that the reader has seen before (viz. in Arrow's original proof of his impossibility theorem). There is one person who prefers $x$ to $y$ to $z$, a second person prefers $y$ to $z$ to $x$, and a third person prefers $z$ to $x$ to $y$. Let us write this in the following form:

$$xP_1 yP_1 z$$

$$yP_2 zP_2 x$$

$$zP_3 xP_3 y.$$

This profile of preferences is called a 'latin square' and yields the famous paradox of voting or Condorcet paradox (Condorcet was an influential mathematician, statistician and social scientist in France in the second half of the eighteenth century). Applying the simple majority rule to the preference profile above leads to the following social relations: $x$ is preferred to $y$, $y$ is preferred to $z$, and $z$ is preferred to $x$. These preferences clearly violate the transitivity property. In other words, the application of the simple majority rule to 'certain' preference profiles yields intransitivity. If we only considered the preferences of persons 1 and 2, we would still obtain an intransitive relation, viz. intransitivity of social indifference.

## 3.2. **Single-peaked preferences**

We just said that the simple majority rule has problems with some preference patterns but not with others. Can this be made more precise? Is there a way (or are there ways) to depict 'those other' preference profiles in a useful way and add some reasonable interpretation? Our first example in chapter 2 described a situation where one 'strange' individual had unacceptable views on the issues at stake, preferences that were not shared by the other members of the society. Let us generalize this situation and assume that in the given society, there are several people who share unacceptable views which culminate in a unanimous preference ordering and the rest of the society has just the opposite of these preferences. This clearly is a domain restriction for the social aggregation function but note that the method of majority decision would have no problems with such a preference constellation.

Let us discuss more interesting cases. Consider a student who wants to live as closely to the university as possible or a frequent traveller who wants to have an apartment as close to the central railway station as possible. Both individuals will have decreasing preferences for locations further away from their optimal site. Or consider three individuals with low, medium and high income, respectively, who plan to purchase cars. Let us assume that there are three categories of cars, a low-priced small car, a medium-priced and medium-sized car and an expensive large car. The person with the low income will 'most probably' prefer the small car to the medium-sized car and prefer the latter to the large vehicle. The person with the high income will 'most probably' have the inverse ordering. The individual with the medium income will 'most likely' prefer the medium-priced car most and show a declining preference towards both the small and the large car.

The preferences of these three persons are what Black (1948) and Arrow (1951, 1963) called single-peaked preferences. There is a peak, the point of highest desirability, and on either side of this peak, given that the peak does not lie at the extreme left or the extreme right of the spectrum of objects, individual desirability declines. There is no cardinality involved – the framework is purely ordinal. Figure 3.1 depicts our last example. The lines between the symbols have no meaning. They simply help to interpret the structure of points as single-peaked. Note that the arrangement of the options along the horizontal axis seems natural in our car example. This may be less so in situations where the alternatives are defined more abstractly. Please also note – we shall be more explicit in a few moments when we discuss constellations depicted by figures 3.3 and 3.4 below – that a rearrangement of the alternatives along the line may drastically change the 'picture'.

The paradox of voting with its latin square structure clearly is not single-peaked, as can be seen from figure 3.2.

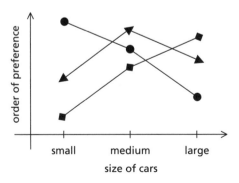

**Figure 3.1.**

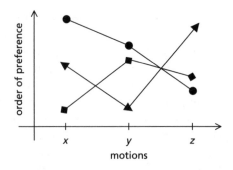

**Figure 3.2.**

We now have to become more formal. What we want to show on the following pages is that the simple majority rule becomes a social welfare function in the sense of Arrow for any number of alternatives provided that the number of individuals is odd and the property of single-peakedness is fulfilled for every triple of alternatives. We shall follow the demonstrations of both Arrow (1951, 1963) and Kelly (1988).

We hasten to add that the oddness requirement that we just mentioned refers to the number of so-called concerned voters, i.e. those individuals who, for a given set of options, are not indifferent between every pair of elements in this set. Those persons who are totally indifferent ('unconcerned') do not enter the oddness requirement understandably and will be unconsidered in what follows.

In order to define the notion of single-peakedness properly, we have to introduce an ordering, viz. a strict ordering among the set of alternatives that is not a preference relation. It is an ordering among the 'labels', so to speak, along the horizontal line in figures 3.1 and 3.2. It could be an ordering from left to right in the political sphere or, for example, an ordering over colours from light to dark. So if $S$ stands for such a strict ordering, we obtain for any $x, y \in X$ with $x \neq y$ that either $xSy$ or $ySx$, and for any $x, y, z$ from $X$ that are all distinct from each other that if $xSy$ and $ySz$, then $xSz$.

Having defined such a strong ordering which, as Arrow explains, is analogous to the relation of 'less than' in the domain of real numbers, we can define the notion of 'betweenness' with respect to $S$. We let $B(x, y, z)$ mean that $y$ is between $x$ and $z$. This means that either $xSy$ and $ySz$ or $zSy$ and $ySx$. Clearly, with $x, y, z$ being distinct elements of $X$, exactly one of the following holds: $B(x, y, z)$, $B(x, z, y)$, $B(y, x, z)$.

With these notions, we can now define Black's concept of single-peaked preferences.

**Condition of single-peakedness.** A profile $(R_1, \ldots, R_n)$ of individual preferences satisfies the property of single-peakedness if there exists a strong ordering $S$ such that for all $i$, $xR_iy$ and $B(x, y, z)$ imply $yP_iz$, where $B(x, y, z)$ is the betweenness relation derived from $S$.

It becomes clear from this definition that single-peakedness imposes a particular property on each individual ordering. The possibility theorem by Black and Arrow reads

**Theorem 3.2 (A possibility theorem for single-peaked preferences).** Provided the number of concerned voters is odd, the majority decision rule is a social welfare function for any number of alternatives if the individual orderings satisfy the property of single-peakedness over each triple of alternatives.

The requirement of single-peakedness is a sufficient condition on the set of individual preferences. This means that whenever a set of individual preferences satisfies this condition, the social relation generated by the method of majority decision is an ordering, given the oddness requirement. It also means that single-peakedness is not a necessary condition in order to obtain an ordering (see Sen and Pattanaik (1969) for the precise meaning of necessary and sufficient conditions in the present context).

*Proof.* We have to show that under the assumption of single-peaked preferences the social relation that is generated by the method of majority decision is an ordering, i.e. satisfies completeness and transitivity. For any $x, y \in X$, let $N(xR_iy)$ again be the number of people who find $x$ at least as good as $y$ and let $N(xP_iy)$ be the number of voters who strictly prefer $x$ to $y$. Clearly, $N(xR_iy) \geq N(xP_iy)$.

Completeness. For any $x, y \in X$, it is obvious that either $N(xR_iy) \geq N(yR_ix)$ or $N(yR_ix) \geq N(xR_iy)$. Under the method of majority decision, this, however, means that for any $x, y$ either $xRy$ or $yRx$, and this is the definition of completeness of a binary relation.

Transitivity. We have to show that $R$ is transitive. We assume that $zRy$ and $yRx$ and have to prove that $zRx$ where $x, y$ and $z$ are all distinct. Under the majority rule, $zRy$ and $yRx$ correspond to $N(zP_iy) \geq N(yP_iz)$ and $N(yP_ix) \geq N(xP_iy)$. With respect to betweenness, we have to consider three cases: (1) $B(x, y, z)$, (2) $B(x, z, y)$, (3) $B(y, x, z)$.

**Case 1:** $B(x, y, z)$.
By single-peakedness, $zR_iy$ implies $yP_ix$. Due to transitivity of the individual preference relation, we obtain $zP_ix$ so that $zR_iy$ implies $zP_ix$. Therefore, $N(zP_ix) \geq N(zR_iy) \geq N(zP_iy)$. From our supposition, we also have $N(zP_iy) \geq N(yP_iz)$.

From $[zR_iy \rightarrow zP_ix]$, we can infer that (not $zP_ix$) implies (not $zR_iy$), i.e. $yP_iz$. Therefore, (not $zP_ix$), i.e. $xR_iz$ implies $yP_iz$. Hence $N(yP_iz) \geq N(xR_iz) \geq N(xP_iz)$. Finally, from the three steps above, we obtain

$N(zP_ix) \geq N(zP_iy) \geq N(xP_iz)$, so that $zRx$ under the majority rule, as was to be shown.

**Case 2:** $B(x, z, y)$.
By single-peakedness, $xR_iz$ implies $zP_iy$ so that, together with transitivity, we obtain that $xR_iz$ implies $xP_iy$. Therefore, $N(xP_iy) \geq N(xR_iz)$. Since according to our supposition, $N(yP_ix) \geq N(xP_iy)$, $\frac{1}{2} \cdot |N| \geq N(xP_iy)$. Consequently, $\frac{1}{2} \cdot |N| \geq N(xR_iz)$. Since $N(xR_iz) \geq N(xP_iz)$, clearly $\frac{1}{2} \cdot |N| \geq N(xP_iz)$.

$N(zP_ix) = |N| - N(xR_iz)$. Since, as we have seen, $N(xR_iz) \leq \frac{1}{2} \cdot |N|$, $|N| - N(xR_iz) \geq |N| - \frac{1}{2} \cdot |N| = \frac{1}{2} \cdot |N|$. Therefore, $N(zP_ix) \geq \frac{1}{2} \cdot |N|$. Combining the last two steps, we obtain that $N(zP_ix) \geq N(xP_iz)$ so that, again, $zRx$ under the majority rule.

**Case 3:** $B(y, x, z)$.
We shall show that this case cannot occur under the supposition that $zRy$ and $yRx$ and under the hypothesis in the theorem that the number of voters is odd, an assumption that we have not yet used so far.

By single-peakedness, $yR_ix$ implies $xP_iz$ so that, using transitivity, we obtain that $yR_ix$ implies $yP_iz$. Therefore, $N(yP_iz) \geq N(yR_ix)$. But $zRy$ from our supposition so that $N(yP_iz) \leq \frac{1}{2} \cdot |N|$. Therefore, $N(yR_ix) \leq \frac{1}{2} \cdot |N|$. But, again, from our hypothesis $yRx$ so that $N(yR_ix) \geq \frac{1}{2} \cdot |N|$. Combining the last two results, we get $N(yR_ix) = \frac{1}{2} \cdot |N|$. This, however, implies that $\frac{1}{2} \cdot |N|$ must be integer valued. Then $|N|$ has to be even, contrary to the hypothesis in the theorem.

Therefore, in all situations in which it was possible to have $zRy$ and $yRx$, we could show that $zRx$. This proves the transitivity of $R$ and the proof is complete.

Three points before we continue. The mirror image of single-peakedness, sometimes called single-cavedness or single-troughedness, would lend itself to exactly the same result. A single trough would, for example, manifest itself in the preferences of three individuals who have in common a strong dislike for a particular location. However, their dislike concerns different locations. One of the three wants to live as far away as possible from a nuclear power plant (a), for the second person it is a huge shopping centre (b), for the third one it is an arterial road (c) that they most disprefer. Single-troughedness is depicted in figure 3.3.

The second point refers to the ordering along the horizontal line, an issue that was already briefly mentioned above.

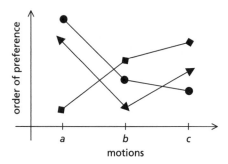

**Figure 3.3.**

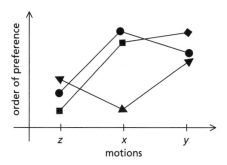

**Figure 3.4.**

The preference profile

$$xP_1yP_1z$$

$$yP_2zP_2x$$

$$yP_3xP_3z$$

can, for $B(z, x, y)$, be depicted as in figure 3.4.

The structure here looks like the structure in the case of the paradox of voting. However, a rearrangement of the alternatives along the horizontal line can either produce single-peakedness (viz. for $B(x, y, z)$) or single-troughedness (viz. for $B(y, z, x)$). Such a rearrangement would be of no help in the case of the paradox of voting. The structure of figure 3.2 would remain the same under all possible rearrangements.

The profile

$$wP_1yP_1zP_1x$$

$$zP_2xP_2yP_2w$$

$$yP_3zP_3xP_3w$$

looks 'rather wild' when you choose the strict ordering $xSy \land ySz \land zSw$ along the horizontal line but can be turned into a single-peaked structure for a different arrangement of alternatives along the line (which one?).

The profile

$$yP_1zP_1xP_1w$$

$$xP_2yP_2zP_2w$$

$$wP_3yP_3zP_3x$$

can for the four alternatives $x$, $y$, $z$ and $w$ neither be arranged in a single-peaked fashion nor in a single-troughed way. However, each of the triples within the quadruple can be depicted in a single-peaked way so that the Black–Arrow theorem applies: the method of majority decision generates a social ordering, since single-peakedness is satisfied for every triple of alternatives.

The third point refers to what, in the theory of voting, is known as Black's (1948) median voter theorem. This concept will be taken up again in chapter 5. The idea is very simple. If the voters' preference orderings can be depicted along a single dimension, the size of some public park, let's say, the equilibrium outcome according to the simple majority rule lies at the preference peak of the median voter. In figure 3.1 above, the voting outcome with three persons is 'medium'. More generally, if there are $n + 1$ voters, all of them showing single-peaked preferences and all of them in favour of a different most preferred size $s_i$ of the park, the voting equilibrium is given by the median value of the $s_i$'s. The median voter is characterized by the fact that $n/2$ of the voters want a smaller size and $n/2$ want a larger size. The median voter balances the diverging interests, so to speak.

## 3.3. **Other domain conditions: qualitative and quantitative**

We have seen above that both for single-peaked and for single-troughed individual preferences, the simple majority decision rule is an Arrovian social welfare function. Can this result be generalized even further? The answer was given by Sen (1966) with his concept of value-restricted preferences.

**Condition of value restriction.** In a triple $(x, y, z)$ there is some alternative, say $x$, such that all concerned individuals agree that it is not worst, or agree that it is not best, or agree that it is not in the middle, i.e. for all concerned voters,

$$\text{for all } i : xP_iy \text{ or } xP_iz \qquad \text{or}$$

$$\text{for all } i : yP_ix \text{ or } zP_ix \qquad \text{or}$$

$$\text{for all } i : [xP_iy \text{ and } xP_iz] \text{ or } [yP_ix \text{ and } zP_ix].$$

The resulting theorem then says

**Theorem 3.3 (A possibility theorem for value-restricted preferences).**   If the set of individual orderings satisfies for every triple of alternatives the condition of value-restricted preferences, the majority rule is a social welfare function, provided the number of concerned voters is odd.

The oddness requirement may seem to be an 'odd' demand. What happens when we drop this requirement? It can be shown that with an even number of concerned individuals, pairwise majority voting ensures that the social preference relation is quasi-transitive, i.e. the strict part of the preference is transitive. In such cases, there always exists at least one best element, an element that according to the majority rule beats or ties every other element in a pairwise comparison. In the voting literature, such an element is called a Condorcet winner, a candidate that is at least as good as every other candidate. We shall come back to this concept in Chapters 5 and 6. For many choices, it may be fully sufficient to guarantee the existence of such a Condorcet winner.

One could argue – this is now an aside – that a completely specified ordering over all alternatives may sometimes appear superfluous. One could even permit preference cycles 'down the line'. Imagine, for example, that in the case of the Condorcet paradox, described in section 3.1, all three individuals would have a unanimous strict preference for $w$ over $v$, and both alternatives would be unanimously preferred to $x, y$, and $z$. Then we would obtain a 'bottom cycle' but also, clearly, a best element ($w$). A 'top cycle' must be prevented from occurring.

Value restriction is a sufficient condition for the existence of a Condorcet or majority winner. It is not necessary. There are various other sufficient conditions under the majority rule. We will only pick one of them, Inada's (1969) so-called dichotomous preferences.

**Condition of dichotomous preferences.**   For all $i \in \{1, \ldots, n\}$, $R_i$ is transitive and for some distinct $a, b$ in $(x, y, z)$, $aI_ib$.

Note that the pair of alternatives between which the persons are required to be indifferent must not necessarily be the same for each individual.

Inada showed that for any number of individuals who all have dichotomous preferences over each triple of alternatives, the majority decision rule is a social welfare function in the sense of Arrow. For Inada's result, the oddness requirement is not at all required.

A common feature of the domain restrictions that we have discussed so far was that certain individual preferences were not allowed to occur at all (as in the case of Inada's condition just discussed) or were excluded in the presence of other preference relations. On the other hand, once a preference profile satisfies, say, single-peakedness, the existence of a Condorcet winner under the majority rule is given for any number of voters. There is no restriction in terms of numbers of individuals having a particular preference.

Let us denote conditions such as value restriction and dichotomous preferences as *qualitative* domain conditions. We now want to introduce just one *quantitative* condition, a restriction in terms of numbers, and point out a logical relationship between this condition and Inada's dichotomous preferences.

In order to do this, we go back to a profile that generates the Condorcet paradox under the majority decision rule, viz.

$$xP_1yP_1z$$
$$yP_2zP_2x$$
$$zP_3xP_3y.$$

For any ordered triple $(x, y, z)$ of alternatives, Saposnik (1975) denoted this preference structure as 'the clockwise cycle' of individual orderings. 'The counterclockwise cycle' of individual orderings then is

$$zP_4yP_4x$$
$$xP_5zP_5y$$
$$yP_6xP_6z.$$

Note that $xP_1yP_1z$ and $zP_4yP_4x$, for example, are 'inverse' to each other. Under simple majority voting, these two strict orderings alone would yield total social indifference, viz. $xIyIz$.

According to Saposnik, 'cyclical balance' of the voters' preference profile is given iff there is the same number of individual rankings constituting the clockwise cycle and the counterclockwise cycle, i.e. $n_1 + n_2 + n_3 = n_4 + n_5 + n_6$, where $n_i$, $i \in \{1, \ldots, 6\}$, stands for the number of persons having the $i$'th strict ordering.

Saposnik's result is

**Theorem 3.4 (A possibility result for cyclical balance).**  Under the majority decision rule the social preference relation is transitive if the individual preference relations are cyclically balanced.

The domain of cyclically balanced preferences may appear rather small but Saposnik observed that in his set-up the distribution of voters over the subset of orderings with at least one indifference has no effect on the issue of social transitivity. Consider, for example, the following profile: $n_1 = 2$ for $xP_1yP_1z$, $n_6 = 2$ for $yP_6xP_6z$, one individual has $yI_izP_ix$ and two persons have $zP_ixI_iy$. Then, clearly, cyclical balance is given, Saposnik's sufficient condition is satisfied and the social ordering reads: $yPxPz$. Now reduce $n_6$ by one voter to $n_6 = 1$. Cyclical balance is no longer fulfilled. The social relations are: $xIy$, $xIz$ and $yPz$. The social relation is not 'fully' transitive any more, i.e. transitivity of the indifference relation is no longer obtained.

What is the 'mystery' around this point? Gaertner and Heinecke (1977) have proved that Saposnik's condition of cyclical balance is a rather unique property in the sense that if and only if cyclical balance is satisfied, individual orderings with at least one indifference over each triple of alternatives can be added or taken away from a profile arbitrarily without affecting the transitivity of $R$. Why is this so? Note that in the example above with $n_6 = 1$, we no longer obtained the full transitivity of $R$, but we would achieve transitivity again if we dropped, for example, the dichotomous preference relation $yI_izP_ix$.

In order to answer the question just posed, we come back to our earlier observation that $xP_1yP_1z$ from the clockwise cycle and $zP_4yP_4x$ from the counterclockwise cycle, under the majority rule, yield $xIyIz$ for $n_1 = n_4$. We denoted these two orderings as inverse to each other. Furthermore, pairs of non-inverse strict orderings belonging to different cycles can be transformed into dichotomous preference relations. The pair $yP_2zP_2x$ and $yP_6xP_6z$ with $n_2 = n_6$, for example, can be transformed into the dichotomous ranking $yPxIz$ and in order to preserve the underlying majorities between the pairs of alternatives, $yPxIz$ would have to be counted $(2 \cdot n_6)$ times.

The point now is that in cases where cyclical balance is satisfied, *all* strict preference orderings can either be deleted directly (or turned into complete social indifference) since they are inverse to each other or can eventually be transformed into dichotomous rankings, as in the case above. Thus, for a preference profile with a subset of strict individual preference relations that satisfy Saposnik's cyclical balance, and an additional arbitrary number of dichotomous preferences, we can be sure that after performing the transformations described above, we definitely arrive at a set of preferences that contains *only* dichotomous preferences. And for these, we know from Inada's theorem that the application of the simple majority rule yields a fully transitive social relation. Thus, we have the explanation of Saposnik's assertion that in the case of cyclical balance the number of individual rankings that are dichotomous has no bearing on the issue of social transitivity.

Our last observation on the simple majority rule. Recently, Maskin (1995) has come up with a characterization of simple majority voting that is different in perspective from May's seminal work. Maskin focuses on the widest domains of preferences on which the majority rule is defined, and he offers a defence of this voting rule in terms of a criterion that he calls 'robustness'.

For which restricted domains of individual preferences does a voting scheme such as the majority rule become an Arrow social welfare function? For the case of individual weak orderings, we have seen that there is not a unique answer. The situation becomes simpler when we require that all individual orderings be strict and that, in addition, there be an odd number of voters. Then Sen's (1966) value restriction condition is necessary and sufficient for the method of majority decision to be an Arrow social welfare function. Maskin has shown the following.

Let $g$ be any social aggregation function that is anonymous, neutral and positively responsive (and therefore fulfils the Pareto condition). Given the two requirements of oddness and strict individual preferences, if $g$ is transitive on a particular domain, then simple majority rule is transitive on this domain as well. Moreover, unless $g$ itself is the simple majority rule, there exists a domain of individual orderings on which the majority rule is transitive but $g$ is not. Among all aggregation rules that fulfil the properties given above, simple majority rule is the only one that is transitive on the widest class of domains. In this sense the majority rule is robust.

## 3.4. **A short summary**

The importance of Arrow's impossibility theorem is its generality. Therefore, it is essential to know what is possible and what the requirements for such possibilities are. The majority rule is a prominent and often used decision rule in public voting. Many people will agree that it reflects democratic values, at least to a certain degree. The majority rule treats persons and alternatives equally and it is responsive to changes in the underlying preference profile. Of course, minorities may consider this rule unfair under particular circumstances.

Unfortunately, simple majority voting has problems with certain preference profiles. The so-called Condorcet paradox is the by far best-known example for this. Preference cycles are a 'disaster' for decision makers. Single-peakedness is a qualitative property which imposes a particular 'regularity' on each individual's ordering and by doing so also on the preference profile of society. Single-peakedness not only avoids the 'cyclic dilemma', it also lends itself to a straightforward interpretation. It seems to be a condition that people satisfy under various circumstances. There is a generalization of this requirement, viz. Sen's value restriction, which is still quite intuitive, as well as various other properties which, unfortunately, are less easy to interpret. We therefore left them out in our presentation. The property of single-peakedness will reappear in other chapters, again to yield positive results. It is interesting to see that there are logical relationships between qualitative conditions on preferences and certain quantitative requirements on profiles.

## ☐ RECOMMENDED READING

Kelly, J. S. (1988). *Social Choice Theory. An Introduction,* chapters 1–3. Berlin, Heidelberg, New York: Springer-Verlag.

May, K. O. (1952). 'A Set of Independent Necessary and Sufficient Conditions for Simple Majority Decision'. *Econometrica,* 20: 680–84.

Sen, A. K. (1970b). *Collective Choice and Social Welfare,* chapter 10. San Francisco, Cambridge: Holden-Day.

Sen, A. K. and P. K. Pattanaik (1969). 'Necessary and Sufficient Conditions for Rational Choice under Majority Decision'. *Journal of Economic Theory,* 1: 178–202.


## ☐ HISTORICAL SOURCES

Arrow, K. J. (1951, 1963). *Social Choice and Individual Values* (2nd edn), chapters 5 and 7. New York: John Wiley.

Black, D. (1948). 'On the Rationale of Group Decision Making'. *The Journal of Political Economy,* 56: 23–34.

May, K. O. (1952). See above.


## ☐ MORE ADVANCED

Gaertner, W. (2001). *Domain Conditions in Social Choice Theory,* chapters 3 and 5. Cambridge: Cambridge University Press.

# 4 Individual rights

## 4.1. **Sen's impossibility of a Paretian liberal**

Chapter 2 has taught us that a set of rather mild-looking conditions imposed on an Arrovian social welfare function creates the dictatorship of one person. Whenever this individual prefers any $x$ over any $y$ from the set of alternatives $X$, society prefers $x$ over $y$ by necessity, and this holds for all pairs of alternatives from $X$ and for all profiles in the domain of the social welfare function. Arrow called such an individual a dictator, and most people will agree that a person with such wide-ranging power is unacceptable for a democratic society. The reader should remember that this dictatorial power refers to all-encompassing social alternatives. We do not want one person to decide whether or not our country goes to war, we do not want this person to decide all by himself whether the country pursues a policy that benefits a few and makes many citizens suffer nor do we want one single person to determine that our country execute a cultural revolution.

There are, however, good arguments for allowing citizens to exercise 'local decisiveness', i.e. be dictatorial with respect to narrowly defined spheres which are the citizens' private business. This idea can be found in J.S. Mill's *On Liberty* where the author speaks about a circle around every human being upon which nobody should trespass. We do not want the government to decide which religion we practise nor do we want a busybody to determine whether we read *Playboy* or not. It is a distinct feature of a democratic society that its members are free to exercise certain rights over private spheres. In other words, local decisiveness not only makes a lot of sense but it is also a vital characteristic of a liberal society.

Sen (1970a,b) was the first to model the exercise of individual rights within the social choice context and to derive what has become known as 'the impossibility of a Paretian liberal'. Let us assume that each individual $i \in N$ has a 'protected or recognized private sphere' $D_i$ consisting of at least one pair of personal alternatives over which this individual is decisive both ways in the social choice process, i.e. $(x, y) \in D_i$ iff $(y, x) \in D_i$ with $x \neq y$. $D_i$ is called symmetric in this case. And decisiveness means that whenever $(x, y) \in D_i$ and $xP_iy$, then $xPy$ and whenever $(y, x) \in D_i$ and $yP_ix$, then $yPx$ for society. Clearly, the alternatives in each pair should be distinct. Note that with the introduction of individual decisiveness, neutrality as defined in section 3.1 is no longer given.

Note that the present notation with respect to decisiveness is slightly different from that in Chapter 2 but the meaning is exactly the same. A rights system then is an assignment of ordered pairs of states to individuals, viz. an $n$-tuple $D = (D_1, D_2, \ldots, D_n) \in \Omega(n)$, where $\Omega(n)$ stands for the $n$-fold cartesian product of $\Omega$, the set of all non-empty subsets of $X \times X$. A short example may help to illustrate. Let us assume that $X = \{a, b, c, d\}$ and that there are only two individuals. Then a rights system $D = (D_1, D_2)$ for this two-person society could be such that $D_1 = ((a, b), (b, a))$ and $D_2 = ((c, d), (d, c))$. So individual 1 would possibly be decisive both ways over the pair $(a, b)$ and the same would hold for person 2 over the pair $(c, d)$. In this case, there would, for example, be no individual rights over the pairs $(b, c)$ and $(a, d)$.

In his original presentation of the 'liberal paradox', Sen (1970a) used the concept of a social decision function. This is a collective choice rule or social aggregation mechanism, the range of which is restricted to social preference relations that generate a choice function. The latter concept was introduced in chapter 1. The reader will remember that a necessary and sufficient condition for a choice function to be defined over a finite set $X$ is that the binary relation $R$ be reflexive, complete and acyclical over $X$.

Sen required the collective choice rule to satisfy the following three properties:

**Condition $U$ (Unrestricted domain).**  The domain of the collective choice rule includes every logically possible set of individual orderings on $X(\mathcal{E}' = \mathcal{E})$.

**Condition $P$ (Weak Pareto principle).**  For any $x, y$ in $X$, if every member of society strictly prefers $x$ to $y$, then $xPy$.

Note that conditions $U$ and $P$ have the same definition as in chapter 2.

**Condition $L$ (Liberalism).**  For each individual $i$, there is at least one pair of personal alternatives $(x, y) \in X$ such that the individual is decisive both ways in the social choice process. Therefore, $(x, y) \in D_i$ and $xP_iy$ imply $xPy$ and $(y, x) \in D_i$ and $yP_ix$ imply $yPx$ for society.

The reader should note that Sen never claimed that condition $L$ would adequately describe the multifaceted character of the concept of liberalism. Sen (1970a) wrote that this condition 'represents a value involving individual liberty that many people would subscribe to' (p. 153).

In order to strengthen his impossibility result, Sen weakened the condition of liberalism further. He required that the decisiveness over at least one pair of alternatives be given not to all members of society but to at least two individuals. Sen called this condition 'minimal liberalism' (condition $L^*$).

The result then is

**Theorem 4.1 (Sen's impossibility of a Paretian liberal (1970)).**  There is no social decision function that satisfies conditions $U$, $P$ and $L^*$.

*Proof.* The proof is very simple. We shall suppose that person $i$ is decisive over $(x, y)$ and person $j$ is decisive over $(z, w)$, i.e. $(x, y) \in D_i$ and $(z, w) \in D_j$. We shall assume that these two pairs have no element in common (the other cases are as easy to treat as this one). Let us suppose that $xP_iy$, $zP_jw$ and for all $k \in \{1, 2\}$ :   $wP_kx$ and $yP_kz$. From condition $L^*$, we obtain $xPy$ and $zPw$. From condition $P$, we get $wPx$ and $yPz$ so that we arrive at $xPy, yPz, zPw$ and $wPx$. This outcome clearly violates the property of acyclicity of the social preference relation so that no social decision function exists that fulfils conditions $P$ and $L^*$ under unrestricted domain.

Sen's own illustration of his impossibility theorem has won certain fame over the decades. His example, in contrast to the case in the proof above, contains only three alternatives, with some overlap in the decisiveness structure. There are three alternatives revolving around reading a copy of *Lady Chatterley's Lover* by D.H. Lawrence. Alternative $a$ says that Mr A, the prude, reads this copy. Alternative $b$ prescribes that Mr B, the lascivious, reads the book, and alternative $c$ specifies that neither A nor B studies the novel. Mr A prefers most that nobody reads the book, next that he reads the book and last that Mr B reads the novel. Therefore, $cP_AaP_Ab$. Mr B has the preference $aP_BbP_Bc$. There are no other individuals in this society.

Sen now assumes that $(c, a) \in D_A$ and $(b, c) \in D_B$. Sen writes that a liberal argument can be made for the case that given the choice between A reading the book and no one reading it, A's preference should be turned into a social preference. Likewise, B's preference should be made the social preference for the case between B reading the novel and nobody reading it. Therefore, we arrive at $cPa$ and $bPc$, and $aPb$ due to the Pareto principle. These preferences manifest a case of cyclicity of the social relation so that no social decision function exists.

Note that decisiveness in one direction only would have been enough to generate an impossibility result. From a conceptual point of view, however, decisiveness both ways is much closer to the idea that individuals have a certain degree of autonomy.

## 4.2. **Gibbard's theory of alienable rights**

Sen's negative result had a tremendous impact on the imagination of many researchers in social choice theory. How can this impossibility result be turned into a possibility theorem? It seems obvious that there are many ways to achieve this, among them the suggestions to introduce domain restrictions of individual preferences, to constrain the Pareto principle or to weaken the condition of liberalism. Of course, all three paths will successfully eliminate

Sen's negative result – at some price, however. As a matter of fact, a bit further on we shall briefly consider the idea to weaken the libertarian claim. We shall not elaborate on the suggestion to constrain the Pareto rule though Sen's *Lady Chatterley* story may be a good case against applying the Pareto principle 'automatically'.

For reasons below where we shall focus on choice functions and the existence of non-empty choice sets, we shall slightly redefine what it means for an individual to be decisive. We have said above that whenever $(x, y) \in D_i$ and $xP_iy$, then $xPy$ socially. We will now say that individual $i$ is decisive over the pair $(x, y)$, i.e. $(x, y) \in D_i$ and $xP_iy$, if $y$ will never be socially chosen when $x$ is available and $i$ strictly prefers $x$ to $y$. Kelly (1988) speaks of exclusionary power in this context. In other words, whenever $(x, y) \in D_i$ and $xP_iy$, then $y$ will not be an element of the choice set $C(S)$, the set of socially chosen states from $S$, where $S \in K$ denotes a set of implementable social states and $K$ stands for the family of all finite non-empty subsets of the set $X$ of social alternatives. Sen's original result would now assert that under conditions $U$, $P$, and $L^*$ (respectively $L$), the set of socially chosen states can be the empty set. In other words, a social decision function does not exist for all profiles $(R_1, \ldots, R_n)$.

In what follows, we wish to discuss Gibbard's (1974) theory of alienable rights. In this approach the libertarian claim of an individual is not *directly* constrained, i.e. made dependent on some feature within the individual's own preference ordering but it is shown that under well-defined conditions, a person may find it advantageous to forgo certain assigned rights. Thus, in the case of *Lady Chatterley's Lover*, prude Mr A may be willing to waive his right to $c$ over $a$, since given the unanimous preference for $a$ over $b$, Mr B's right to $b$ over $c$ will make it impossible for him to obtain $c$ anyway. By waiving his rights, he will be able to secure that $a$ is socially chosen and not $b$ which would be his worst outcome.

Let us motivate Gibbard's suggestion a bit more by presenting his own Angelina–Edwin case. Gibbard's starting point for this particular proposal to reconcile the exercise of individual rights with the Pareto principle is that 'there is a strong libertarian tradition of free contract, and on that tradition, a person's rights are his to use or bargain away as he sees fit' (1974, p. 397).

There are three persons, Angelina, Edwin and 'the judge'. Angelina would like to get married to Edwin but would settle for the judge who is happy with whatever she wants. Edwin would like to remain single but would rather marry Angelina than see her marry the judge. There are three alternatives: Edwin and Angelina get married ($x$); Angelina and the judge marry and Edwin remains single ($y$); both Edwin and Angelina (and, of course, the judge) remain single ($z$). Angelina has the preference $xP_AyP_Az$. Edwin has the ordering $zP_ExP_Ey$.

Gibbard argues that Angelina has a right to marry the judge instead of remaining single. So Angelina has a libertarian claim over the pair $(y, z)$. Edwin has the right to remain a bachelor rather than marry Angelina. So he has a claim over the pair $(z, x)$. And finally, Edwin and Angelina have a unanimous preference for $x$ over $y$. Thus, the combination of the weak Pareto principle and the two libertarian claims leads to a preference cycle, viz. $yPz$, $zPx$ and $xPy$.

In order to avoid Sen's impossibility result, the cycle has to be broken somewhere, but where? Gibbard argues that Edwin, of course, has the right to remain single, but he should think twice about exercising this right. 'He can bargain it away to keep Angelina from marrying the judge' (p. 398). Though Edwin prefers $z$ over $x$ and has the chance to avoid $x$ by exercising his right over $(z, x)$, Angelina has a right over $(y, z)$ and prefers $y$ to $z$. This, however, means that when Edwin exercises his right, at the end of the day he will see Angelina wedded to the judge. And this would be worse for Edwin (we apologize for this phrase) than arriving at state $x$. Therefore, it will be to Edwin's own advantage to waive his right over $(z, x)$ in favour of the Pareto preference $xPy$.

The idea behind this story is the source of Gibbard's general solution to which we now turn in detail. Let there be a rights system $D = (D_1, \ldots, D_n)$ and a finite set $S = \{x, y, \ldots\}$ of feasible alternatives. We define a subset $W_i(R|S)$ of the set of protected pairs $D_i$ for each individual $i$ – let us call it the 'waiver set' of person $i$ – by the following condition:

$(x, y) \in W_i(R|S)$ iff there exists a sequence $\{y^1, y^2, \ldots, y^\lambda\}$ of states in $S$ such that

1. $y^1 \neq y$
2. $y^\lambda = x$
3. $yR_iy^1$ and
4. $\forall t \in \{1, 2, \ldots, \lambda - 1\}$, at least one of the following holds:
   $\forall j \in \{1, \ldots, n\} : y^t P_j y^{t+1}$,
   $\exists k \in \{1, \ldots, n\}, k \neq i : (y^t, y^{t+1}) \in D_k$ and $y^t P_k y^{t+1}$.

Note that given the set of feasible alternatives, the decision to waive or not to waive one's right(s) strongly depends on the preferences of the other persons. With the help of the idea of a sequence of alternatives in $S$, Gibbard formulates the following libertarian claim.

**Condition GL (Gibbard's libertarian claim for alienable rights).** For every preference profile $(R_1, \ldots, R_n)$, every $S \in K$, every $i \in N$, and every pair $(x, y) \in X$, if $(x, y) \in D_i$ and $xP_iy$ and $(x, y) \notin W_i(R|S)$, and furthermore $x$ is in $S$, then $y$ is not an element of the choice set $C(S)$.

The following possibility result is then obtained.

**Theorem 4.2 (Gibbard's rights-waiving solution).** There exists a collective choice rule that satisfies conditions $U$, $P$ and $GL$.

We abstain from presenting a proof of this result. The basic idea should have become clear from the two illustrations above. The central role of the waiver set is to break a cycle whenever there is one. Gibbard's resolution scheme is quite mechanistic and places heavy demands on information holding and processing. The individual who has to decide whether to waive some right or not has to calculate sequences that comprise pairs of unanimous strict preferences and pairs over which other persons exercise their decisiveness. These sequences can be quite long. But Gibbard's scheme is effective, no doubt about that.

## 4.3. **Conditional and unconditional preferences**

We started this chapter by claiming that in a liberal society each person $i$ has a protected or recognized private sphere $D_i$ with at least one pair of personal alternatives over which this person is decisive. In the two illustrations by Sen and Gibbard, it was assumed that the spheres of the persons involved had exactly this property. In his paper from 1974, Gibbard was very formal when he specified the private spheres of the members of society. His idea was that social states can be decomposed into different components representing aspects within the recognized spheres of the individuals. More precisely, if $X_i$ stands for the set of feature alternatives $x_i$ of person $i$, the state space $X$ is given by the full cartesian product $X_1 \times \cdots \times X_n$, if the society considered comprises $n$ individuals. There could also be a set $X_0$ of public feature alternatives which would represent aspects outside the private spheres of the individuals, but in the sequel we shall omit this component for the sake of simplicity. A particular social state $x$ can then be written as $x = (x_1, \ldots, x_i, \ldots, x_n)$, where $x_i \in X_i$ for all $i$. Gibbard assumed that $|X_i| \geq 2$ for all $i \in \{1, \ldots, n\}$. Individual $i$'s recognized private sphere can then be identified as $D_i = \{(x, y)|x_k = y_k$ for $k \neq i$, and $x_i \neq y_i\}$. The elements of $D_i$ are called $i$-variants. They only differ with respect to the specification of $i$'s personal component.

Gibbard formulated the following libertarian claim which is much stronger than Sen's original condition of liberalism.

**Condition GL′.** For every individual $i$ and for all distinct social alternatives $x$ and $y$, if $x$ and $y$ differ only with respect to something in $i$'s recognized private sphere, then $i$ is decisive over $(x, y)$, i.e. if $xP_iy$ and $x$ is in $S$, $y$ is not chosen from $S$ [$y \notin C(S)$] and if $yP_ix$ and $y$ lies in $S$, $x \notin C(S)$.

Gibbard demands that person $i$ be decisive over every pair of $i$-variants within the private sphere. Sen required decisiveness for at least one pair of alternatives. For his own libertarian claim, Gibbard could show the following

**Theorem 4.3 (Gibbard's conditional preferences).**   There exists no collective choice rule that satisfies conditions $U$ and $GL′$.

*Proof.* Let us assume that there are two private features $b$ and $w$ that can be independently chosen by two individuals 1 and 2. We consider four states: $x = (bb)$, $y = (wb)$, $z = (bw)$, and $v = (ww)$, where in each tuple, the first (second) component refers to person 1(2). Thus $S = \{x, y, z, v\}$ and the private spheres of persons 1 and 2 are $D_1 = \{(x, y), (z, v)\}$ and $D_2 = \{(x, z), (y, v)\}$. The preferences of the two persons are assumed to be

|     |     |     |     |
|-----|-----|-----|-----|
| 1 : | *ww* | 2 : | *bw* |
|     | *bb* |     | *wb* |
|     | *bw* |     | *ww* |
|     | *wb* |     | *bb* |

According to condition $GL'$, person 1 eliminates alternatives $y$ and $z$ from the choice set $C(S)$. Person 2 eliminates alternatives $x$ and $v$ from the choice set so that $C(S) = \emptyset$.

A closer look at the preferences of the two persons reveals that both persons have so-called conditional preferences. Given that person 2 picks $w$, person 1 prefers component $w$ to feature $b$. Given that person 2 picks $b$, person 1 prefers $b$ to $w$. Person 1 can be called a conformist, person 2 then is a non-conformist. Imagine that persons 1 and 2 are two young ladies who are invited to a dinner party. Let us suppose that each of the two owns a black dress and a white dress. Person 1 prefers that they both wear the same colour, be it white or black. Person 2 prefers that they wear different colours. It is assumed that both women take their decision independently. There is no coordination (could there be one?).

Perhaps a possibility theorem for conditional preferences is too much to ask for. Gibbard examined so-called unconditional preferences next.

**Definition 4.1 (Unconditional preferences).** Individual $i$ has unconditional preferences with respect to his or her recognized private sphere $D_i$ if for all $(x, y) \in D_i$, whenever $xP_iy$, then $(x_i, z)P_i(y_i, z)$ for all $z$, where $(x_i, z)$ is short for $(z_1, \ldots, z_{i-1}, x_i, z_{i+1}, \ldots, z_n)$ and $(y_i, z)$ stands for $(z_1, \ldots, z_{i-1}, y_i, z_{i+1}, \ldots, z_n)$.

The vector $z$ comprises the personal features of all the other individuals in the society considered. Whenever person $i$ has manifested a strict preference for $x_i$ over $y_i$ for some constellation $z$, this strict preference is required to hold for any constellation of features of the other individuals. A preference profile that satisfies the property of unconditionality will be given in the proof of the next theorem.

Earlier on in this chapter, we mentioned that at some point we would discuss a weakening of the libertarian claim. Here is Gibbard's version.

**Condition GL″.** For every individual $i$ and for all distinct social alternatives $x$ and $y$, if $(x, y) \in D_i$ and $xP_iy$ and furthermore, individual $i$'s preferences are unconditional, then $[x \in S \rightarrow y \notin C(S)]$.

The reader should note that this is not a domain condition on preferences. It is a restriction on individual rights. The exercise of individual rights depends on the fulfilment of certain requirements within the individuals' preferences. Gibbard mentions that as long as the number of issues on which individuals are allowed to be decisive is as great as the number of individuals in the society, no consistency problem arises. However, the combination of condition $GL″$ and the weak Pareto rule yields another impossibility result.

**Theorem 4.4 (Gibbard's unconditional preferences).** There exists no collective choice rule that satisfies conditions $U, P$ and $GL″$.

*Proof.* We assume again that there are four social states: $x = (bb)$, $y = (wb)$, $z = (bw)$, and $v = (ww)$. Also, the private spheres are the same as before: $D_1 = \{(x, y), (z, v)\}$; $D_2 = \{(x, z), (y, v)\}$. According to condition $U$, we can admit the following preferences for persons 1 and 2.

$$
\begin{array}{llll}
1: & ww & 2: & bb \\
   & bw &    & bw \\
   & wb &    & wb \\
   & bb &    & ww
\end{array}
$$

The orderings of both individuals satisfy the property of unconditionality. Therefore, due to condition $GL″$, alternatives $z$ and $v$ are eliminated by person 2, $x$ and $z$ are eliminated by person 1 and the Pareto condition (appropriately redefined in terms of choices) prohibits the choice of $y$. Thus, $C(S) = \emptyset$.

## 4.4. Conditional and unconditional preferences again: matching pennies and the prisoners' dilemma

Let us have a second look at theorems 4.3 and 4.4, from a different perspective so to speak (see Gaertner (1993) for further details). In connection with the proof of theorem 4.3, we presented an illustration where two young ladies were, independent of each other, choosing their personal or private features, viz. $b$ or $w$. The four social states $x, y, z$ and $v$ obviously are the outcome of these independent choices. Given the conditional preferences of the two women used in the proof of theorem 4.3, we can depict this situation via the matrix in figure 4.1.

| 1 \ 2 | w | b |
|-------|------|------|
| w | 4 , 2 | 1 , 3 |
| b | 2 , 4 | 3 , 1 |

**Figure 4.1.**

The entries in the four cells of the matrix are meant to represent the ordinal preferences of the two women (no cardinality is involved here). The first number refers to person 1, the second number to person 2. The reader should check that the numbers in the cells match the rankings postulated in the proof of theorem 4.3. The matrix representation in figure 4.1 is well known from non-cooperative game theory. It depicts the 'matching pennies' case and it is common knowledge that no Nash equilibrium in pure strategies exists for such a situation.

Since this is a book on social choice and not on non-cooperative game theory, a few explanations may be in order at this point. We wish to define a game form (a) as a set $N$ of $n$ players; (b) a set $S_i$ of (pure) strategies for each player $i \in N$ with $s_i \in S_i$, and $s = (s_1, \ldots, s_n)$ as a vector of strategies with $s \in \prod_{j=1}^{n} S_j$; (c) a set $X$ of feasible outcomes; and (d) an outcome function $h$ which maps $\prod_j S_j$ into $X$ (exactly one outcome is specified for each element of $\prod_j S_j$). In the situation given by figure 4.1, there are four strategy vectors, viz. $(w, w), (w, b), (b, w)$ and $(b, b)$, and four outcome vectors, corresponding to these four strategy vectors. We define a strategy vector $\hat{s} = (\hat{s}_1, \ldots, \hat{s}_n)$ as a (non-cooperative) Nash equilibrium, if for each player $i$ with $s_i \in S_i$, the following holds: $h(\hat{s}) R_i h(\hat{s}_1, \ldots, \hat{s}_{i-1}, s_i, \hat{s}_{i+1}, \ldots, \hat{s}_n)$.

A Nash equilibrium represents a strategy vector where each and every player has given the best response to the strategies of all the other players so that there is a situation of simultaneous best responses. Obviously, in the 'matching pennies' game, at each cell in the matrix either player 1 or player 2 can do better by switching to the other strategy. This means that there is no Nash equilibrium in pure strategies. There is, however, a mixed-strategy equilibrium which is based on the idea that positive probabilities are attached to the pure strategies.

Obviously, the objectives of the conformist and the non-conformist do not match – there is no equilibrium strategy for the two 'players'. What does this mean within our context of social choices? The non-existence of an equilibrium point (in pure strategies) apparently translates into the Gibbardian result that the choice set is empty. But the 'game' that the two women play would have an outcome or result in real life, wouldn't it?

Let us now examine theorem 4.4 and the preference structure used in the proof. In this situation, we obtain the matrix in figure 4.2.

| 1 \ 2 | w | b |
|---|---|---|
| w | 4 , 1 | 2 , 2 |
| b | 3 , 3 | 1 , 4 |

**Figure 4.2.**

In this case where both persons display unconditional preferences, a dominant strategy Nash equilibrium exists. Person 1 prefers her personal feature $w$ to $b$ independently of whether person 2 chooses $w$ or $b$. And person 2 prefers her private aspect $b$ to $w$ independently of what person 1 does. Both persons obviously possess a dominant strategy which yields an equilibrium point (viz. $wb$ with the outcome vector $(2,2)$) that is Pareto inferior to the strategy combination $bw$ with its outcome $(3,3)$. This is the 'classical' structure of the prisoners' dilemma game. The inefficiency of the Nash equilibrium translates within the Gibbardian social choice context into a clash between condition $GL''$ and the Pareto condition with the result that, again, the choice set is empty. In this situation as well, there will be an outcome in real life. Don't you agree?

## 4.5. **The game form approach to rights**

On the following pages we wish to discuss whether Sen's conception of individual rights as well as Gibbard's stronger notion correspond to our intuitive idea of what it means for an individual to have and exercise a right. Remember that according to Sen's definition every individual (or at least two individuals) is (are) decisive over a pair of distinct social states as long as these states differ only with respect to some private aspect. Decisiveness over a pair $(x, y)$ for individual $i$ means that if $xP_iy$, then the social preference is $xPy$ or, formulated in terms of choices, if $xP_iy$, then $y$ will be eliminated from the choice set for society, i.e. $y \notin C(S)$. Do individuals really have the power to eliminate social states from further consideration? Except for some very special cases to which we will turn towards the end of this section, this exclusionary power does not correspond to our intuitive conception of what it means for an individual to have a right. Let us be more specific.

In Sen's as well as in Gibbard's formulation, individual rights are seen as restrictions on social choice. These constraints on social choice are linked to the individuals' preferences over some pairs of social states. Gaertner, Pattanaik and Suzumura (GPS for short) have proposed an alternative formulation of rights in terms of game forms. In their approach from 1992, individual rights are formulated by specifying the admissible strategies or actions of each player and the complete freedom of each player to pick any of the permissible strategies and the obligation not to choose a non-admissible strategy (for more details on this, see Fleurbaey and Gaertner (1996)). In the case of the two young ladies, choosing black or choosing white were both admissible strategies. There were no non-admissible strategies. Under the GPS proposal, the exercise of particular rights determines *particular features* of a social state.

An early forerunner of this idea was Nozick (1974) who argued that 'individual rights are co-possible; each person may exercise his rights as he chooses. The exercise of these rights fixes some features of the world. Within the constraints of these fixed features, a choice can be made by a social choice mechanism based on a social ordering, if there are any choices left to make!' (p. 166). Obviously, Nozick, unlike Sen, did not see individual rights linked to individual preferences as constraints on social choice. Under Nozick's conception, the individual's act of choice from among several available options fixes only some features of the social states. And it is this and not the individual's preferences over some pairs of social states that imposes a constraint on social choice.

We consider the following example. The reader will remember the conformist and the non-conformist from the proof of theorem 4.3. Each woman has two dresses, a white one and a black one. Both women are completely ignorant of each other's preferences, and when each woman makes her choice (either white or black), she has absolutely no clue as to what the other will do. We assume again that all the other aspects which shape a social state have already been determined. For simplicity reasons, we disregard these aspects altogether. The preference orderings of the conformist (person 1) and the non-conformist (person 2) then are as before:

$$
\begin{array}{llll}
1: & ww & 2: & bw \\
   & bb &    & wb \\
   & bw &    & ww \\
   & wb &    & bb
\end{array}
$$

According to Sen's condition of liberalism and the idea of an individual's recognized private sphere, at least one of the following cases (a) and (b) and also at least one of the cases (c) and (d) must be satisfied:

(a) $(ww, bw) \in D_1$ and $(bw, ww) \in D_1$;
(b) $(bb, wb) \in D_1$ and $(wb, bb) \in D_1$;

(c) $(bw, bb) \in D_2$ and $(bb, bw) \in D_2$;
(d) $(wb, ww) \in D_2$ and $(ww, wb) \in D_2$.

Given these personal spheres and given the potential decisiveness of the two women, Sen's formulation of individual rights as well as Gibbard's formulation run into several difficulties.

**Difficulty 1.** Suppose that case (a) holds. Let the two young ladies freely choose their dresses without knowing the other's preferences and her actual choice. GPS argue that given such ignorance, each woman may apply the 'maximin principle' (in this case, choosing that colour which avoids the worst outcome) and therefore, 1 picks $b$ and 2 chooses $w$. Clearly, this result is inconsistent with Sen's condition of liberalism and person 1's decisiveness over the pair $(ww, bw)$, for Sen's condition would declare $bw$ as socially dispreferred. In the choice function formulation, $bw$ would be eliminated from the set of chosen elements. Given that $bw$ is the strategy combination of the two women's free choices of their respective dresses, 'very few people would be willing to say that there was a violation of the right of any individual' (1992, p. 165) to choose her dress. And GPS go on saying that 'the fact that each individual is free to choose... without any external constraint seems to capture the entire intuitive content of our conception of the right under consideration' (p. 165).

The inconsistency that we have just derived would also hold for cases (b), (c) and (d). We would only have to change the individuals' preference orderings and then use the hypothesis of maximin behaviour in a similar way as above. Since Sen's formulation of rights demands that at least two individuals be decisive over at least one pair, there will necessarily be a violation of Sen-type rights even though, from our intuitive point of view, no individual's right has been infringed. Maximin behaviour makes a lot of sense in the situation considered, but other choice rules (maximax behaviour of a risk-prone individual, for example) would have generated the same kind of inconsistency if we had modified the individual orderings appropriately.

**Difficulty 2.** What happens when we allow a person to be decisive over both pairs? Sen requires decisiveness over at least one pair, so decisiveness over both pairs is not excluded by him. Gibbard's condition $GL'$ demands decisiveness over every pair of $i$-variants. This type of power leads to an inconsistency that clashes even more with our intuition.

Take person 1 and suppose that she is decisive both over the pair $(ww, bw)$ and the pair $(bb, wb)$. Given her preferences as stated above, person 1 would be able to eliminate strategy combination $bw$ as well as $wb$. But this is rather strange. In the current situation where each of the two women is choosing either a white dress or a black dress, not knowing what the other person will do, person 1, under our intuitive conception, can either choose white or black. By picking *w*, person 1 can secure that the strategy combinations *bb* and *bw* will be excluded. By choosing *b*, she can make sure that the strategy combinations *ww* and *wb* will be eliminated. But person 1 has no power to ensure that *bw* and *wb* will be excluded. How on earth could she achieve this? Yet this is exactly the power that person 1 has under cases (a) and (b), given Sen's formulation of liberalism (slightly extended, of course, by appropriating two pairs of states) and given Gibbard's condition *GL'*.

To be more concrete, let us look at our example of the conformist and the non-conformist again. Gibbard's preference-based scheme of rights assignment is unintuitive. In most rights systems, there is no legal claim to match another person in terms of colour (or habit) nor is there a right to be different. By eliminating *bw* and *wb*, person 1 would exactly have this power. She would be able to exclude non-conformity. An analogous argument would have applied if we had allowed person 2 to be decisive over two pairs. In the latter case, person 2 would have had the power to exclude conformity, given her preferences. All this sounds extremely unintuitive.

**Difficulty 3.** What happens when we allow both persons to be decisive over two pairs each? It would be very unnatural indeed if we granted this possibility to one of the two persons but not to the other. In this situation where cases (a)–(d) are satisfied, the choice set will be empty under the stated preferences, as we know from Gibbard's theorem 4.3. On the other hand, there will, of course, be a social outcome after all. This, however, is tantamount to saying that the decisiveness of one of the two persons must have been broken inevitably. Again, there is a clash between our intuition and the Sen-Gibbard claim of rights-exercising. We do not know which outcome will come about eventually. Sure enough, it will be disappointing for one of the two women. But this is perfectly understandable given the preferences of the two young ladies. Actually, the game-theoretic analysis shows, as pointed out above, that there is no equilibrium in pure strategies in such a conflict of conformity vs. non-conformity. There is, however, a mixed-strategy equilibrium (where each of the two women chooses each of her two actions with non-zero probability), and this seems to make a lot of sense in the given conflict.

Let us reiterate that the main difference between the Sen–Gibbard approach and the GPS approach is that in the former the constraints on social choice are linked to the individuals' preferences over pairs of social states whereas in the latter the individuals merely choose aspects of social states that fall within their recognized private sphere. It is only in rather special cases that the choice of an aspect of a social state is linked to exactly one state. Let us assume that only two strategy combinations are available, say *ww* and *bw*. This means that person 1 has the choice between aspects $w$ and $b$ while person 2 has no choice at all. For her, only a white dress is available. Let us further assume that this information is also known to person 1. Then, if person 1 prefers $ww$ to $bw$, the choice of aspect $w$ automatically means that $bw$ has been eliminated. Therefore, in such a case there is a direct link between person 1's preference and a constraint on social choice. Person 1 has exclusionary power. This argument would also apply in a case where the second woman, let's say, has already picked her colour and woman 1 has been informed of this choice.

There is yet another constellation with a direct link between individual preferences and the elimination of complete social states. It is the case where both women have a dominant strategy. If person 1, let's say, always chooses $w$ irrespective of what person 2 does, and the latter always picks $b$ irrespective of what person 1 decides and if this information is common knowledge, three of the four strategy combinations will be directly excluded. For each person there is an 'as if' choice situation. Each woman is choosing her aspect as if the other woman had already fixed hers. Person 2 knows that since woman 1 will never choose $b$, strategy combinations $bw$ and $bb$ will not come about. Woman 1 knows that person 2 will never pick $w$ so that combinations $ww$ and, again, $bw$ will not occur. These inferences are perfectly plausible within the GPS formulation.

GPS emphasize that the game form formulation while corresponding to our intuition about individual rights does not heal the conflict between the exercise of those rights and the requirement of Pareto efficiency and that this problem appears to persist 'under virtually every plausible concept of individual rights that we can think of' (1992, p. 161). Particular domain conditions of the individuals' preferences would be able to achieve the compatibility of Pareto efficiency and the requirement of individual rights over private issues, given some notion of equilibrium, but these domain restrictions would, of course, need justification (see Gaertner (1993), and Gaertner and Krüger (1981)). Deb et al. (1997) have analysed the conflict between individual decisiveness over personal spheres and the Pareto principle in a general way, viz. for different notions of equilibria in games. Their first proposition, for example, states a necessary and sufficient condition for a dominant strategy equilibrium to have an outcome that is not Pareto efficient (see section 4.4 above).

## 4.6. **A short summary**

Not all societal issues should be resolved by using the majority rule or some variant of the latter. My decision in an $n$-member society to worship the Christian God as everybody else does in this community or to worship Buddha instead should entirely be taken by myself. There should be a certain degree of autonomy in decisions, at least as long as these decisions do no create severe negative externalities for others.

Can this issue of local decisiveness be dealt with within the Arrovian set-up of collective choice? Sen's answer to this question and that of many other scholars was in the affirmative. Sen clothed his idea of a certain degree of decisional autonomy in his condition of liberalism, added the requirements of Pareto efficiency and unrestricted domain of individuals' preferences, and came up with a surprise, an impossibility result. This negative finding stimulated many scholars, among them Sen himself, to look for a way out. Over the last three decades, there have been literally hundreds of serious contributions to this problem, ranging from restricting individual preferences over constraining the Pareto principle to modifying the condition of liberalism or autonomy.

Most of these proposals for resolution are interesting in themselves but do they conform to our intuitive idea of what it means for an individual to have *ad personam* rights over certain private matters and exercise them? In Sen's formulation, individual rights are viewed as restrictions on social choice. Gaertner et al. have proposed an alternative formulation of rights in terms of game forms. In this approach, individual rights are formulated by specifying the admissible strategies of each actor and the complete freedom of each actor to choose any of the permissible strategies and the obligation not to pick a non-admissible strategy. This formulation appears to be closer to what we observe in real life. It does not mean, however, that the game form analysis by itself will heal the conflict between the exercise of personal rights and the requirement of Pareto efficiency.

## RECOMMENDED READING

Gaertner, W., Pattanaik, P.K. and Suzumura, K. (1992). 'Individual Rights Revisited'. *Economica*, 59: 161–77.
Gibbard, A. (1974). 'A Pareto-Consistent Libertarian Claim'. *Journal of Economic Theory*, 7: 388–410.
Sen, A. K. (1970b). *Collective Choice and Social Welfare*, chapter 6. San Francisco, Cambridge: Holden-Day.

## HISTORICAL SOURCES

Nozick, R. (1974). *Anarchy, State and Utopia*, chapter 7. New York: Basic Books.
Sen, A.K. (1970a). 'The Impossibility of a Paretian Liberal'. *The Journal of Political Economy*, 78: 152–57.

☐ **MORE ADVANCED**

Deb, R., Pattanaik, P. K. and Razzolini, L. (1997). 'Game Forms, Rights, and the Efficiency of Social Outcomes'. *Journal of Economic Theory*, 72: 74–95.

Peleg, B. (1998). 'Effectivity Functions, Game Forms, Games, and Rights'. *Social Choice and Welfare*, 15: 67–80.

# 5 Manipulability

## 5.1. The underlying problem

Up to this chapter, it has always been assumed that individuals who were asked to state their preferences, reported them truthfully. This is a nice assumption, but does it hold in general, i.e. in reality? The reader may have a gut feeling that any system that can be manipulated is an unsatisfactory or even unacceptable scheme. The word 'manipulative' clearly has a negative connotation. A voting system that cannot be manipulated seems to be straightforward and transparent. To admit that there is strategic voting is tantamount to saying that there are people who spend energy and resources on manipulative activities. Since manipulative skills will not be spread evenly across the population, some agents may gain certain advantages solely because of their special talents in these activities. Also, some agents (chairpersons, for example) may be in the position to alter the agenda, whereas others are not, and this can significantly affect the final outcome. One may find this undeserved and undesirable from a social (choice) perspective.

Dummett and Farquharson (1961, p. 34) assert in a rather prosaic way that 'we cannot assume that each voter's actual strategy will be determined uniquely by his preference scale. This would be to assume that every voter votes 'sincerely', whereas it seems unlikely that there is any voting procedure in which it can never be advantageous for any voter to vote 'strategically', i.e. non-sincerely'. Of course, in order to manipulate successfully, one has to have a clear picture of the preference orderings of the others. One could argue that since knowledge about individual preferences is an example of private information – each individual just knows his or her preferences, other people have hardly any information about them – the phenomenon of strategic misrepresentation, though theoretically interesting, loses much of its relevance in practical situations. However, there are important cases where knowledge of each other's preferences may be rather complete. Think of decision-making in committees where voting typically occurs at the end of a longer debate that sufficiently revealed the preferences of the other committee members.

What does it mean for an agent to successfully manipulate? Let there be a set of choosable elements $S$ and a social choice function $C$ that for any $S' \subseteq S$ generates a unique non-empty choice or outcome (the latter is a simplification that makes 'life' much easier), given any preference profile of society. Consider two preference profiles $u$ and $\hat{u}$ that are $i$-variants, i.e. they only differ at the $i$th place (the reader will remember that we introduced this notion in the previous chapter):

$$u = (R_1, \ldots, R_{i-1}, R_i, R_{i+1}, \ldots, R_n)$$

$$\hat{u} = (R_1, \ldots, R_{i-1}, \hat{R}_i, R_{i+1}, \ldots, R_n).$$

Since, due to our assumption, choices are singleton sets, we can, without having to introduce additional notation, write, let's say, $C(S, \hat{u}) \, P_i \, C(S, u)$, meaning that agent $i$ strictly prefers the outcome under profile $\hat{u}$ to the outcome under $u$, given the feasible set $S$. We can now state that a choice function or choice rule $C$ is manipulable by agent $i$ at profile $u$, given set $S$, if there is an $i$-variant profile $\hat{u}$ such that $C(S, \hat{u}) \, P_i \, C(S, u)$, where $P_i$ is the strict part of agent $i$'s sincere preference ordering $R_i$ belonging to profile $u$. A choice rule is strategy-proof if for no preference profile and for no given set of alternatives some individual can improve upon the social outcome relative to his or her truthful ordering by misrepresenting the preferences.

Are there any strategy-proof voting rules in spite of Dummett's and Farquharson's conjecture? Yes, there are, but they are highly unattractive. Consider, for example, a choice rule that always picks $x \in S$ where $S$ comprises more than one option, whatever the preferences of the members of society are. Or consider a rule that for any set of alternatives $S \supset \{x, y\}$ only focuses on the majorities between $x$ and $y$, totally neglecting the votes with respect to the other alternatives in $S$. Both rules are strategy-proof, but they profoundly violate our intuition about how social choice rules should reflect the underlying preferences of the voters. The latter rule, for example, violates a requirement that in the social choice literature is called 'voters' sovereignty'. A choice mechanism should not a priori or by imposition exclude certain alternatives from being selected by society. On the other hand, Gibbard's (1974) theory of alienable rights is highly susceptible to manipulation. As we saw in section 4.2, Gibbard proposed a mechanism that makes persons alienate some of their rights under certain conditions. These conditions are brought about by particular preferences of *other* agents. It can be shown (Gaertner, 1986) that it may be in the interest of the latter, given their true preferences, to state preferences such that these conditions are met.

Dummett's and Farquharson's assertion above implicitly presupposed an unrestricted domain of preference profiles. If this condition is upheld and if, in addition, the range of the social aggregation function comprises at least three outcomes, we run into a general impossibility result that will be explained and discussed in the next section. In section 5.3 we shall ask whether there are relevant circumstances under which the structure of the alternatives suggests 'natural' restrictions on preference domains such that strategy-proof aggregation functions exist. Of course, in such situations, social choice rules that become available, should be acceptable, i.e. they should not violate some very basic properties (as in the two examples mentioned above).

Under unrestricted domain of preference profiles and given the fact that 'almost all social choice rules are highly manipulable' (Kelly, 1993), the question this author posed was whether there are ways to measure the degree of manipulability of certain aggregation rules. Kelly suggested that aggregation rule $f_1$, let's say, is more manipulable than another rule $f_2$ if there are more preference profiles at which $f_1$ is manipulable. Kelly showed that the Borda rank-order rule which we shall discuss in chapter 6, though having the fame of being highly manipulable, does not fare so badly after all in comparison with many other aggregation rules. This verdict gets even more positive when one realizes that some of the rules which are less manipulable are blatantly insensitive to changes in the underlying preferences of the voters.

Manipulability is not a phenomenon that was discovered only recently though; clearly, its deeper theoretical analysis started roughly 40 years ago and culminated in the Gibbard–Satterthwaite (1973, 1975) theorem to be presented in the next section. Farquharson (1961) began his book on voting by discussing a voting situation to be found in the *Letters of Pliny the Younger* (around AD 90). In a letter to Titus Aristo, Pliny described the fate of a Roman consul where it was uncertain whether the latter killed himself or whether he died by the hands of his freedmen, and furthermore, whether they killed him from a spirit of malice or of obedience. In the Roman senate, there were three opinions about what one should do with the freedmen: they should be sentenced to death, should be banished or should be acquitted. Those who were in favour of an entire acquittal were the most numerous so that others who favoured the death penalty were worried that total acquittal would win in pairwise comparison. Therefore, these senators desisted from their first preference and voted for banishment.

The incentive to falsely report one's own preferences does, in general, not only depend on the other persons' preferences but also on the voting method used and on the sequence of voting comparisons. Take the Latin square structure of Condorcet's paradox representing the preferences of three voters, use simple majority rule and assume that in the first round, there is a comparison between $x$ and $y$. At the second stage, the winner between $x$ and $y$ will be compared to $z$. If person 1 prefers $x$ to $y$ and $y$ to $z$, with the other two persons having $yPzPx$ and $zPxPy$, respectively, person 1 should report $yPxPz$ instead of her true preference ordering. She will then achieve $y$ as the social outcome. This is better for her than $z$ which would have been the result under honest reporting. Also this sequential aspect of strategic voting has been known for a long time.

The truthful revelation of agents' preferences not only plays an important role in voting situations but also in other cases where individuals interact strategically. We shall briefly discuss problems in the allocation of public and private goods. Pure public goods have the property of being non-excludable and non-rival. Examples are, among others, lighthouses, national defence and clean air. When I enjoy the clean air in a city centre, you can enjoy it as well, and to the same degree. Who should bear the costs for providing these goods? One answer is that those who enjoy these public goods should pay for them. We could tax them according to their willingness to pay. We could, for example, ask agents to reveal their marginal rates of substitution between public and private goods. But there is a problem. Would individuals reveal their willingness to pay for a particular public good in terms of some private good with which they will have to pay for the public good – an amount depending on their willingness to pay? When I have reliable information that many other people who also live in my city, urgently want a considerable improvement of the air in the city centre, I could always understate my true preferences without endangering the realization of this environmental measure.

Clarke (1971), Groves (1973), and others have come up with very clever demand revealing mechanisms which have the characteristic that truth telling becomes a dominant strategy. However, a restricted domain of quasi-linear preferences (the reader will remember these from the microeconomics and public finance classes) is required for such positive results. Some of the first proposals used the idea of side payments that individuals receive when a certain public good is provided. Actually, the side payments for each agent were equal to the aggregate bids or values that the other agents declared. Unfortunately, this method, though it induces individuals to reveal their true preferences, can become very costly. Refinements were designed where the side payments were considerably reduced, but not to zero, unfortunately. In these proposals, agents never receive a positive side payment. Agents are taxed if their individual bid changes the social decision, either in the sense of inducing a public good to be provided or exactly the opposite of this. In other words, an individual is required to pay for the harm or externality that is imposed on the other agents' welfare by his or her own bid. Such a design has sometimes been called a pivotal mechanism.

In a broader analysis of informationally decentralized and 'incentive-compatible' processes, Hurwicz (1972) showed that the Walrasian mechanism for the allocation of private goods is not immune to strategic manipulability either. Hurwicz was primarily interested in truthful revelation in connection with non-cooperative Nash equilibria, but this should not bother us too much. Consider the following simple pure exchange situation with two agents and two commodities. Let each person $i \in \{1, 2\}$ have the same true Cobb–Douglas utility function $u^i = x_1^i \cdot x_2^i$. Assume that person 1 has one unit of the second commodity as her initial endowment, while person 2 owns one unit of the first commodity at the outset. The reader knows from the undergraduate microeconomics course that in this situation, the competitive allocation à la Walras is in the centre of the Edgeworth box which is a square in the given

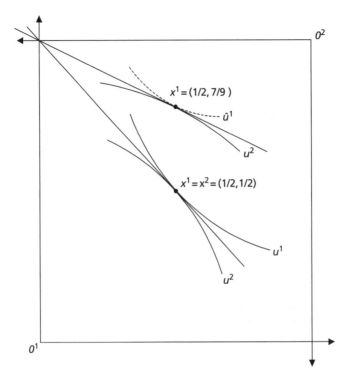

$$x^1 = (1/2, 7/9)$$

$$\hat{u}^1$$

$$u^2$$

$$x^1 = x^2 = (1/2, 1/2)$$

$$u^1$$

$$u^2$$

$$0^2$$

$$0^1$$

**Figure 5.1.**

situation. Both persons receive half of each of the two commodities. The equilibrium price ratio $p_1/p_2$ is equal to one.

Hurwicz demonstrated that it will be advantageous for the first agent to announce a fictitious utility function instead of the true one, given the truthful utility function of the second agent. If person 1 announces $\hat{u}^1 = x_2^1 - (1 + x_1^1)^{-1}$ instead of the true function, a straightforward calculation shows that person 1 receives the equilibrium allocation $(1/2, 7/9)$, person 2 gets $(1/2, 2/9)$, at the competitive price ratio $p_1/p_2 = 4/9$. Person 1 now achieves, according to her sincere preferences, a higher utility level than under an honest reporting of preferences (see figure 5.1). In other words, the Walrasian mechanism is not incentive-compatible or strategy-proof. This is bad news since as we said above, the personal preferences of traders are private information. Hurwicz argued that since no privacy-preserving mechanism can implement the Walrasian outcome, an agency should be created 'whose task will be to acquire information about the individual characteristics ... of the participants and to enforce price-taking behavior' (1972, p. 333).

In retrospect, Hurwicz's findings may be considered to have been the starting point for an important research programme under the heading of implementation theory and mechanism design that aims at designing strategy-proof mechanisms for different economic environments. We refer the interested reader to a longer survey by Jackson (2001).

## 5.2. **The Gibbard–Satterthwaite theorem**

In this section we wish to state and prove a fundamental result by Gibbard (1973) and Satterthwaite (1975) that strategy-proof and non-dictatorial allocation mechanisms do not exist in general. Meanwhile the reader can find quite a few proofs of this theorem. Gibbard's (1973) original proof establishes a close relation between strategy-proof social choice functions and Arrovian social welfare functions under the assumption of unrestricted domain. The main idea is that from every strategy-proof social choice function $h$ one can construct, via a binary relation on the alternatives that is shown to be transitive, a social welfare function. This function will satisfy the Pareto condition and independence of irrelevant alternatives over the range of $h$. Therefore, if this range comprises more than two alternatives, the social welfare function will be dictatorial, as we know from Arrow's theorem, and the same then holds for the social choice function from which the welfare function was derived.

We shall present Reny's (2001) proof which was inspired by ideas from both Geanakoplos (1996) and Muller and Satterthwaite (1977). Reny's proof closely follows his proof of Arrow's impossibility theorem which we presented in chapter 2 so that the reader gets the chance to see the similarities and differences between the two proofs. Before going into details, let us first introduce some notation and definitions.

A finite set of alternatives will be denoted by $S$. $\Sigma$ stands for the set of all strict linear orderings on $S$. Let there be $n$ individuals. A function $h: \Sigma^n \to S$ will be called a social choice function. A member of $\Sigma^n$ is called a profile of linear orderings with its $i$th component being individual $i$'s strict ranking that we shall denote by $P_i$. The function $h$ is onto or surjective, if every element of $S$ will be chosen for some profile.

A social choice function $h: \Sigma^n \to S$ is

- *Pareto efficient* if whenever alternative $a$ is at the top of every individual $i$'s ordering $P_i$, then $h(P_1, \ldots, P_n) = a$;
- *monotonic* if whenever $h(P_1, \ldots, P_n) = a$ and for every individual $i$ and every alternative $b$ the ordering $P'_i$ ranks $a$ above $b$ if $P_i$ does, then $h(P'_1, \ldots, P'_n) = a$;
- *dictatorial* if there exists an individual $i$ such that $h(P_1, \ldots, P_n) = a$ if and only if $a$ is at the top of $i$'s ordering $P_i$.

The reader will realize that Pareto efficiency and the concept of dictator-ship – though considerably weaker here – correspond to the requirements in Arrow's theorem, reformulated, of course, in terms of a choice function. The monotonicity condition represents a very weak form of responsiveness. Its role will become clear in the proof.

We now state the following variant of the Gibbard–Satterthwaite theorem.

**Theorem 5.1.** Let $h$ be a social choice function defined on an unrestric-ted domain of strict linear preferences. If the range of $h$ contains at least three alternatives and $h: \Sigma^n \rightarrow S$ is onto and strategy-proof, then $h$ is dictatorial.

*Proof.* The proof is split into two parts. We begin with part (a).

**Result (a).** If there are at least three alternatives and if the social choice function $h: \Sigma^n \rightarrow S$ is Pareto efficient and monotonic, then $h$ is dictatorial.

In step 1, we consider any two distinct alternatives $a, b \in S$ and a profile of strict rankings in which $a$ is ranked highest and $b$ is ranked lowest by every individual $i \in \{1, \ldots, n\}$. Pareto efficiency implies that the social choice for this profile is $a$.

We now change individual 1's ordering by raising $b$ one position at a time. Due to monotonicity, the social choice is still equal to $a$ as long as $b$ is below $a$ in 1's ordering. But when $b$ finally rises above $a$ and, therefore, is at the top of 1's ranking, monotonicity implies that the social choice either switches to $b$ or remains equal to $a$. If the latter holds, raise $b$ in individual 2's ordering until it reaches the top, then do the same for the third, fourth, . . . individual ranking, until for some individual $m$, the social choice does change from $a$ to $b$, when $b$ has risen above $a$ in $m$'s ordering. We know that there must be such an individual $m$, because alternative $b$ will 'in the end' be at the top of every individual's ranking and then, by Pareto efficiency as defined above, the social choice will definitely be alternative $b$. Figures 5.2 and 5.3 show the situation just before and just after $b$ was raised to the top of individual $m$'s strict ordering $P_m$.

| $P_1$ | $\ldots$ | $P_{m-1}$ | $P_m$ | $P_{m+1}$ | $\ldots$ | $P_n$ | social choice |
|---|---|---|---|---|---|---|---|
| $b$ | $\ldots$ | $b$ | $a$ | $a$ | $\ldots$ | $a$ | $a$ |
| $a$ | | $a$ | $b$ | $\cdot$ | | $\cdot$ | |
| $\cdot$ | | $\cdot$ | $\cdot$ | $\cdot$ | | $\cdot$ | |
| $\cdot$ | | $\cdot$ | $\cdot$ | $\cdot$ | | $\cdot$ | |
| $\cdot$ | | $\cdot$ | $\cdot$ | $b$ | | $b$ | |

**Figure 5.2.**

| $P_1$ | | $P_{m-1}$ | $P_m$ | $P_{m+1}$ | | $P_n$ | social choice |
|---|---|---|---|---|---|---|---|
| $b$ | ... | $b$ | $b$ | $a$ | ... | $a$ | $b$ |
| $a$ | | $a$ | $a$ | . | | . | |
| . | | . | . | . | | . | |
| . | | . | . | . | | . | |
| . | | . | . | $b$ | | $b$ | |

**Figure 5.3.**

In step 2, we introduce the following changes into figures 5.2 and 5.3. We move alternative $a$ to the lowest position of individual $i$'s ranking for $i < m$ and move $a$ to the second lowest position in the rankings of persons $i > m$. This is depicted in figures 5.4 and 5.5.

| $P_1$ | | $P_{m-1}$ | $P_m$ | $P_{m+1}$ | | $P_n$ | social choice |
|---|---|---|---|---|---|---|---|
| $b$ | ... | $b$ | $a$ | . | ... | . | $a$ |
| . | | . | $b$ | . | | . | |
| . | | . | . | . | | . | |
| . | | . | . | $a$ | | $a$ | |
| $a$ | | $a$ | . | $b$ | | $b$ | |

**Figure 5.4.**

| $P_1$ | | $P_{m-1}$ | $P_m$ | $P_{m+1}$ | | $P_n$ | social choice |
|---|---|---|---|---|---|---|---|
| $b$ | ... | $b$ | $b$ | . | ... | . | $b$ |
| . | | . | $a$ | . | | . | |
| . | | . | . | . | | . | |
| . | | . | . | $a$ | | $a$ | |
| $a$ | | $a$ | . | $b$ | | $b$ | |

**Figure 5.5.**

What will be the effect of these changes? The answer is that there will be no effect at all on the social outcome. Why is this so? Note first that the social choice in figure 5.5 must be $b$ because the social choice in figure 5.3 is $b$. This is due to monotonicity and the fact that no person's ordering of $b$ versus any other alternative changes during the move from figure 5.3 to figure 5.5. Next note that the profiles of figures 5.4 and 5.5 are identical except for the ranking of person $m$. Therefore, since the outcome in figure 5.5 is $b$, the outcome in figure 5.4 must, by monotonicity, be either $a$ or $b$. But if the result in figure 5.4 were $b$, then, due to monotonicity, the same result would have to occur in figure 5.2. This, however, would lead to a contradiction since the social choice in figure 5.2 is $a$. Therefore, the result in figure 5.4 is $a$.

In step 3, we focus on any third alternative $c \in S$ which is distinct from $a$ and $b$. In figure 5.6 we now construct a profile where the ranking of $a$ versus any other alternative in any individual's ordering is not changed at all in relation to the situation in figure 5.4. In the latter situation, the outcome is $a$, as just argued. Therefore, by monotonicity, the result in figure 5.6 is also $a$.

| $P_1$ | ... | $P_{m-1}$ | $P_m$ | $P_{m+1}$ | ... | $P_n$ | social choice |
|---|---|---|---|---|---|---|---|
| . | ... | . | $a$ | . | ... | . | $a$ |
| . | | . | $c$ | . | | . | |
| $c$ | | $c$ | $b$ | $c$ | | $c$ | |
| $b$ | | $b$ | . | $a$ | | $a$ | |
| $a$ | | $a$ | . | $b$ | | $b$ | |

Figure 5.6.

In step 4, we modify the preference profile from figure 5.6 in the following way, and this is the only change: for individuals $i > m$, we reverse the ordering of alternatives $a$ and $b$. The outcome in figure 5.6 is $a$. The outcome in figure 5.7 will also be $a$, but we have to show that it cannot be either $b$ or $c$ or any other alternative $d$. Assume that it were $c$. Then, due to monotonicity, the outcome in figure 5.6 would also have to be $c$, but we know that in the latter situation, it is $a$. Can it be $b$? If the outcome in figure 5.7 were $b$, though alternative $c$ is ranked above $b$ in all individual orderings, then this result would continue to hold, due to monotonicity, even if $c$ were raised to the top of every individual's ranking. Then, however, we would get a contradiction with Pareto efficiency. Could the choice be anything different from $a$, $b$, or $c$? Suppose that in figure 5.7, the choice is $d$, different from $a$. In going from figure 5.7 to figure 5.6, $d$ does not fall in anyone's ordering below $a$ or $b$ or $c$, so by monotonicity, $d$ would have to be chosen in figure 5.6, a contradiction. Therefore, the social choice in figure 5.7 is $a$.

| $P_1$ | ... | $P_{m-1}$ | $P_m$ | $P_{m+1}$ | ... | $P_n$ | social choice |
|---|---|---|---|---|---|---|---|
| . | ... | . | $a$ | . | ... | . | $a$ |
| . | | . | $c$ | . | | . | |
| $c$ | | $c$ | $b$ | $c$ | | $c$ | |
| $b$ | | $b$ | . | $b$ | | $b$ | |
| $a$ | | $a$ | . | $a$ | | $a$ | |

Figure 5.7.

In the final step 5, we start from the situation in figure 5.7 and construct an arbitrary profile of orderings with $a$ at the top of person $m$'s ordering. Note that all these profiles have the characteristic that the ranking of $a$ versus any other alternative in any individual's ordering is nowhere reduced. Because of this, monotonicity yields the result that the social choice must be $a$ whenever $a$ is at the top of person $m$'s ranking. Therefore, person $m$ appears to be a dictator for alternative $a$. Since $a$ was chosen arbitrarily, it has been shown that for each alternative $a \in S$, there is a dictator for $a$. Can there be different dictators for different alternatives? Clearly not, since our social choice mapping produces a unique outcome for every set of alternatives. Therefore, only one person can dictate the social outcome. In other words, there is a single dictator for all alternatives.

**Result (b).** If $h: \Sigma^n \rightarrow S$ is strategy-proof and onto, then $h$ is Pareto efficient and monotonic.

Before we have a look at the proof of this part, let us explain two things. What does it mean in the present context that the social choice function $h$ is onto or surjective? It simply means that for each singleton set $S' \subseteq S$, there exists a profile $(P_1, \ldots, P_n)$ such that $h(P_1, \ldots, P_n) = S'$. This property, to which we referred earlier as voters' sovereignty, disallows that some $S' \subseteq S$ will never be chosen via $h$.

We have already defined what it means for a choice function to be strategy-proof. In the present context, using our current notation the social choice function $h: \Sigma^n \rightarrow S$ is strategy-proof if for every individual $i$, every profile $(P_1, \ldots, P_n) \in \Sigma^n$, and every $P_i' \in \Sigma$, $h(P_i', P_{-i}) \neq h(P_1, \ldots, P_n)$ implies that $h(P_1, \ldots, P_n)$ is ranked above $h(P_i', P_{-i})$ according to $P_i$, the honest strict preference of person $i$, where $P_{-i} = (P_1, \ldots, P_{i-1}, P_{i+1}, \ldots, P_n)$. Clearly, if $h(P_1, \ldots, P_n)$ were ranked below $h(P_i', P_{-i})$, there would be room for successful manipulation, given preference $P_i$. Also, of course, strategy-proofness requires that $h(P_i', P_{-i})$ is ranked above $h(P_1, \ldots, P_n)$ according to $P_i'$.

Now we turn to part (b) of the proof. Let us assume that $h(P_1, \ldots, P_n) = a$ and that for every alternative $b$, the ordering $P_i'$ ranks $a$ above $b$ when $P_i$ does. We have to show that $h(P_i', P_{-i}) = a$. Let us suppose to the contrary that $h(P_i', P_{-i}) = b \neq a$. Then strategy-proofness implies that $a = h(P_1, \ldots, P_n)$ is ranked above $h(P_i', P_{-i}) = b$ according to $P_i$ (since if not, there would be a case for profitable manipulation). But since the ranking of $a$ does not fall in the move to $P_i'$, it follows that $a = h(P_1, \ldots, P_n)$ must also be ranked above $b = h(P_i', P_{-i})$ according to $P_i'$. This, however, is in contradiction with strategy-proofness (for it would be profitable for person $i$ to switch from $P_i'$ to $P_i$ and then reach $a$). Therefore, $h(P_i', P_{-i}) = a = h(P_1, \ldots, P_n)$.

Suppose next that $h(P_1, \ldots, P_n) = a$ and that for every person $i$ and every alternative $b$, the ordering $P_i'$ ranks $a$ above $b$ whenever $P_i$ does. When we now move from $(P_1, \ldots, P_n)$ to $(P_1', \ldots, P_n')$ by changing the ordering of each person $i$ from $P_i$ to $P_i'$ one at a time, we must obtain $h(P_1', \ldots, P_n') = h(P_1, \ldots, P_n)$, because in the previous step it was shown that the social outcome must remain unchanged for every such change. Therefore, $h$ is monotonic.

Choose $a \in S$. Because the mapping $h$ is surjective or onto, there is some profile $(P_1, \ldots, P_n) \in \Sigma^n$ such that $h(P_1, \ldots, P_n) = a$. Due to monotonicity, the social choice remains equal to $a$ when $a$ is raised to the top of every individual's ordering. And because of monotonicity, the social choice must remain $a$ independently of how the alternatives below $a$ are ranked by each individual. This, however, means that whenever $a$ is at the top of every person's ordering, the social outcome is $a$. Since $a$ was arbitrarily chosen, it is shown that $h$ is Pareto efficient.

Let us now string things together. Result (b) says that if $h$ is strategy-proof and surjective, then $h$ satisfies Pareto-efficiency and monotonicity. Result (a) has shown that with the latter two properties, $h$ is dictatorial. Therefore, results (a) and (b) together prove Theorem 5.1, the stated variant of the Gibbard–Satterthwaite impossibility result. In the following section, we shall explore under what restrictions on preference domains, reasonable social choice rules exist that are immune to strategic misrepresentation.

## 5.3. **Strategy-proofness and restricted domains**

Let us come back to Chapter 3 where we saw, among other things, that if there is an odd number of concerned voters and if all voters have single-peaked preferences over each triple of alternatives, the rule of simple majority decision is a social welfare function for any number of alternatives (theorem 3.2). We also saw that if oddness of the number of concerned voters is not satisfied, a Condorcet (majority) winner exists, a candidate that is at least as good as every other candidate in pairwise choice. Of course, if oddness is fulfilled, the Condorcet winner will be unique.

Let us now assume that there is a unique Condorcet winner generated by the majority rule. Then this voting rule is strategy-proof. Why is this? If $x$, let's say, is a unique Condorcet winner, $x$ has a strict majority over all other alternatives. Then it is not possible that there exists a coalition of one or several voters who prefer some $y$ to $x$ and bring about $y$. For a coalition of one person, this is immediately evident. If a coalition of several voters brings about $y$, some persons who voted for $x$, must now vote for $y$, if $y$ becomes a Condorcet winner. But this would be against the own interest of these voters. Therefore, it is not possible that there will be a coalition that brings about $y$ and thereby makes every member of the coalition better off. This was clearly seen by Dummett and Farquharson already in 1961; they talked about 'stability' of a voting situation.

We stated above that under a single-peaked domain, simple majority voting leads to a social ordering if the number of voters is odd. The (then unique) Condorcet winner is the most preferred alternative in this ordering. Moulin (1988, p. 264) showed that this unique Condorcet winner is the median peak of the individual orderings. This is easily demonstrated as well but before going on, the reader may want to revert to the end of section 3.2 where we introduced the notion of a median voter.

Denote by $a_i$ the peak of agent $i$'s single-peaked preferences and arrange the $n$ individuals by increasing peaks (think of a location problem in terms of distance, for example), along the given ordering of the alternatives. We then obtain $a_1 \leq a_2 \leq \ldots \leq a_n$. Since $n$ is odd, the number $m = \frac{1}{2}(n + 1)$ is an integer and $a_m$ is the median peak. Clearly, the voters whose peak is not smaller than $a_m$ form a strict majority (for $n = 9$, for example, $m = 5$, and persons with peaks $a_5, a_6, \ldots, a_9$ form a strict majority), and the same holds true for those voters whose peaks are not greater than $a_m$. Moulin calls them 'the rightists' and 'the leftists', respectively. Agent $m$ belongs to both groups. When outcome $a_m$ is confronted with a larger outcome (peak) $a$, i.e. $a_m < a$, the leftist majority (viz. those with peaks $a_1, a_2, \ldots a_5$) support $a_m$ against $a$, due to their single-peaked preferences. An analogous argument holds, when $a_m$ is opposed to a smaller outcome. This shows that the median peak represents the unique Condorcet winner. When there is an even number of voters, we no longer obtain a unique or strict Condorcet winner. However, there is no other outcome that will overrule the Condorcet winners by a strict majority.

Let us illustrate the foregoing discussion by means of a concrete example. We assume that there is the following profile of single-peaked strict preferences, graphically depicted in figure 5.8 (the preferences are to be read from left to

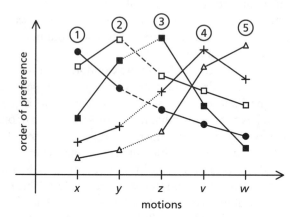

**Figure 5.8.**

right – we have omitted the symbol $P$ for strict preference):

$$1: \quad xyzvw$$
$$2: \quad yxzvw$$
$$3: \quad zyxvw$$
$$4: \quad vwzyx$$
$$5: \quad wvzyx$$

According to simple majority rule, the social ordering is $zyxvw$. The unique Condorcet winner is alternative $z$.

Let us assume that there is a coalition that brings about $y$ as the Condorcet winner. This coalition will, of course, comprise persons 1 and 2 and is in need of a third agent. If person 4 or person 5 'strategically' voted for $y$ against $z$, the coalition would indeed bring about $y$ as the Condorcet winner but persons 4 and 5 would be worse off in terms of their sincere preferences. Why should one of them join this coalition?

Outcome $z$, the unique Condorcet winner, is the median peak. In a comparison with outcome $y$, for example, a strict majority of persons 3–5 'defends' $z$ against $y$ (the single-peaked structure of the preferences shows why the word 'defend' is not totally inappropriate). An analogous argument holds for a vote between $z$ and $v$, viz. persons 1–3 would vote against $v$. None of the alternatives obtains a majority against $z$.

Over the domain of single-peaked preferences, there are various other rules which are strategy-proof or non-manipulable. Consider the leftist rule (Moulin, 1988) where each person reports her own peak, and the smallest peak with respect to the given ordering of the alternatives is chosen. In figure 5.9 where alternatives are arranged in increasing magnitude from left to right, would persons 1 or 2 or 3 or 4 report a lower peak than the true

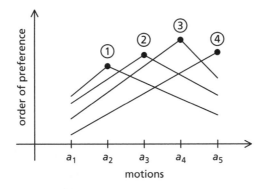

**Figure 5.9.**

one? Single-peakedness shows that this would be against their own interest. To pretend to have a peak at $a_1$ would be worse for all, to announce to have a peak at $a_2$ would be worse for persons 2–4, etc. A rightist rule would have the same properties.

Another strategy-proof social choice rule can be found in Barberà (2001). Assume that a finite number of alternatives lies in an interval $[a, b]$ = $\{a, a+1, \ldots, b\}$. Furthermore, individuals have single-peaked preferences over the alternatives in this interval. There are two individuals. An alternative $p$ in interval $[a, b]$ is fixed. The individuals are asked to vote for their most preferred alternative. The outcome is the median of $p$ and the two most preferred options. The median is uniquely defined since there is an odd number of values, viz. the best options of agents 1 and 2 and the fixed value $p$. The latter value is called a 'phantom'.

Moulin (1980) characterized the class of all strategy-proof voting rules in the framework of single-peaked preferences. This set of rules can be viewed as the class of generalized Condorcet winners. We have seen above that in the context of Condorcet winners, the individual peaks (their best alternatives) are what counts. Therefore, in Moulin's approach, each agent's message is reduced to announcing the peak of the respective individual ordering. The class of generalized Condorcet winners is as follows. Given $n$ voters, $n - 1$ outcomes specifying the peaks of some $n - 1$ phantom voters are arbitrarily fixed. Then every genuine voter is asked to cast a vote for his or her peak alternative. To these $n$ votes, the $n - 1$ peaks of the phantom voters are added. The outcome is the overall Condorcet winner from the $2n - 1$ votes. Notice that a unique result is obtained since $2n - 1$ is an odd number. This method can be called a generalized median voter scheme. It is strategy-proof among the real voters. Moulin shows that it is also anonymous and efficient in the sense of selecting a Pareto optimal alternative.

**Theorem 5.2 (The class of generalized Condorcet winners).** For all profiles of single-peaked preferences, the generalized median voter scheme is anonymous, efficient and strategy-proof.

Since the proof of this result is rather lengthy, it will not be given here. A natural question to ask is what the meaning and role of the $n - 1$ phantom voters is. Notice first that a unanimous vote of the $n$ real agents can always override the voting power of the phantoms.

Let us imagine that there is a legislative body of $n$ representatives which is cautious in the sense that it keeps records of $n - 1$ votes on various issues that concerned the previous legislative body. Whenever there is a new round of decision-making, it will, for each issue on the agenda, take the $n - 1$ votes of the previous body on this issue (if they exist) and add these to the current $n$ votes. An extreme case is the situation where the previous votes were concentrated in one point (peak) on the interval of ordered alternatives. Then one agent from the new body can align with these unanimous votes and out-vote all the other members of the current body. If the previous body was unanimously leftist (rightist), one left-(right-)wing person can successfully restore the previous situation. 'Normally', the $n - 1$ phantom votes will be spread over the whole interval of options. In this way, they will act as arbitrators.

Up to this point, it was assumed that both the true preferences of the agents and their professed preferences belong to the domain of single-peaked orderings. Zeckhauser (1973) had conjectured that single-peakedness of the true or sincere individual preferences alone would be sufficient to eliminate any incentive for a voter to misrepresent his or her preferences, whenever simple majority decision is used as the aggregation rule. Unfortunately, this conjecture is false (see Blin and Satterthwaite (1976) and Pattanaik (1976)). In order to secure strategy-proofness, it is neither sufficient that the sincere preferences are single-peaked and the professed preferences, the cast ballots, are unrestricted, nor it is enough that the cast ballots are single-peaked and the sincere preferences are unrestricted. In other words, and this is what was assumed in the results by Dummett and Farquharson, Moulin and others, both profiles have to satisfy the property of single-peakedness. Let us explain this in more detail.

Consider again our example from above with single-peaked preferences over the set of alternatives $\{x, y, z, v, w\}$. Assume that person 1 announces the ordering $xyvzw$ instead of $xyzvw$. Under the simple majority rule, the insincere ordering of agent 1 turns the original profile into a non-single-peaked profile and generates, together with the other orderings, a 'top cycle', comprising $x, y, z$ and $v$. Only if person 1 is utterly pessimistic or extremely risk-averse, believing that a random mechanism applied to the elements in the cycle will 'automatically' yield the worst outcome for her, will this agent abstain from misrepresenting her preference. Otherwise, she has a chance to obtain $x$ or $y$ which are better for her than the outcome under sincere preferences. The examples that Blin and Satterthwaite present in relation to Zeckhauser's conjecture are similar to the above example in the sense that a voting cycle occurs that has to be resolved 'some way'. Blin and Satterthwaite apply the Borda count which will be discussed in the next chapter. Pattanaik's counter-examples to the conjecture are somewhat different. In his examples, the aggregation function produces socially indifferent alternatives, and he proposes that whenever this occurs, the agents follow the maximin rule, an extremely risk-averse behavioural rule that we already employed in section 4.5.

Pattanaik showed something else. He proved that if the social preference relation, generated by a binary aggregation rule, is transitive in its strict part and yields a unique outcome for the sincere situation, then strategy-proofness or stability of the aggregation function is given. No coalition of voters will be able to bring about a more preferred unique outcome by misrepresenting its preferences. This result, however, does not carry over to cases where social outcomes both under sincere and strategic voting are no longer unique.

Dutta (1977) and Sengupta and Dutta (1979) asked under what restrictions of true preferences stability will be secured when the reported preferences are unrestricted. The answer that they give is based on the assumption that all individual preferences are strict. The result is that stability of the social aggregation function is achieved whenever every set of sincere strict preference orderings satisfies 'restricted Pareto optimality' over the set of alternatives. This condition is very stringent indeed. It demands that in each set of feasible objects, the number of Pareto-optimal alternatives be at most two. This means nothing else but requiring a high degree of similarity among the individuals' sincere preferences. A little more can be said again in the case of unique social outcomes (see Gaertner (2001, chapter 4.4)).

Let us digress for a moment and pick up a point that could have been discussed already in Chapter 3 when we presented various domain restrictions. We shall come back to the issue of manipulability in a moment. We saw earlier on that under single-peaked preferences and for an odd number of voters, the unique Condorcet winner is the median peak of the individual orderings. The majority preference relation is the same as the ordering of the median voter and the Condorcet winner is the median of the voters' best or ideal points. In economic theory and political science (see, e.g. Roberts (1977) and Gans and Smart (1996)), another restriction on individual preferences has been proposed that is somewhat closer to the political sphere than the single-peakedness property. This restriction is called single-crossing. It combines an ordering over alternatives with an ordering over individuals.

We shall use an example from politics to describe this property. Let there be a set of policy alternatives $A$ and let its elements be ordered completely and transitively, from left to right so that for any $a$, $b$ from $A$, '$a < b$' means that option $a$ is to the left of option $b$ in the space of political alternatives.

It is now assumed that the voters are also ordered completely and transitively, let's say from 'leftist' to 'rightist' in some political spectrum and we will write '$i < j$' to indicate that person $i$ is to the left of person $j$ in this political spectrum. This ordering over the voters means that a voter who is leftist tends to prefer a left-wing policy more than voters who are rightist in the political spectrum, and vice versa. Roberts refers to a voting over alternative tax rates, where high-income receivers will prefer a lower income tax rate to a higher rate, while low-income receivers may have the opposite preference. It is obvious that the income receivers can be ordered along the real line. More formally, and we again use the analogy from politics, for any two voters $i$ and $j$ such that $i < j$ and for any two policy alternatives $a$ and $b$ from $A$ such that $a < b$, a profile is called single-crossing if $u_i(b) > u_i(a)$ implies $u_j(b) > u_j(a)$, and $u_j(a) > u_j(b)$ implies $u_i(a) > u_i(b)$, where $u_i(\cdot)$ and $u_j(\cdot)$ are the utility evaluations of voters $i$ and $j$.

It has now been shown that for an odd number of voters and if all voters' preference relations are complete and transitive, the ideal point of the median voter is a Condorcet winner with respect to $A$, if the single-crossing property is fulfilled. Since, as we asserted above, the property of single-crossing combines an ordering over alternatives with an ordering over voters, while single-peakedness requires an ordering over the elements of a set of alternatives only, the two conditions are logically independent. Both properties, however, yield the result that the ideal point of the median voter is a Condorcet winner.

To point out the structural difference between single-crossing and single-peakedness, consider the following example. Let there be three individuals 1, 2 and 3 with increasing incomes so that there is an ordering $1 < 2 < 3$. There are three options, i.e. income tax rates, $a$, $b$ and $c$ such that $a > b > c$. Assume that the three individuals have the following preferences:

$$
\begin{array}{ccccc}
1 & : & a & b & c \\
2 & : & a & c & b \\
3 & : & c & b & a.
\end{array}
$$

It is easily seen that for any ordering of the alternatives along the real line, single-peakedness is violated. However, the profile is single-crossing over $\{a, b, c\}$. Person 2 'already' prefers $c$ over $b$ and the highest income receiver 3 prefers $c$ over $b$ a fortiori. Person 2 prefers $a$ over $c$ and the lowest income receiver also prefers $a$ over $c$. The Condorcet winner is alternative $a$, the majority ordering is $acb$.

It has recently been shown by Saporiti and Tohmé (2004), and now we come back to the issue of strategy-proofness, that over the domain of single-crossing preferences, the generalized median voter scheme, as proposed by Moulin, is not strategy-proof in general. We know from theorem 5.2 above that strategy-proofness is given for all profiles of single-peaked preferences, and there were no restrictions imposed on the distribution of the phantom voters. Saporiti and Tohmé show that for the case of single-crossing preferences, Moulin's result only holds if the peaks of the phantom voters (the fixed ballots) take their values at the extremes of the real line. The authors give a reason for this. If any possible distribution of the phantom voters is admissible, the socially chosen alternative for such arbitrary distributions need not be the most preferred alternative of a real voter. 'However, without this information, single-crossing cannot rule out manipulation' (p. 13).

Is there a chance to generalize our results on strategy-proof social choice rules in the sense of going from one dimension to higher dimensions? The answer is 'yes', but the analysis becomes much more intricate and therefore goes well beyond the confines of a primer. Nevertheless, we want to point out a few things.

The notion of single-peaked preferences was hitherto restricted to preferences along the real line. This is adequate in quite a few problems such as the choice of distance between my flat and the university or the choice of a political party in the left–right spectrum. However, parties are normally represented by a political programme, and in all serious instances, such programmes consist of different issues concerning, for example, interior policy, foreign policy, economics, and other dimensions.

Barberà, his collaborators, and others (see, e.g. Barberà et al. (1991, 1993)) have formalized multidimensional social choices in the following way. Let $K$ denote a finite number of dimensions. Each dimension $k$ from the index set $[K]$ stands for one relevant characteristic of the choice problem. Each dimension is represented by an admissible interval $B_k = [a_k, b_k]$. Then the set of alternatives can be determined as the cartesian product $B = \prod_{k=1}^{K} B_k$. Barberà speaks of sets like $B$ as $K$-dimensional boxes. Within each dimension, the alternatives are linearly ordered. The voters are assumed to have a unique top or ideal point and, in close analogy to single-peakedness in one dimension, if $z$ is between $x$ and the ideal point, $z$ is preferred to $x$. Without going into details, we can now speak of generalized single-peakedness. Reduced to one dimension, we are back to standard single-peakedness.

One way to choose from $K$-dimensional boxes is to apply $K$ generalized median voter schemes, one for each characteristic or dimension. When each individual is asked to name his or her ideal alternative, the $k$th component of this point is combined with the $k$th component of the other persons. All this information is used to make a choice, based on the specific generalized median voter scheme that is attached to the $k$th component. In the same way, the values of the other components or dimensions are computed, and the resulting $K$-tuple of values is taken as the social outcome. For such a $K$-dimensional generalized median voter scheme, the authors obtain strategy-proofness, given that the aggregation rule is defined on the set of generalized single-peaked preferences over the $K$-dimensional box (Barberà et al., 1993).

Admittedly, the last few pages were somewhat more abstract than most of the other pages in this chapter. Therefore, a second reading may be required in order to 'grasp' the various subtleties discussed in the paragraphs above. The reader may prefer to do this at a later stage and should not worry too much at this point. The main message of this chapter, however, is the pervasiveness of the Gibbard–Satterthwaite result and, again, the importance of single-peaked preferences as a structural condition to yield positive results.

## 5.4. A short summary

Social choice theory has acquired a certain 'fame' for producing impossibility theorems. There are indeed many negative results in this field, and the reader by now is familiar with various forms. It is probably uncontroversial to assert that the most important, i.e. most influential impossibility results are Arrow's theorem, Sen's impossibility of a Paretian liberal, and the result by Gibbard and Satterthwaite that we discussed in this chapter. Just to repeat, if there are at least three alternatives, then under an unrestricted domain of individual preferences, a social choice function is either dictatorial or manipulable. Gibbards's own proof of this result shows a close relationship with Arrow's theorem.

Why should one worry about the lack of strategy-proofness? One could argue that if people have the opportunity to manipulate (in order to achieve a better outcome for themselves), just let them manipulate. Along this line, one could view social aggregation and public voting as a non-cooperative 'game' where agents behave strategically. One may, perhaps, see social choice this way but we mentioned above that strategic voting presupposes that (some) people spend energy and resources in order to manipulate successfully. Once it has become evident that some people try to vote insincerely, others who have seen through this game, will keep their own preferences and intentions in disguise. Such a situation is perfectly natural and, therefore, understandable in contested markets but would one want to argue that such a 'climate' should also prevail in committees, legislative bodies and other assemblies?

Anyway, the reader has seen that strategy-proofness can be restored under domain restrictions, and it is again the property of single-peakedness which leads to positive results.

## ☐ RECOMMENDED READING

Kelly, J. S. (1988). *Social Choice Theory. An Introduction,* chapter 10. Berlin, Heidelberg, New York: Springer-Verlag.
Reny, Ph. J. (2001). 'Arrow's Theorem and the Gibbard–Satterthwaite Theorem: A Unified Approach'. *Economics Letters*, 70: 99–105.

## ☐ HISTORICAL SOURCES

Dummett, M. and Farquharson, R. (1961). 'Stability in Voting'. *Econometrica*, 29: 33–43.
Farquharson, R. (1969). *Theory of Voting.* New Haven: Yale University Press.

## ☐ MORE ADVANCED

Barberà, S. (2001). 'An Introduction to Strategy-Proof Social Choice Functions'. *Social Choice and Welfare,* 18: 619–653.

Gaertner, W. (2001). *Domain Conditions in Social Choice Theory,* chapter 4. Cambridge: Cambridge University Press.

Gibbard, A. (1973). 'Manipulation of Voting Schemes: A General Result'. *Econometrica,* 41: 587–602.

Pattanaik, P.K. (1978). *Strategy and Group Choice,* chapters 4–7. Amsterdam: North-Holland Publishing Company.

# 6 Escaping impossibilities: social choice rules

## 6.1. The Pareto-extension rule and veto power

Impossibility theorems are ubiquitous in social choice theory. By now, the reader has encountered several of these, among them the famous impossibility results by Arrow, Sen, and Gibbard and Satterthwaite. We think that it is high time to study various possibility results. Of course, this has a price: at least one of Arrow's conditions must be weakened and the reader has to ask himself or herself whether in each individual case, the ensuing possibility is worth its price.

In Chapter 4, we extensively used the concept of a social decision function. Just to refresh the reader's memory, a social decision function is a social aggregation rule, the range of which is restricted to social preference relations $R$ that generate a choice function $C(S, R)$ for every finite $S$ contained in the set $X$ of all conceivable social states.

Let us consider the following social relation proposed by Sen (1969):

$$xRy \leftrightarrow \neg[\text{for all } i \in N : yR_ix \text{ and there exists at least one } j \in N : yP_jx].$$

Sen proves the following result that may be surprising at the first glance.

**Theorem 6.1.** There exists a social decision function that satisfies Arrow's conditions $U, P, I$ and $D$ for any finite set $X$.

A first thought the reader may have could be: 'Ah, at long last, a counter-example to Arrow's negative result'. But this is not so, as we will see in a few moments. Let us have a look at Sen's proof (Sen, 1970b, pp. 52–53).

*Proof (by example).* Consider the social preference relation $R$ given above that is generated by the social decision function. It is easy to see that $R$ is reflexive and complete. It is also obvious that the social decision function fulfils properties $P, I$ and $D$. For example, if for all $i \in N, xP_iy$, then $xRy$ according to Sen's definition above. Furthermore, it is not the case that $yRx$. However, $xRy \land \neg yRx$ is equivalent to $xPy$ (see section 1.3). Therefore, condition $P$ is satisfied. That there is no Arrovian dictator is also clear immediately. Consider the following situation and generalize it to other cases: $xP_1y$, $xP_2y$ and $yP_3x$ for any three individuals 1, 2 and 3. According to the definition of $R$, we obtain $xRy \land yRx$

which is equivalent to $xIy$. Nobody dictates his or her strict preference. Finally, the construction of $R$ is such that if the decision is between $x$ and $y$, let's say, so-called irrelevant alternatives are never considered.

We now show that $R$ is quasi-transitive but it is not fully transitive. Assume that $xPy \land yPz$. From this follows, according to the definition of $R$, that [for all $i$ : $xR_iy$ and for at least one $j$ : $xP_jy$] and [for all $i$ : $yR_iz$]. Since each $R_i$ is assumed to be complete and transitive, we obtain [for all $i$ : $xR_iz$ and for at least one $j$ : $xP_jz$]. This, however, means that $xRz \land \neg zRx$, which is equivalent to $xPz$. This shows that quasi-transitivity is fulfilled.

Sen shows in his proof furthermore that if $R$ is reflexive, complete and quasi-transitive over a finite set $X$, no domain restriction is needed for the social decision function to exist. In other words, condition $U$ is also fulfilled, and this completes the proof of the theorem.

For the last step, the reader may want to go back to theorem 1.1 in the introduction which uses the property of acyclicity to prove the existence of a choice function. Note that acyclicity is a weaker requirement than quasi-transitivity.

We still want to demonstrate that the social preference relation established above satisfies quasi-transitivity as just proved, but not full transitivity. Consider two individuals with the preference orderings $yP_1z \land zP_1x$ and $zP_2x \land xP_2y$, over elements $x$, $y$, $z$. We obtain $xIy$, $yIz$ and $zPx$ according to $R$. This shows that the indifference relation is not transitive (a fact which is not compatible with Arrow's concept of a social welfare function). In the situation of the so-called voting paradox (section 3.1), the social decision function from above yields $xRy \land yRx$, $yRz \land zRy$ and $xRz \land zRx$, so that there is complete social indifference among the three alternatives $x$, $y$ and $z$.

Based on the social preference relation defined at the beginning of this chapter, Sen (1969, 1970b) proposed the so-called Pareto-extension rule as a social choice rule. It says that

$$\forall x, y \in X : xRy \leftrightarrow \neg(y\bar{P}x),$$

where $y\bar{P}x$ means that [(for all $i$ : $yR_ix$) $\land$ (for at least one $j$ : $yP_jx$)]. As an example, for three individuals and two alternatives $x$ and $y$, $xRy$ would not hold if $yR_1x$, $yR_2x$ and $yP_3x$. Both $xRy$ and $yRx$ would hold if $xP_1y$, $xR_2y$ and $yP_3x$.

Obviously, we have a possibility result here. The Pareto-extension rule is a social aggregation rule which exists for all possible profiles. But is it satisfactory? Clearly, this social choice rule resolves all conflicting preference constellations by ranking alternatives equally. This aggregation mechanism satisfies the Pareto principle. Actually, it is based on it (therefore its name). This rule is complete and quasi-transitive, as we have demonstrated above. Sen (1970b, pp. 76–77) characterized the Pareto-extension rule. He showed (but we shall omit the proof) that for a social aggregation rule that always generates a quasi-transitive and complete social preference relation, conditions $U$ and $I$, together with anonymity $A$ (section 3.1) and a strict Pareto principle $SP$, are necessary and sufficient for the aggregation rule to be the Pareto-extension rule. The strict Pareto principle $SP$ says that for all $x, y \in X$, $xRy$ if $xR_iy$ for all $i \in N$. If moreover, $xP_jy$ for some $j \in N$, then $xPy$.

Our last example above demonstrated that the Pareto-extension rule does not satisfy the condition of positive responsiveness ($PR$), defined and used in section 3.1. For if instead of $xR_2y$, we were to have $xP_2'y$, the social result would still be $xIy$. Furthermore, the strict opposition of a single individual is sufficient to generate social indifference. Or turned around, the strict preference of a single individual over any pair $(x, y)$ will always achieve social indifference between $x$ and $y$ and a strict social preference if all members of society agree with this individual. This means that a single person achieves veto power. His or her strict preference achieves social indifference even if *all* the other individuals in society have an opposite strict preference. Kelly (1988, p. 66) describes this phenomenon which applies to every single member of society as 'inclusionary power'. Subsequently, this individual power will be termed 'weak dictatorship'. Let us discuss the latter point in more detail. We follow Mas-Colell and Sonnenschein (1972). In the sequel, we only consider social decision functions that are quasi-transitive. We learned above that they are defined over all possible profiles.

**Definition 6.1.** Person $i$ is called a weak dictator if for all $x, y \in X$, $xP_iy$ implies $xRy$.

**Condition WD (No weak dictatorship).** There does not exist a weak dictator.

Note that this condition is stronger than Arrow's requirement of non-dictatorship. Mas-Colell and Sonnenschein prove the following result.

**Theorem 6.2.** There does not exist a quasi-transitive social decision function that satisfies conditions $P$, $I$ and $WD$.

The proof uses two lemmata.

**Lemma 6.1.** If there is a quasi-transitive social decision function that satisfies conditions $P$ and $I$, and if there is some individual $j$ who is almost decisive for some $x$ against some $y$, then person $j$ is a dictator.

*Proof of lemma.* We can fully refer to lemma 2.1 in chapter 2. Arrow had shown this result for his concept of a social welfare function, but in his proof, only the property of quasi-transitivity of $R$ was used, not full transitivity (please check this by having another look at the proof of lemma 2.1). Therefore, this result carries over to quasi-transitive social decision functions.

The following definition is not completely new for the reader who studied the last part of Arrow's original proof.

**Definition 6.2.** Let $a, b \in X$ and assume that some set of individuals $V \subset N$ is almost decisive for $a$ against $b$. If for some $x, y \in X$, some set of individuals $W \subset N$ is almost decisive for $x$ against $y$, then $V$ is called a smallest almost decisive set, if the number of persons in $W$ is at least as large as the number of persons in $V$.

**Lemma 6.2.** Let there be a quasi-transitive social decision function that satisfies conditions $P$, $I$ and $D$. Assume that $V$ is a smallest almost decisive set with respect to $a$ and $b$. Then

(a) $V$ contains at least two persons, and
(b) every person in $V$ is a weak dictator.

*Proof of lemma.* Part (a) follows directly from lemma 6.1 and condition $D$. If $V$ contained only one individual, lemma 6.1 would establish the existence of a dictator, and this would contradict the hypothesis in lemma 6.2.

To prove part (b), it is shown first that if $i \in V$, then

$$xP_iy \rightarrow xRy \quad \text{for some } x \text{ and } y \text{ in } X. \tag{1}$$

Suppose not; then for $a$ and some arbitrary $z \in X$, there exists a set of individual preference orderings of the form

| $\{i\}$ | $N\backslash\{i\}$ | |
|---|---|---|
| $a$ | some $(n - 1)$-tuple of individual orderings between | (2) |
| $z$ | $z$ and $a$ (not necessarily the same for each person) | |

such that $zPa$. We will see that this leads to a contradiction. Let $W \subset V$ and $V = \{i\} \cup W$.

| $\{i\}$ | $W$ | $N\backslash V$ | |
|---|---|---|---|
| $a$ | the same orderings | $b$ | |
| $b$ | between $z$ and $a$ | the same orderings | (3) |
| | as in (2) | between $z$ and $a$ | |
| | | as in (2) | |
| $z$ | $b$ | | |

Since $V$ is almost decisive with respect to $a$ and $b$ according to the supposition, we obtain $aPb$ and, furthermore from (2), $zPa$. Therefore, due to quasi-transitivity and the independence condition, we arrive at $zPb$. But this implies that $W$ is almost decisive. This, however, contradicts the assumption that $V$ is the smallest almost decisive set. Therefore, it is shown that (1) holds.

Next, it has to be shown that if $i \in V$, then for all $s$, $t$ in $X$,

$$sP_i t \rightarrow sRt. \tag{4}$$

Mas-Colell and Sonnenschein argue that it is enough to prove

$$[xP_i y \rightarrow xRy] \rightarrow [\text{for all } s \in X : sP_i y \rightarrow sRy], \tag{5}$$

$$[xP_i y \rightarrow xRy] \rightarrow [\text{for all } t \in X : xP_i t \rightarrow xRt]. \tag{6}$$

A repeated use of (5) and (6) will establish (4).

Let us just consider one case of (5). Assume that (5) does not hold. Then there is a set of individual preference orderings such that $xP_i y$ implies $xRy$; furthermore $sP_i y$ for some $s \in X$ but not $sRy$.

| $\{i\}$ | $N\backslash\{i\}$ | |
|---|---|---|
| $s$ | some $(n-1)$-tuple of possibly | (7) |
| $x$ | different orderings between $y$ and $s$ | |
| $y$ | $x$ | |

For this preference constellation, we have $xRy$ and $yPs$ by assumption, and $sPx$ due to the weak Pareto principle $P$. Quasi-transitivity yields $yPx$ but this is in contradiction with $xRy$. Therefore, we have shown that for some $s \in X$, $sP_i y$ implies $sRy$.

The proof of (6) for some $t \in X$ is similar. A repeated use of this type of proof for all $s \in X$ and all $t \in X$ proves lemma 6.2.

*Proof of theorem 6.2.* We already noted that condition *WD* is stronger than condition *D*. Therefore, *WD* implies *D*. Thus if a quasi-transitive social decision function exists that satisfies *P*, *I* and *WD* (and, therefore, *D*), lemma 6.2 tells us that there must exist a weak dictator. This, however, contradicts condition *WD* in the theorem.

It is interesting to compare theorems 6.1 and 6.2. With theorem 6.1, we obtained a possibility result within the Arrovian set-up by weakening the rationality requirements (quasi-transitivity instead of full transitivity), but leaving all the other conditions untouched. We get back to an impossibility result by strengthening one of the Arrovian conditions, in this case going from non-dictatorship to a condition which forbids the existence of weak dictators.

We already noted that the Pareto-extension rule violates the requirement of positive responsiveness (*PR*). Therefore, again using theorem 6.1 as a point of reference, we obtain another impossibility result by requiring additionally that the quasi-transitive social decision function be positive responsive. Mas-Colell and Sonnenschein (1972, p. 188) point out that this result only holds if there are at least three individuals.

**Theorem 6.3.** There does not exist a quasi-transitive social decision function that fulfils conditions $P, I, D$ and $PR$, when there are at least three individuals.

For two persons, the method of majority decision is a quasi-transitive social decision function that satisfies all the conditions in theorem 6.3.

## 6.2. **Scoring functions and the Borda rule**

In this section, we shall discuss what Young (1974, 1975) and others call scoring functions, among them the well-known Borda rank-order method. Imagine that there is a committee of voters who consider a finite set of alternatives $S = \{a_1, a_2, \ldots, a_m\}$ for election. Each voter is assumed to rank the elements of $S$ according to his or her preferences in a strict linear order (this is a simplification – weak orders would make the analysis a bit more cumbersome). We again use the concept of a social choice rule or social decision function which, as the reader remembers, is a mapping from the set of all preference profiles to the family of non-empty subsets of $S$. In other words, this function is a rule that assigns, to every finite committee of voters with specified linear preferences, a non-empty subset of $S$, interpreted as the set of winning alternatives. We want the social choice rule to satisfy the properties of anonymity and neutrality (see section 3.1), i.e. a permutation of name-tags among voters should have no effect on the social decision, and if the name-tags of alternatives were permuted on the level of individual orderings, the same permutation would have to occur on the level of social preference. The reader, of course, remembers that the simple majority rule fulfils these two properties.

We now introduce a condition which relates choices made by subsets of voters to choices made by their union. This implies that we allow the number of voters to vary. Imagine that, say, $C'$ is the choice set of a group of voters $V' \subset N$, and $C''$ is the choice set of another group of voters $V'' \subset N$, where $V' \cap V'' = \emptyset$. It is now required that if $C' \cap C'' \neq \emptyset$, then the larger group $V' \cup V''$ should select exactly the options in $C' \cap C''$. More precisely:

**Condition *CONS* (Consistency).** Let $h$ be a social choice rule. This rule is consistent if whenever $w', w''$ are preference profiles for disjoint voter sets $V'$ and $V''$, then $h(w') \cap h(w'') \neq \emptyset$ implies $h(w') \cap h(w'') = h(w' + w'')$, where $w' + w''$ is the profile on $V' \cup V''$ that agrees with $w'$ on $V'$ and with $w''$ on $V''$.

This condition of consistency with respect to sets of voters is not to be confounded with consistency requirements in the sense of rationality conditions discussed in section 1.3. The following example may help to illustrate. Let $V'$ and $V''$ consist of three voters each, i.e. $V' = \{1, 2, 3\}$, $V'' = \{4, 5, 6\}$. We assume the following subsets $w'$ and $w''$ of strict orderings to be read in a perpendicular way:

|  | $V'$ |  |  | $V''$ |  |
|---|---|---|---|---|---|
| 1 | 2 | 3 | 4 | 5 | 6 |
| $a_1$ | $a_2$ | $a_4$ | $a_3$ | $a_1$ | $a_4$ |
| $a_2$ | $a_3$ | $a_1$ | $a_1$ | $a_4$ | $a_3$ |
| $a_3$ | $a_1$ | $a_2$ | $a_2$ | $a_3$ | $a_1$ |
| $a_4$ | $a_4$ | $a_3$ | $a_4$ | $a_2$ | $a_2$ |

Let the choice sets be $h(w') = \{a_1, a_2\}$ and $h(w'') = \{a_1, a_3\}$. Then consistency requires that $h(w' + w'') = \{a_1\}$.

A social choice rule on $m$ alternatives is called a scoring function if in a profile of strict orderings a score of $s_i$ ($s_i$ is a real number) is assigned to each voter's $i$th most preferred alternative and the choice set consists of the alternative(s) with the highest total score. One of the results in Young (1975) which is stated without proof is the following.

**Theorem 6.4.**   A social choice function is anonymous, neutral and consistent if and only if it is a scoring function.

One example in this class of scoring functions is the so-called plurality rule, where each voter casts one vote for his or her most preferred alternative, and the choice set consists of the alternative(s) with the highest total number of votes. Expressed in terms of scores, one can say that in the plurality function, a score of 1 is assigned to each voter's most preferred alternative and a score of 0 to all the other options.

Another example in this class is the Borda rank-order rule where for $m$ alternatives, a score of $m - 1$ is assigned to each voter's most preferred altern- ative, a score of $m - 2$ to the second most preferred option and, in general, a score of $m - i$ to the $i$th most preferred alternative. Also for the Borda rule, the choice set consists of the alternative(s) with highest total score. Note already at this point that the Borda method is based on an equally distanced weight- ing scheme which means that the difference in weights or scores between two neighbouring or adjacent positions is the same everywhere in an individual's strict ordering. This feature does not apply to the plurality rule nor to the 'anti- plurality' rule (Saari, 1995, p. 102) where the voter is asked to vote for all but one candidate so that in the case of three alternatives, for example, the scoring vector would read $(s_1, s_2, s_3) = (1, 1, 0)$. Saari (p. 102) draws attention to the fact that in this case of three alternatives, the scoring vector according to Borda is just the sum of the scoring vectors for the plurality and the antiplurality rule. Since the Borda rule perhaps is the most prominent scoring rule, let us define it more formally.

We denote, for a given preference profile $w$ and a fixed set of alternatives $S$, the Borda rule or Borda choice function as $h^B(w, S)$. The Borda ranks or Borda scores will be denoted by $r_j^B(a_i)$ for person $j$'s rank of alternative $a_i$. Given $w$ and $S$, the set of chosen elements according to Borda is

$$h^B(w, S) = \left\{ a_i \in S \middle| \sum_{j=1}^{n} r_j^B(a_i) \geq \sum_{j=1}^{n} r_j^B(a_k) \text{ for all } a_k \in S \right\}.$$

For a society with $n$ individuals, $\sum_{j=1}^{n} r_j^B(a_i)$ is the total rank sum for alternative $a_i \in S$ according to the Borda method. Check that in our example used in relation to the consistency condition, the choice sets $h(w')$ and $h(w'')$ were determined by their Borda scores.

Which set of axioms characterizes the Borda rank-order method? Several scholars have answered this question (see, e.g. Gärdenfors (1973)). We decided to follow Young (1974). The latter defines a social choice function to be faithful if 'socially most preferred' and 'individually most preferred' have the same meaning when society comprises just one person. More technically, $h(w) = \{a_i\}$ when $w$ represents the ordering of a single individual whose most preferred alternative is $a_i$. If social choice rule $h$ is faithful and consistent, then $h$ satisfies the weak Pareto principle. This means that $h(w) = \{a_i\}$ for any profile $w$ in which $a_i$ is preferred to all other alternatives by every individual.

**Cancellation property** (*CP*). A social choice rule $h$ is said to fulfil the cancellation property if, whenever there is a profile $w$ such that for all pairs of alternatives $(a_i, a_j)$ from $S$, the number of voters preferring $a_i$ to $a_j$ equals the number preferring $a_j$ to $a_i$, then $h(w, S) = S$.

Any profile that satisfies the cancellation property will be called balanced. The following example shows that the Borda rule satisfies condition *CP*, but the plurality rule does not.

| 1 | 2 | 3 | 4 |
|---|---|---|---|
| $a_1$ | $a_1$ | $a_3$ | $a_3$ |
| $a_2$ | $a_2$ | $a_2$ | $a_2$ |
| $a_3$ | $a_3$ | $a_1$ | $a_1$ |

It is immediate that $h(w, \{a_1, a_2, a_3\}) = \{a_1, a_2, a_3\}$ under the Borda rule, but $h(w, \{a_1, a_2, a_3\}) = \{a_1, a_3\}$ under the plurality rule. Note that the method of majority decision also satisfies condition *CP*.

Since the proof is quite lengthy, we just state Young's (1974) characterization of the Borda rule.

**Theorem 6.5.** For any fixed number $m$ of alternatives, there is one and only one social choice function that is neutral, consistent, faithful and has the cancellation property. It is the Borda rank-order rule.

Young has also shown that any choice rule that is consistent and has the cancellation property, is anonymous.

Above, we have specified the scoring method for the Borda rule. Actually, the one given is the version originally proposed by Borda himself. However, an infinite number of different scoring vectors is as good as (or equivalent to) the original one (see Saari (1995, pp. 104–105)). Let $s_1^m$ be a scoring vector for $m$ alternatives, i.e. $s_1^m = (s_1^1, s_1^2, \ldots, s_1^m)$. Define $s_2^m = a \cdot s_1^m + b(1, 1, \ldots, 1)$ for scalars $a > 0$ and $b$, where $(1, 1, \ldots, 1)$ is also an $m$-vector. Then, for any profile $w$, the Borda winner for $h(w; s_1^m)$ agrees with that for $h(w; s_2^m)$. Saari draws attention to the fact that the antiplurality scores $(1, 1, \ldots, 1, 0)$ are equivalent to $(0, 0, \ldots, 0, -1)$ by choosing $a = 1$ and $b = -1$ in the above formula. The latter vector expresses the fact that the antiplurality rule puts 'all the blame' on the bottom-ranked alternative. Furthermore, a scoring vector $s^3 = (s^1, s^2, s^3)$ for the case of three alternatives corresponds to the Borda method if and only if $s^1 - s^2 = s^2 - s^3$, i.e. if and only if the difference between successive scores is fixed (earlier on, we called such a scheme equally distanced).

The next point we want to discuss will by no means surprise the reader, but it is very important: different voting procedures will in general lead to different outcomes. This is crucial for everyone who participates in voting procedures. One should be sceptical and very cautious when some member of a voting committee emphatically proposes a particular voting method. The offering of some voting procedure could simply be a particular voting strategy in disguise. On the other hand, it can also be said that the outcomes according to different procedures are not totally arbitrary or volatile. Can one be more precise? We start again with an illustration. We consider the strict preferences of five committee members over four alternatives:

| 1 | 2 | 3 | 4 | 5 |
|---|---|---|---|---|
| $a_1$ | $a_3$ | $a_4$ | $a_2$ | $a_2$ |
| $a_2$ | $a_1$ | $a_1$ | $a_4$ | $a_3$ |
| $a_3$ | $a_2$ | $a_2$ | $a_1$ | $a_1$ |
| $a_4$ | $a_4$ | $a_3$ | $a_3$ | $a_4$ |

Alternative $a_1$ is the Condorcet winner. Alternative $a_2$ is the Borda winner and also the plurality winner. One important finding from this example is that the Condorcet winner (if it exists) and the Borda winner can be different alternatives. Can one say more? Saari (1995, p. 157) shows that a Condorcet winner is never bottom-ranked according to the Borda method, and a Condorcet loser (a candidate that loses in pairwise contest against all other alternatives) is never top-ranked according to the Borda count. Saari also proves that a Condorcet winner always receives more than a third of the assigned Borda rank-order points while a Condorcet loser always receives less than a third of the assigned Borda points. Clearly then, a Condorcet winner is always ranked above a Condorcet loser according to the Borda method. These results should give some comfort to those readers who were worried about the use of the word 'volatile' a few passages above. The Condorcet winner is based on pairwise majority voting, the Borda rule counts positions which can be interpreted as an aggregated version of pairwise voting (Saari, 1995, p. 156), and the plurality rule restricts its attention to top elements. The latter procedure neglects to an extremely high degree information that is contained in the individual rankings.

In order to see that the Borda method can be viewed as an aggregated version of pairwise voting, consider the following simple example. Let there be five voters who prefer $a_1$ to $a_2$, $a_2$ to $a_3$ (and $a_1$ to $a_3$) and another three voters who prefer $a_2$ to $a_3$, $a_3$ to $a_1$ (and $a_2$ to $a_1$). Clearly, $a_1$ is the Condorcet winner in pairwise voting. The Borda score for $a_1$ is 10; $a_2$ reaches a score of 11 so that $a_2$ is the Borda winner. The point we wish to make is that 5 is the number of votes that $a_1$ obtains in pairwise comparison with $a_2$ and 5 is also the number of votes that $a_1$ gets in pairwise comparison with $a_3$. The total is 10, and this is $a_1$'s Borda score as we know. Alternative $a_2$ receives 8 votes against $a_3$ and 3 votes in pairwise comparison with $a_1$, a total of 11, which is $a_2$'s Borda score.

What happens when the Borda scores are no longer equally distanced? The answer is: 'more or less anything'. Let us consider another example with four voters having the following strict orderings:

| 1 | 2 | 3 | 4 |
|---|---|---|---|
| $a_1$ | $a_1$ | $a_3$ | $a_4$ |
| $a_2$ | $a_2$ | $a_2$ | $a_2$ |
| $a_3$ | $a_3$ | $a_4$ | $a_3$ |
| $a_4$ | $a_4$ | $a_1$ | $a_1$ |

We begin by using the typical Borda scores, i.e. $(3, 2, 1, 0)$. The Borda winner is alternative $a_2$. Let us now use the scoring vector $(1, 1/2, 1/4, 0)$. In this case, the winners are $a_1$ and $a_2$ with an equal score. Finally, pick the scoring vector $(1, 1/4, 1/5, 0)$. In this situation, the unique Borda winner is $a_1$. All of the scoring vectors above satisfy the condition that $s^i \geq s^{i+1}, i \in \{1, \ldots, n-1\}$, and $s^1 > s^n$ which are very natural requirements within a scoring system. Otherwise, however, those scores chosen after the usual Borda ranks were somewhat arbitrary. Saari (1995, p. 106) writes that to justify a particular scoring vector, 'just concoct a convincing argument why that … choice is the "correct one"'. Since, as we have just seen, different scoring vectors in general lead to different outcomes, the choice and defence of particular scores can also, at least to some degree, be seen under the aspect of manipulation. Gaertner (1983) proposed non-linear transformations of the Borda scores for profiles of individual orderings that focus on the positions of agents under different social alternatives. In order to reflect equity considerations, a class of strictly concave transformations of the original Borda ranks was proposed with the effect that rank differences among higher positions are smaller than rank differences among lower positions. Note that elements of this class do not satisfy the cancellation property any longer.

Just one final word on the issue of manipulation in relation to the Borda rank-order method. There is the famous exclamation by Borda himself who declared that his rule was designed for honest men only. In section 5.1 we referred to an investigation by Kelly (1993) who showed that the Borda method, though easily manipulable, does not fare so badly after all when compared with other aggregation rules that are also sensitive to changes in the voters' preference orderings. This is an important aspect. If the degree of manipulability is the issue, the Borda rule and other scoring rules should not be compared to voting rules that can hardly be manipulated because they are highly insensitive to alterations in the voters' preferences. Insensitivity renders these aggregation rules very unattractive. Saari (1995, p. 12) writes that 'manipulative behavior is important, but it must never be the single deciding factor in choosing a system'.

Our final point in this section refers to two versions of the Borda method, viz. the broad and the narrow Borda rule. The first variant always uses the ranks or scores assigned to the alternatives in superset $S$, viz. score $m - j$ for the $j$th ranked alternative in a set of $m$ alternatives. This means that when the choice is over any subset $S' \subset S$, the choice set for $S'$ is based on the Borda scores for $S$. The narrow Borda rule uses, for a choice over $S' \subset S$, the Borda scores based on the rankings of the elements in $S'$. The score is still $m - j$ for the $j$th ranked alternative, but $m$ now stands for the number of alternatives in $S'$.

Does this make a difference? It does indeed, as will be shown subsequently. We shall argue by several examples. Consider $S = \{x, y, z, v\}$ and the following profile $w$ for three individuals:

| 1 | 2 | 3 |
|---|---|---|
| $x$ | $y$ | $z$ |
| $y$ | $z$ | $v$ |
| $z$ | $v$ | $x$ |
| $v$ | $x$ | $y$ |

According to the broad Borda rule, the choice set is $h^{BB}(w, S) = \{z\}$. For $S' = \{x, y, v\}$, the result is $h^{BB}(w, S') = \{y\}$.

Let us modify the above profile to profile $w'$ in the following way:

| 1 | 2 | 3 |
|---|---|---|
| $x$ | $y$ | $v$ |
| $z$ | $v$ | $x$ |
| $y$ | $x$ | $z$ |
| $v$ | $z$ | $y$ |

According to the broad Borda rule, the choice set now is $h^{BB}(w', S) = \{x\}$. For $S' = \{x, y, v\}$, the outcome is $h^{BB}(w', S') = \{x\}$. So far, so good.

Note, however, that the two profiles $w$ and $w'$ are exactly the same over the set $S'$, viz.

|   | 1 | 2 | 3 |
|---|---|---|---|
|   | $x$ | $y$ | $v$ |
|   | $y$ | $v$ | $x$ |
|   | $v$ | $x$ | $y$ |

We clearly obtain $h^{BB}(w, S') \neq h^{BB}(w', S')$, where $w = w'$ over $S'$. This means that the Arrovian independence condition is violated, appropriately redefined for rank-order rules or scoring functions. Obviously, the broad Borda method has no problems with contraction consistency (note that the Borda rule actually generates an ordering over all alternatives). Since the scores from the superset are used for each possible subset, an alternative that scored highest in the superset will always be chosen in a subset, as long as it belongs to this subset. This characteristic does not apply to the narrow Borda rule, as the following example will show for $S = \{x, y, z\}$ and profile $w''$ for three individuals:

|   | 1 | 2 | 3 |
|---|---|---|---|
|   | $x$ | $y$ | $z$ |
|   | $y$ | $z$ | $x$ |
|   | $z$ | $x$ | $y$ |

This is, of course, the paradox of voting. The outcome according to the narrow Borda method is $h^{NB}(w'', S) = \{x, y, z\}$. When $z$ is dropped, the choice over $S' = \{x, y\}$ is $h^{NB}(w'', S') = \{x\}$, which violates contraction consistency (e.g. property $\alpha$ from section 1.3). Some form of expansion consistency is not satisfied either. Consider profile $w$ above and construct the choice set over $\{y, z, v\} = S''$. One obtains $h^{NB}(w, S'') = \{y, z\}$. The choice set for $S \supset S''$ is $h^{NB}(w, S) = \{z\}$ so that property $\beta$ is not satisfied.

The narrow Borda rule has no problem at all with the independence condition. If every voter's ranking over $S' \subset S$ is the same in two profiles $w$ and $w'$, the narrow Borda score is, of course, the same for every alternative, which means that the choice set is identical over $S'$.

We do hope that the passages above, together with the various voting situations that we presented, were not too confusing for the reader. We repeat what we have asserted a few pages above: different voting procedures will in general yield different results. Is this a dilemma? To some degree, it is. Therefore, as in all other axiomatic analyses, one has to look 'behind the curtain' and discuss and debate the underlying properties of the various voting methods. This will most probably *not* lead to a unanimous verdict among the participants in such a discussion, but it will certainly render the arguments pro and con more transparent. This already is, we believe, some achievement.

## 6.3. **Other social choice rules**

At different instances in this primer, we 'stumbled' over the paradox of voting. How can such a voting constellation be resolved? The binary relation based on the simple majority rule is cyclical in this case so that there does not exist a non-empty choice set. The Borda rule with its equidistanced weighting scheme assigns the same rank-total to all the alternatives in the last example of the previous section. Note that other weighting schemes would do exactly the same in this particular situation of three alternatives and three individuals (or four alternatives with four persons, etc. all showing the fully symmetric Latin square structure). So, according to Borda, all alternatives are socially equivalent. There is a method which is based on pairwise majority voting, that also leads to social indifference in these, but also other cases. It is the transitive closure method.

For any finite set $S$ of alternatives and any given preference profile $w$, the choice set $h^{TC}(w, S)$ according to the transitive closure method is defined by

$$h^{TC}(w, S) = \{x \in S| \text{ for every } y \in S, \text{ there exist alternatives } y_1, y_2, \ldots, y_m$$
$$\text{in } S \text{ such that } N(xR_iy_1) \geq N(y_1R_ix), N(y_1R_iy_2)$$
$$\geq N(y_2R_iy_1), \ldots, N(y_mR_iy) \geq N(yR_iy_m)\},$$

where $N(xR_iy_1)$, as before, stands for the number of persons who declare that $x$ is at least as good as $y_1$. In the typical paradox of voting profile, $x$ beats $y$ majority-wise in a direct comparison, but $y$ also beats $x$ majority-wise through a sequence, i.e. $y$ beats $z$ and $z$ beats $x$. So, by applying the transitive closure method to all alternatives involved, we obtain $h^{TC}(w, S) = \{x, y, z\}$ in the paradox-of-voting case.

Is this method a satisfactory choice rule? Like the Borda method, it avoids the non-existence of a choice function. It does this at the cost of declaring all elements whenever involved in a majority cycle as equivalent. Therefore, it does this more often than the Borda method which can already be seen from the following simple example with five persons and $S = \{x, y, z\}$:

| 1 | 2 | 3 | 4 | 5 |
|---|---|---|---|---|
| x | x | y | y | z |
| y | y | z | z | x |
| z | z | x | x | y |

The transitive closure method leads to $h^{TC}(w, S) = S$; the Borda rule yields $h^B(w, S) = \{y\}$.

The transitive closure method has one rather unpleasant characteristic – it can include a Pareto-dominated alternative in its choice set. Consider profile

$w$ we have used before with $S = \{x, y, z, v\}$:

| 1 | 2 | 3 |
|---|---|---|
| $x$ | $y$ | $z$ |
| $y$ | $z$ | $v$ |
| $z$ | $v$ | $x$ |
| $v$ | $x$ | $y$ |

The result is that $h^{TC}(w, S) = S$. This set includes alternative $v$ which all persons consider less desirable than $z$.

We could now do the same as in the case of the Borda rule, viz. introduce a broad and a narrow variant of the transitive closure method. But we shall abstain from this and simply appeal to the reader's imagination. Analogous to what we saw in the Borda case, the broad version of the closure method has problems with the independence condition; the narrow variant runs into problems with contraction consistency. The latter point can be immediately inferred from the previous example. Here we have seen that $h^{TC}(w, \{x, y, z, v\}) = \{x, y, z, v\}$, but over the pair $(z, v)$, the narrow variant would 'honour' the weak Pareto principle, i.e. $h^{NTC}(w, \{z, v\}) = \{z\}$. Alternative $v$ which was chosen before and still is feasible, will no longer be picked.

Let us look at some other choice rules. The Copeland method is based on pairwise contests, typically applying the simple majority rule. For each alternative $x$ in a set $S$ of options, a score $s(x)$ is calculated which represents the number of other alternatives that $x$ beats or ties in a pairwise comparison. The choice set according to the Copeland procedure consists of those elements $x$ in $S$ for which $s(x)$ is maximal. For profile $w$ above, the choice set according to Copeland would be $h^{CO}(w, \{x, y, z, v\}) = \{y, z\}$. If the Copeland scores are calculated for each $S' \subseteq S$, then going from subsets to the superset may lead to a violation of expansion consistency. Kelly (1988, pp. 54–55) shows that the Copeland method violates the condition of consistency of sets of voters that we discussed in connection with Young's characterization of the Borda method. On the other hand, Copeland's rule always picks a Condorcet winner, if it exists, and never chooses a Pareto-dominated alternative.

Dodgson (1876) – alias Lewis Carroll – suggested for the case that no Condorcet winner exists, that for each alternative $x \in S$, the number of binary preference reversals be calculated such that $x$ becomes a Condorcet winner. A binary preference reversal is an interchange or switch between two adjacent positions. Those alternatives should eventually be chosen for which the number of binary preference reversals is minimal. To illustrate this procedure, let us go back to profile $w$ with $S = \{x, y, z, v\}$ from above:

| 1 | 2 | 3 |
|---|---|---|
| $x$ | $y$ | $z$ |
| $y$ | $z$ | $v$ |
| $z$ | $v$ | $x$ |
| $v$ | $x$ | $y$ |

It is easily seen that one binary preference reversal will turn alternative $z$ into a Condorcet winner. This preference reversal could 'happen' either in person 1's or in person 2's ordering. However, one preference reversal (either in the first or the third ordering) would also make $y$ a Condorcet winner. Alternative $x$ would need two preference reversals, alternative $v$ more than two. Therefore, according to Dodgson, $h^{DO}(w, \{x, y, z, v\}) = \{y, z\}$. Which of Arrow's conditions is violated by this rule? It is the independence condition (just form a new profile $\hat{w}$ where in the third ordering above, $x$ and $y$ are reversed).

Dodgson's proposal to look for the minimal number of binary preference reversals such that a Condorcet winner arises, when there was no Condorcet winner before the preference inversions, is an interesting one. This method can be interpreted as some sort of a distance minimization procedure, although it has to be admitted that at this point we have not yet clarified what a distance function could look like when its domain are binary relations on the set of alternatives.

We mentioned in our introduction that Condorcet was well aware of cyclical majorities. Condorcet proposed a resolution scheme for such cases but his arguments remained fragmentary. At one instance, however, Condorcet argued that in a situation where, let's say, a majority prefers $x$ to $y$, $y$ to $z$, and $z$ to $x$, the proposition with the smallest majority should be deleted and that alternative should be picked which comes out as the winner under the two remaining propositions. This seems to indicate that Condorcet wanted his proposal to be based on maximal support of propositions that express preferability of different options. For the general case of $k$ alternatives, Condorcet's suggestion would imply to count the support provided by the voters to each of $k!$ collective rankings (if only strict orderings are considered) and choose the one with largest support. Nurmi (2002) quotes Michaud (1985) and Young (1988) when he argues that 'what Condorcet had in mind as a general method of voting' (2002, p. 65) was a procedure that is known in the modern voting literature as Kemeny's (1959) rule.

Kemeny's procedure looks for a ranking to be viewed as a unanimous social preference ordering that is closest to a given preference profile. Being closest is meant in the sense of requiring the smallest number of inversions in the individual orderings such that this ranking becomes a common ranking for all members of society. This rule is computationally rather complex so that some more explanation and an example may help to clarify what is going on.

Let us start out from a given preference profile. Kemeny suggests to construct, for a given number of alternatives, all complete and transitive preference rankings, decompose them into pairs of alternatives and then compare these pairs, for each ordering in turn, with the given preference profile of society. More concretely, for the ordering $x$ preferred to $y$ preferred to $z$, one considers the ordered pairs $(x, y)$, $(y, z)$ and $(x, z)$ and checks for the number of instances where the strict preference for $x$ over $y$, for $y$ over $z$, and for $x$ over $z$ occur in a given profile for society.

In order to illustrate Kemeny's rule in detail, we use an example from Nurmi (2002, p. 67). Though we are primarily interested in deriving the Kemeny ranking, this example contains a couple of other aspects which should not remain unnoticed. First of all, there is a Condorcet winner, viz. $z$, which, however, is not chosen by plurality voting. Actually, plurality voting leads to the choice of a Condorcet loser. Alternative $x$ loses against $y$ and $z$ in pairwise majority contests. Here is the profile:

| 1–4 | 5–7 | 8–9 |
|-----|-----|-----|
| $x$ | $y$ | $z$ |
| $z$ | $z$ | $y$ |
| $y$ | $x$ | $x$ |

Obviously, four voters have the first strict preference, three voters the second, and two voters the third. We now compute the Kemeny ranking as the unanimous ordering closest to the given profile. There are six possible orderings (if we only consider strict preferences), which receive the following amount of support from the profile:

$$
\begin{aligned}
x \succ y \succ z: &\quad 4 + 3 + 4 = 11 \\
x \succ z \succ y: &\quad 4 + 6 + 4 = 14 \\
y \succ x \succ z: &\quad 5 + 4 + 3 = 12 \\
y \succ z \succ x: &\quad 3 + 5 + 5 = 13 \\
z \succ x \succ y: &\quad 5 + 4 + 6 = 15 \\
z \succ y \succ x: &\quad 6 + 5 + 5 = 16
\end{aligned}
$$

Thus, the strict preference of $z$ over $y$, for example, is supported at six instances (persons 1–4 and persons 8–9), $y$ strictly preferred to $x$ is supported at five instances and the same holds for the strict preference of $z$ over $x$. Taking all frequencies into account, we see that the unanimous ranking according to Kemeny is $z \succ y \succ x$, which is just the opposite of a ranking based on the plurality rule. The ordering $z \succ y \succ x$ receives maximal support from the given profile or, turned around, this ordering has the smallest distance to the preferences of the nine voters. Thus, Kemeny's rule minimizes the distance between a preference ordering and the underlying preference profile, applying an inversion metric where pairwise preference reversals are the units. It can be shown that whenever a Condorcet winner exists, it is the top element in the Kemeny ranking (Nurmi, 2002, p. 31). Saari and Merlin (2000) have demonstrated that the Condorcet loser is always ranked last in the Kemeny ranking. Both results are good arguments in favour of the Kemeny procedure.

We want to be more precise about the Kemeny metric. In order to do this, we have to introduce the notion of a distance function. Let $\mathcal{R}$ stand for the set of all complete binary relations $R$ on $X$, the set of alternatives. $R, R', R''$ are subsets of ordered pairs in the product $X \times X$. A function $d : \mathcal{R}^2 \to \mathbb{R}_+$, which assigns a non-negative real number to all pairs of binary relations on $X$ will be called a distance function on $\mathcal{R}$. We now define a metric on $\mathcal{R}$ as a distance function $d$, defined on pairs of binary relations, which has the following properties for all $R, R', R'' \in \mathcal{R}$:

1. $d(R, R') = 0$ if and only if $R = R'$;
2. $d(R, R') = d(R', R)$;
3. $d(R, R'') \leq d(R, R') + d(R', R'')$.

The first requirement is obvious. The second requirement says that distance is symmetric. The third requirement says that the distance between two relations $R$ and $R''$ cannot be made any smaller by passing through any third relation $R'$.

The Kemeny metric $d^K$ on $\mathcal{R}$ can be defined as follows for any $R, R' \in \mathcal{R}$: $d^K(R, R') = |(R - R') \cup (R' - R)|$. This means that Kemeny's metric defines a distance between two binary relations $R$ and $R'$ as the number of elements, i.e. ordered pairs, which belong to one set without belonging to the other set. As we can see from the example above, the Kemeny distance reflects the minimum number of binary preference changes or inversions needed to render a ranking unanimously accepted.

The idea of distance or proximity of preference relations and preference profiles is an interesting one which was discussed by Nitzan (1981) and Baigent (1987a,b), among others. We shall come back to this issue in Chapter 10. Nitzan has shown that finding the Borda winner, i.e. determining the alternative with the largest Borda score, is equivalent to finding the alternative that can be made the unanimity winner with the smallest number of preference reversals. In other words, the Borda winner is the alternative which is closest, in terms of Kemeny's metric, to being first ranked by all voters. Baigent and Klamler (2004) have shown that the transitive closure method that we discussed at the beginning of this section is not distance-minimizing relative to the Kemeny metric.

A few pages above, we said that the Dodgson method can also be seen as a distance minimization procedure. Ratliff (2001) states that while there are similarities between the rules of Dodgson and Kemeny, 'the difference between requiring a complete transitive ranking and requiring only a Condorcet winner leads to tremendous conflict between the Dodgson winner and the Kemeny ranking' (Ratliff, 2001, p. 79). Let us look at the following example given by the author:

| 1–21 | 22–33 | 34–38 | 39–50 |
|:---:|:---:|:---:|:---:|
| $x$ | $z$ | $v$ | $y$ |
| $y$ | $v$ | $z$ | $v$ |
| $z$ | $y$ | $x$ | $x$ |
| $v$ | $x$ | $y$ | $z$ |

The Kemeny ranking in this situation is the strict ordering of voters 1–21. The Dodgson ranking is $y$ preferred to $x$ preferred to $z$ which is indifferent to $v$. This shows that the Dodgson winner is not necessarily ranked first in the Kemeny ranking. Ratliff (2001) shows that in the case of at least four alternatives, there is no connection between the Dodgson winner and the Kemeny ranking. In other words, the Dodgson winner may occur at any position within the Kemeny ranking, even the last position. This means that the Dodgson winner can be the Condorcet loser.

## 6.4. **A parliamentary vote: Berlin vs. Bonn**

In the last section of this chapter, we present a real-life example from recent Parliamentary history, viz. the decision of the German Parliament (the Bundestag) to move the seat of Parliament and the seat of Government from Bonn to Berlin. This was a historic moment in recent German history and happened on 20 June 1991. The decision is carefully presented and analysed by Leininger (1993).

Before going into details, we would like to emphasize that this example from the political sphere makes an issue very transparent that should have become clear during the theoretical analysis in the preceding sections of this chapter: different voting rules can produce vastly different outcomes. However, an additional aspect shows its importance in the present example. The actually chosen sequential procedure (which was multistage and not single-stage) may matter as well.

Parliamentary proceedings that eventually led to the decision in favour of Berlin consisted of several stages and several votes. There were no secret ballots. There was roll-call which made it possible for Leininger, with a few additional assumptions, to reconstruct the rankings of the members of Parliament.

Originally, there were five motions but one of them was later withdrawn. The remaining four motions were:

alternative A: Parliament resides in Berlin, Government resides in Bonn;
alternative B: Both Parliament and Government move to Berlin;
alternative C: Parliament and Government stay in Bonn;
alternative D: Parliament and Government should not be geographically separated.

Note that alternative D does not recommend a specific outcome but manifests a particular stance or view. The Council of Elders suggested the following agenda which was accepted by the Bundestag. A first vote is to be held on alternative A. Should A be approved, the issue is resolved and no further votes should be taken. In case A is not approved, alternative D will be put to the vote. Whatever the outcome of this vote will be, in the following step alternatives B and C and the fifth motion (which, as we already know, was later withdrawn) will be put simultaneously to the vote against each other. If one of the three alternatives receives more votes than the other two together, it will be adopted as the winning alternative. Should this not be the case, there will be a final vote between the two best-placed alternatives.

As it turned out, there were three votes, viz. on alternative A, alternative D, and on alternatives B and C together. From these results, Leininger inferred the preferences of the members of Parliament. There were three 'real' alternatives, viz. options A, B and C. Leininger used information on the three votes cast by each member of Parliament and combined this information with consistency requirements to reconstruct the individuals' rankings.

All six ways in which alternatives A, B and C can be linearly ordered, can be explained via reasonable hypotheses. Hypothesis 1 of Leininger, for example, says that a member of Parliament who approved of alternative A in the first vote *must* give rank 1 to this alternative in his or her preference ordering. A second hypothesis says that a representative who approved of alternative D in the second vote and had rejected alternative A in the first vote *must* give rank 3 to alternative A in his or her ordering. Leininger asserts that these two hypotheses have the following implications:

(i) An individual who approved of A in the first vote and B, respectively C, in the third vote must have the ordering $A \succ B \succ C$, respectively $A \succ C \succ B$.
(ii) A representative who approved of alternative D in the second vote and B, respectively C, in the third vote must have the preference ordering $B \succ C \succ A$, respectively $C \succ B \succ A$.

These inferences allow the identification of the orderings of 425 members of Parliament, out of 659 who cast valid votes in the final ballot between B and C. Additional hypotheses were needed to explain the other rankings. One of these hypotheses appears more debatable than some others so that

Leininger offered an alternative hypothesis. He then demonstrated to which rankings these alternative hypotheses lead. However, we abstain from giving further details.

The results in the three rounds of voting in Parliament were as follows. Both alternative A and alternative D were defeated, the first by 489 to 147 with 18 abstentions, the latter by 340 to 288 with 29 abstentions. Finally Berlin won against Bonn with 338 to 320 votes, with one abstention and one invalid ballot.

According to one set of hypotheses, the subsequent assignment of votes over the six possible rankings can be inferred:

| 116 voters | 30 voters | 81 voters | 140 voters | 140 voters | 150 voters |
|:---:|:---:|:---:|:---:|:---:|:---:|
| A | A | B | B | C | C |
| B | C | A | C | A | B |
| C | B | C | A | B | A |

Given this preference profile, the following statements can be made:

(1) Majority rule over all three alternatives simultaneously with the requirement that one of them receive more votes than the other two together would have been indecisive.

(2) Majority rule with a second round (run-off vote) after eliminating the alternative with the lowest support in the first round (this was alternative A) would have seen alternative B as the winner.

(3) Plurality rule would have chosen alternative C.

(4) There was a Condorcet winner, viz. alternative B.

(5) The Borda rule would have chosen alternative C.

It is quite remarkable to observe that the voting outcome according to statement (2) comes close to the voting result in stage 3 of the actual Parliamentary vote. This outcome was reported above. On the basis of Leininger's reconstruction, B would have gathered 337 votes, C would have received 320 votes. Leininger writes that this result 'supports the view that the procedure adopted can be best thought of as a variant of majority rule with a run-off vote' (Leininger, 1993, p. 12). He goes on to say that the final outcome in favour of Berlin was in some sense 'forced' by the chosen procedure. Plurality rule would have made Bonn a winner. Eliminating alternative A at an early stage helped Berlin. Leininger's assignment of votes shows that only 30 supporters of A had alternative C in second place, while 116 voters had B in second place. Thus, the sequential procedure chosen by the Bundestag may have mattered a lot.

Given the assignment of votes above, Nurmi (2002, p. 70) computed the total pairwise support for each of the six rankings. The ordering $B \succ C \succ A$ receives a pairwise support of 1138, the ordering $C \succ B \succ A$ gets a support of 1121. Thus, the Kemeny ranking of the given profile is $B \succ C \succ A$ which reminds us of the 'fact' that the Condorcet winner is at the top of the Kemeny ranking. But the two numbers just given also demonstrate that the 'race' between Berlin and Bonn was close.

## 6.5. **A short summary**

Requiring less than full transitivity of the social preference relation makes it possible to combine the four original Arrovian conditions and obtain an aggregation rule that does not lead to contradictory statements. True. On the other hand, we have to ask how satisfactory such a scheme is. Sen's Pareto-extension rule is an aggregation mechanism that exists for all possible profiles, but we have seen that it resolves conflicting preference orderings by ranking alternatives equally. In other words, this rule creates a lot of equivalences. More technically speaking, there exist weak dictators.

We have then started an inquiry that we shall resume in a somewhat different way in the next chapter. We enlarged the informational basis and explored its consequences. The Borda rank-order method uses information from positions so that the social ranking between $x$ and $y$, let's say, not only depends on information on how individuals rank $x$ vis-à-vis $y$ but also on information concerning the positions other alternatives have in relation to $x$ and $y$.

There are various other aggregation rules that use more information than is employed by simple majority voting. An important message of this chapter is that different rules may lead to different outcomes. This may be considered to be a dilemma and the vote on Berlin vs. Bonn can be viewed as a striking example, but we have also seen that the outcomes from applying various aggregation methods are not totally arbitrary. There are regularities that we have tried to make more precise. For example, if a Condorcet winner exists, it is the top element in the Kemeny ranking which is based on the idea of proximity or distance between preference relations and profiles. And a Condorcet loser is always ranked last in the Kemeny ranking. This is comforting.

### ☐ **RECOMMENDED READING**

Kelly, J. S. (1988). *Social Choice Theory. An Introduction,* chapters 5 and 6. Berlin, Heidelberg, New York: Springer-Verlag.

Nurmi, H. (2002). *Voting Procedures under Uncertainty,* chapters 3 and 5. Berlin, Heidelberg, New York: Springer-Verlag.

Sen, A. K. (1970b). *Collective Choice and Social Welfare,* chapters 4 and 5. San Francisco, Cambridge: Holden-Day.

## ☐ HISTORICAL SOURCE

Black, D. (1958). *The Theory of Committees and Elections,* part II. Cambridge: Cambridge University Press.


## ☐ MORE ADVANCED

Saari, D. G. (1995). *Basic Geometry of Voting,* chapter IV. Berlin, Heidelberg, New York: Springer-Verlag.

Sen, A. K. (1986). 'Social Choice Theory', in K. J. Arrow and M. D. Intriligator (eds.), *Handbook of Mathematical Economics,* vol. III, chapter 22. Amsterdam: North-Holland.

Young, H. P. (1975). 'Social Choice Scoring Functions'. *SIAM Journal of Applied Mathematics,* 28: 824–838.

# 7 Distributive justice: Rawlsian and utilitarian rules

## 7.1. **The philosophical background**

Over more than two centuries, utilitarianism had been the uncontested school of thought for issues of welfare and redistribution. In Hutcheson's (1725) *An Inquiry into the Original of Our Ideas of Beauty and Virtue*, one can find the utilitarian postulate 'of the greatest happiness of the greatest number' which became famous through Bentham's work (1776) who admitted to have been heavily influenced by Helvétius's writings (1758). In order to decide whether state $x$ is at least as good for society as state $y$ (the reader will hopefully excuse our more prosaic language), utilitarianism prescribes that the utilities that accrue to the individual members of society under the two states be summed or aggregated. So $x$ will be chosen for society if the utility sum under $x$ is at least as large as the utility sum under $y$. Utilitarianism is outcome-oriented and consequentialist in nature. While it focuses on maximizing the sum of individual utilities, it is largely unconcerned with the interpersonal distribution of this sum.

Rawls (1971) developed his concept of justice as fairness, proposing two principles of justice which are meant to be guidelines for how the basic structure of society is to realize the values of liberty and equality. It is probably fair to say that Rawls's work has become a powerful contestant of utilitarianism over the last few decades. In his first principle, Rawls requires each person to have an equal right to the most extensive basic liberty compatible with a similar liberty for others. Basic liberties are political liberty, freedom of speech and assembly, liberty of conscience and freedom of thought, the right to hold personal property, and others. Rawls's second principle, the difference principle, on which economists have focussed in particular, requires that social and economic inequalities are to be arranged so that they are both to the greatest benefit of the least advantaged members of society and attached to offices and positions open to all under conditions of fair equality of opportunity. Rawls argued that benefits should be judged not in terms of utilities but through an index of so-called primary goods which comprise the basic liberties, opportunities and powers, self-respect, and income and wealth. Several of these items are clearly non-welfaristic in character. Rawls's concept of primary goods is chiefly means-oriented. Individuals have rational plans with different final ends. They all require these primary goods for the execution of their plans.

In the following sections, we shall axiomatically describe and compare both utilitarianism and the first half of Rawls's second principle, often called the maximin rule; more precisely, we shall characterize the lexicographic version of this rule. In order to make this comparison as coherent as possible, we shall reformulate Rawls's maximin principle in terms of utilities. We frankly admit that this is a heavy truncation of Rawls's philosophical edifice, but as just said it allows us to make comparisons with utilitarianism; without such a reformulation a comparison would become much harder.

As has become clear from the discussion above, the informational basis of utilitarianism is different from the basis of Rawlsianism. Utilitarianism considers gains and losses across individuals and uses summation. In other words, it is required that utility differences be measurable and comparable interpersonally. Rawls's maximin principle requires that levels of utility be comparable interpersonally but there is no need for measuring utility differences. The following section will make these concepts more precise.

## 7.2. **The informational structure**

Remember that in the third proof of Arrow's theorem in section 2.4, we were exploiting the fact that in a world of ordinal utility with no trace of interpersonal comparability, every individual is perfectly free to map his or her utility scale into another one by a strictly monotone transformation. Informationally speaking, the 'original' utility index and the 'new' one generated by a strictly increasing transformation cannot be distinguished. They belong to the same information set which is very large in this case, since any strictly increasing transformation is as good, informationally wise, as any other. We shall see in due course that with the introduction of various types of comparisons, the size of the class of admissible transformations will shrink. In other words, there is an inverse relationship between the size of the set of transformations that keep information invariant and the amount of usable information.

In the following, we shall largely follow the analysis of D'Aspremont and Gevers (1977). With $N$ being a finite set of individuals and with $X$ being a finite set of conceivable social states, let, for all $i \in N$ and for all $x, y \in X$, $u(x, i), u(y, i)$ be individual $i$'s utility values defined on $X \times N$. The cartesian product $X \times N$ allows us to link individuals $i, j, k$, let's say, to social alternatives $x, y, z, \ldots$ so that the individuals' positions under different social states can be considered (how does individual $i$ in state $x$, for example, fare in comparison to person $j$ under alternative $y$?). The values $u(x, i), u(y, i)$ of individual $i$'s utility are seen either through the eyes of an ethical observer (Harsanyi) or are unanimous evaluations 'under a veil of ignorance' (Rawls). Let $U = (u(\cdot, 1), \ldots, u(\cdot, n))$ be an $n$-tuple of utility functions for the $n$ members of society, a profile for short. The set of all possible profiles will be denoted by $\mathcal{U}$. A social evaluation functional or social welfare functional (see section 2.4 above) is a mapping $F$ from $\mathcal{U}$ to $\mathcal{E}$, the set of all orderings of $X$. This definition implies that the domain of $F$ is assumed to be unrestricted. For every $U^1, U^2 \in \mathcal{U}$, we write $R_{U^1} = F(U^1)$ and $R_{U^2} = F(U^2)$.

Let us now come back to the informational structure. The Arrovian world of ordinally measurable, non-comparable utilities ($OMN$) can be described formally as follows.

OMN. For every $U^1, U^2 \in \mathcal{U}, R_{U^1} = R_{U^2}$ if for every $i \in N$, $\varphi_i$ is a strictly increasing transformation such that, for all $x \in X$, $u^2(x, i) = \varphi_i(u^1(x, i))$ where $u^1(\cdot, \cdot)$ and $u^2(\cdot, \cdot)$ are the utility components of profiles $U^1, U^2$ respectively.

This is the informational set-up of section 2.4. We next wish to introduce interpersonal comparisons of utility levels while preserving ordinal measurability ($OMCL$). Note that this requirement reduces the set of permissible transformations.

OMCL. For every $U^1, U^2 \in \mathcal{U}, R_{U^1} = R_{U^2}$ if $\varphi$ is a strictly increasing transformation such that for all $i \in N$ and for all $x \in X$, $u^2(x, i) = \varphi(u^1(x, i))$.

If individual utilities are transformed, they are subjected to a *common* transformation. Note that level comparisons of individual utilities are possible within this informational requirement since $u^1(x, i) \geq u^1(x, j)$ iff $\varphi(u^1(x, i)) \geq \varphi(u^1(x, j))$ for all $i, j \in N$ and all $x \in X$. Interpersonal comparisons of utility gains and losses are, of course, not possible.

We now introduce cardinal individual utility functions without any interpersonal comparability ($CMN$).

CMN. For every $U^1, U^2 \in \mathcal{U}, R_{U^1} = R_{U^2}$ if there exist $2n$ numbers $\alpha_1, \ldots, \alpha_n, \beta_1 > 0, \ldots, \beta_n > 0$ such that, for all $i \in N$ and for all $x \in X$, $u^2(x, i) = \alpha_i + \beta_i \cdot u^1(x, i)$.

Note that the values for $\alpha_i$ can be positive, negative or zero, whereas the values for $\beta_i$ must be strictly positive ($i \in \{1, \ldots, n\}$). Each individual can choose his or her origin and utility scale independently. This means that neither level comparability nor a comparison of utility gains and losses is possible across individuals. This informational structure will be used in the following chapter on bargaining solutions.

Comparability of both levels and gains and losses would be possible if we required that $\alpha_i = \alpha_j$ and $\beta_i = \beta_j$ for all $i, j \in N$, meaning that both origin and scale unit are the same for everyone. This would be a very severe limitation of admissible transformations but would, of course, render the amount of usable information much richer. However, for our purposes in the sequel, we do not need this restriction of admissible transforms. What we need is the possibility of comparing gains and losses across individuals. This can be achieved by introducing cardinally measurable and unit-comparable utilities (*CMCU*).

*CMCU*. For every $U^1, U^2 \in \mathcal{U}, R_{U^1} = R_{U^2}$ if there exist $n + 1$ numbers $\alpha_1, \dots, \alpha_n$ and $\beta > 0$ such that, for all $i \in N$ and for all $x \in X, u^2(x, i) = \alpha_i + \beta u^1(x, i)$.

The interpersonal comparison of utility differences is now possible; utility levels cannot be compared across individuals.

We have seen above that assumptions of measurability specify which types of transformations may be applied to an individual's utility function *without* altering the individually usable information. Comparability assumptions such as a common scale unit for all $i \in N$ specify *how much* of this information can be used across persons.

Let us recapitulate the different forms of informational set-up in the following scheme:

| | | |
|---|---|---|
| *OMN* | no interpersonal comparisons possible, neither of utility levels nor of gains and losses | ordinal Arrovian approach |
| *OMCL* | interpersonal comparisons of utility levels possible, but not of gains and losses | ordinal Rawlsian approach |
| *CMN* | no interpersonal comparisons possible, neither of utility levels nor of gains and losses | cardinal bargaining approach |
| *CMCU* | an interpersonal comparison of gains and losses possible, not of utility levels | cardinal utilitarian approach |

## 7.3. **Axioms and characterizations**

In this section, we wish to characterize the 'leximin' variant of Rawls's maximin principle and the utilitarian rule. Actually, Rawls (1971, p. 83) provided a verbal statement of the lexicographic version of maximin (which he called the lexical difference principle, referring to a formulation by Sen (1970)) but stated that in his book he would stick to the simpler form. We start by introducing various axioms. Some of these will be known from earlier chapters though, at those instances, they were formulated in terms of orderings and not in terms of utilities.

In section 3.1 when we were discussing simple majority voting, we argued that name-tags of individuals should not matter. Now we shall argue that in each social state only the list of individual utility values should matter, but not the names attached to them. Then we can define anonymity in the following way.

**Anonymity** (*AN*). Let $\sigma$ be any permutation on the set of individuals $N$. For every $U', U'' \in \mathcal{U}, R_{U'} = R_{U''}$ if $U'$ and $U''$ are such that for all $i \in N$ and for all $x \in X, u'(x, i) = u''(x, \sigma(i))$ where $u'(\cdot, \cdot)$ are the utility components of profile $u'$ and $u''(\cdot, \cdot)$ are the utility components after permutation.

It does not matter for the social evaluation whether certain utility values $\bar{u}(x, \cdot)$ and $\bar{\bar{u}}(x, \cdot)$ in state $x$, let's say, are attached to person $i$ and person $k$, respectively, or whether the same utility values are assigned to persons $k$ and $i$ (so that name-tags got permuted).

The next axiom is the strict version of the Pareto principle.

**Strict Pareto** (*SP*). For all $x, y \in X$ and for all $U \in \mathcal{U}, xR_U y$ if, for all $i \in N, u(x, i) \geq u(y, i)$. If, moreover, for some $j \in N, u(x, j) > u(y, j)$, then $xP_U y$.

$R_U$ is the ordering generated by functional $F$ and $xP_U y$ stands for the case that $xR_U y$ and $\neg yR_U x$.

The independence condition, defined in terms of utility values, was informally defined in section 2.4. Here is the more formal version.

**Independence (in utility terms – IU).** For every $U^1, U^2 \in \mathcal{U}$, for all $x, y \in X, R_{U^1}$ and $R_{U^2}$ coincide on $\{x, y\}$, if $x$ and $y$ obtain the same $n$-tuple of utilities in $U^1$ and $U^2$, i.e. $U^1 = U^2$ on $\{x, y\} \times N$.

We mention in passing that *IU* and *SP*, taken together, imply the neutrality property to which we referred at various instances in earlier chapters. Just to remind the reader, neutrality implies that labels of alternatives do not matter. All the relevant information for social evaluation is contained in the given utility values.

In connection with the description of majority voting under restricted domains, we introduced the concept of concerned voters (Sen, 1970, chapter 10), i.e. those voters who are not indifferent between every pair of elements in a given set of alternatives. Unconcerned persons would be those who are indifferent between all given options. Should these individuals have an influence on collective choice? At this point we have not yet properly defined utilitarianism, but from our discussion in the first section of this chapter it should have become clear that voters who are unconcerned between $x$ and $y$, let's say, do not play any decisive rule in the collective decision between $x$ and $y$ under a utilitarian rule. More specifically, these voters increase the sum of utilities both for $x$ and $y$ equally. That is all. Therefore, these people can be 'deleted' in utility calculations. The utility level of unconcerned persons could play a role if complete distributions of utility or welfare levels were evaluated. At this point, however, we shall eliminate the possible influence of unconcerned persons by introducing the following separability requirement.

**Separability of unconcerned individuals (SE).** For every $U^1, U^2 \in \mathcal{U}, R_{U^1} = R_{U^2}$ if there exists $M \subset N$ such that for all $i \in M$ and for all $x \in X, u^1(x, i) = u^2(x, i)$ while for all $h \in N \backslash M$ and for all $x, y \in X, u^1(x, h) = u^1(y, h)$ and $u^2(x, h) = u^2(y, h)$.

Note that $h \in N \backslash M$ are the unconcerned persons. Having the separability axiom in mind, we can consider conflicts between just two individuals over two social states, with all the other individuals being indifferent between these two states. Furthermore, we let one of the two individuals in conflict always be worse-off than the other, no matter whether one or the other of the two states is realized eventually. This leads to an equity axiom which goes back to Sen (1973), Hammond (1976) and Strasnick (1976). The present version in utility terms is taken from D'Aspremont and Gevers (1977).

**Equity (EQ).** For all $U \in \mathcal{U}$, for all $x, y \in X$ and for all $i, j \in N, xP_Uy$ whenever for all $h \in (N \backslash \{i, j\}), u(x, h) = u(y, h)$ and $u(y, i) < u(x, i) < u(x, j) < u(y, j)$.

Clearly, interpersonal comparisons of utility levels are a prerequisite for applying this condition. Given the indifference of persons $h$, it is the worse-off of the two persons $i$ and $j$ who determines the social outcome. Several researchers have circumscribed such a situation by positional dictatorship or rank dictatorship. It is not a particular person who dictates (as in Arrow's set-up), it is a position which is socially decisive, together with the person who holds this position (whoever this person is).

The opposite of a consideration for equity is a focus on inequity, not that appealing admittedly. It is the better-off of the two persons who determines the social preference.

**Inequity (INEQ).** For all $U \in \mathcal{U}$, for all $x, y \in X$ and for all $i, j \in N, yP_Ux$ whenever for all $h \in (N \backslash \{i, j\}), u(x, h) = u(y, h)$ and $u(y, i) < u(x, i) < u(x, j) < u(y, j)$.

D'Aspremont and Gevers state and prove the following result.

**Theorem 7.1.** If $F$ satisfies $IU$, $SP$, $AN$, $SE$ and the informational require-ment $OMCL$, it satisfies either $EQ$ or $INEQ$.

This is an interesting result indeed since it provides a kind of bifurcation. The axiomatic set-up, combined with the informational frame of ordinally measurable and interpersonally comparable utility levels either leads to a focus on the worse-off or to a concentration on the better-off. Our present goal is a characterization of the lexicographic version of Rawls's maximin rule, leximin for short. This principle turns the person holding the least-favoured non-indifferent rank into a positional dictator. Before defining the leximin principle, we have to be somewhat more explicit about the structure of ranks.

Given a vector of utilities $U$ for $n$ individuals, let $r_x(U)$ be the person who holds rank $r(1 \leq r \leq n)$ and is $r$th best-off under state $x$, $1_x(U)$ be the person who holds the first rank and is best-off and $n_x(U)$ be the individual who holds the lowest position and is, therefore, worst-off under $x$ (for simplicity, we omit ties among individuals). As an example, consider the utility vector $U(x) = (2, 6, 4)$, giving the utility values of three persons $1, 2$ and $3$ under state $x$. Then, according to our notation, $1_x(U) = 2$ since person 2 receives the highest utility in a level comparison, $2_x(U) = 3$, and $3_x(U) = 1$. Rawlsian maximin would now require that $xR_Uy$ iff $u(x, n_x(U)) \geq u(y, n_y(U))$. Maximin implies that the $n$th rank or lowest position is a positional dictator. Leximin starts from the very bottom of utility levels (the lowest ranked individual under different social states) and works its way upwards if the utility levels of the lowest ranked persons under the given alternatives are equally low. So under the leximin principle, for all $U \in \mathcal{U}$, for all $x, y \in X$, $xP_Uy$ iff there exists a rank $k$ $(1 \leq k \leq n)$ such that $u(x, k_x(U)) > u(y, k_y(U))$ and $u(x, l_x(U)) = u(y, l_y(U))$ for all $l > k, l \leq n$.

A second example may help. Let us postulate a $U \in \mathcal{U}$ with $U(x) = (5, 3, 6, 2, 1)$ and $U(y) = (1, 2, 4, 3, 6)$. The ranks $r$ in $U(x)$ and $U(y)$ run from 1 to 5 so that $1 \leq r \leq 5$. At the bottom of the hierarchy, we have $r = n = 5$ and $u(x, 5) = u(y, 1)$, then for $r = 4$, we obtain $u(x, 4) = u(y, 2)$, then for $r = 3$, we have $u(x, 2) = u(y, 4)$. For $r = 2$, we get $u(x, 1) > u(y, 3)$ and finally, for $r = 1$, we obtain $u(x, 3) = u(y, 5)$.

The Rawlsian maximin rule would come to the conclusion that $xI_Uy$, since at the lowest level, the utility values under $x$ and $y$ are the same. The lex-imin principle would arrive at $xP_Uy$, since there is a rank $k$, $k = 2$, such that $u(x, k_x(U)) > u(y, k_y(U))$ while for $l > k$, it is always the case that $u(x, l_x(U)) = u(y, l_y(U))$.

The leximax principle starts from the top of utility levels and works its way downwards. Leximax establishes the dictatorship of the most favoured non-indifferent rank. We abstain from providing an explicit definition of this rule.

D'Aspremont and Gevers introduce a minimal equity axiom ($MEQ$) in order to obtain a complete characterization of the leximin principle.

**Minimal Equity ($MEQ$).** The social evaluation functional $F$ is not the leximax principle.

This axiom is very weak indeed. The following characterization of the leximin rule is then established.

**Theorem 7.2.** The leximin principle is characterized by $IU$, $SP$, $AN$, $SE$, the informational requirement $OMCL$ and $MEQ$.

A second characterization of the leximin rule in D'Aspremont and Gevers does without the separability axiom $SE$ and puts the equity axiom $EQ$ to the fore.

**Theorem 7.3.** The leximin principle is characterized by conditions $IU$, $SP$, $AN$ and $EQ$.

Let us come back to the utilitarian rule. We define utilitarianism in this part of the current chapter as the social evaluation functional $F$ which has the property that, for all $U \in \mathcal{U}$ and for all $x, y \in X, x R_U y$ iff $\sum_i^n u(x, i) \geq \sum_i^n u(y, i)$. Clearly, this utilitarian principle satisfies independence, anonymity, strict Pareto and, as mentioned before, separability. When comparing the following characterization of utilitarianism with theorems 7.1 or 7.2 above, the reader will see that the real difference between a utilitarian and a Rawlsian rule stems from the different informational requirements.

**Theorem 7.4.** The utilitarian rule is characterized by conditions $IU$, $SP$, $AN$ and $CMCU$.

Utilitarianism focuses on the sum of utilities without paying special attention to any particular utility value within the sum. The Rawlsian rules, both maximin and leximin, do not consider the sum at all (which constitutes a major part of the criticism against these principles) but focus instead on the lowest level(s) of utility values within the hierarchy of utilities. This does not preclude that in some cases the social decisions under utilitarianism and Rawlsianism are the same. Let us assume for a moment that in our last example, the given utility values were such that comparability of both levels and units would be possible (this type of comparability was briefly mentioned, but not defined in the text above). Then both utilitarianism and leximin yield a strict preference for $x$ against $y$. If the utility vector for $y$ were $U(y) = (1, 2, 4, 3, 8)$, utilitarianism would arrive at $y P_U x$; leximin would achieve the same verdict as before.

## 7.4. **Diagrammatic proofs again**

In the previous section, we have abstained from providing proofs of theorems
7.1–7.4. We have done this for good reasons since proofs for the general case of
more than two individuals become quite complex and would, therefore, go well
beyond the scope of a primer. However, Blackorby, Donaldson and Weymark
(1984) have presented diagrammatic proofs for the case of two individuals. The
theorems which the three authors prove are not fully identical with theorems
7.1–7.4 above, but 'they come close'. We shall be more precise in due course.
Our focus will be on theorems 7.1 and 7.4, in other words, we shall consider
positional dictatorship and utilitarianism. Positional dictatorship will be first.

Theorem 5.1 in Blackorby et al. gives necessary and sufficient conditions for
the occurrence of rank dictatorship for the case of two persons. In section 2.4
above, we explained that if conditions $U$, $I$ and $PI$ are imposed on functional $F$,
then $F$ satisfies a neutrality property such that all non-utility information will
be ignored. In theorem 7.1, $F$ is supposed to satisfy, among other conditions,
$IU$ and $SP$ and it can be shown that if these two conditions are imposed on $F$,
then the same type of neutrality holds. Therefore, the results of both Blackorby
et al. and D'Aspremont and Gevers are established in a welfaristic framework.
Since Blackorby et al. only consider two individuals who are in conflict about
two social states, they can do without the separability axiom which would be
needed for the general case of more than two persons. Also, Blackorby et al. use
the weak Pareto principle instead of the strong version which entered theorems
7.1 and 7.4. The strong version is actually needed to characterize leximin in
theorems 7.2 and 7.3.

We now turn to the details of the diagrammatic proof. Our aim is to show
that either the better-off or the worse-off of the two individuals who are in
conflict will be decisive socially. In other words, there will be a positional
dictatorship. Figure 7.1 provides details.

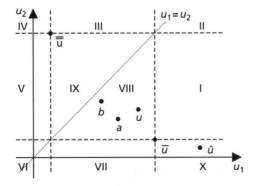

**Figure 7.1.**

D'Aspremont and Gevers show that in the welfaristic framework, there is a mapping from the ordering over alternatives, generated by $F$, to an ordering over utility $n$-tuples in $\mathbb{R}^n$. This result is used by Blackorby et al. It allows them to go from orderings over social states to orderings over $n$-tuples of utility values and examine these exclusively. This will be done in the sequel and was done before in section 2.4 above. As we had mentioned in that section, the requirements on $F$ can be redefined and directly imposed on the ordering over utility $n$-tuples. We abstain from being more specific on this point.

We start from reference point $\bar{u}$. Because of anonymity, $\bar{\bar{u}}$ is indifferent to $\bar{u}$. By strict Pareto, all points in the interior of regions I and II are preferred to $\bar{u}$, and all points in the interior of regions II and III are preferred to $\bar{\bar{u}}$ (for the moment, we leave out points on the horizontal and perpendicular dashed lines). Due to transitivity, points in region III are also preferred to $\bar{u}$. Analogously, utility allocations in the interior of regions V, VI and VII are ranked below $\bar{u}$ and $\bar{\bar{u}}$.

Similar to the proof of Arrow's theorem, we now want to demonstrate that all points in region VIII (and IX due to anonymity) are ranked the same vis-à-vis $\bar{u}$. Because of interpersonal comparability of utility levels, we can assert the following about utility vectors $u$ in region VIII: (i) person 1 is better-off than person 2 since $u_1 > u_2$; (ii) person 1 is worse-off in $u$ than in $\bar{u}$; (iii) person 2 is better-off in $u$ than in $\bar{u}$; (iv) person 1 is better-off in $u$ than person 2 in $\bar{u}$ ($u_1 > \bar{u}_2$); (v) person 2 is worse-off in $u$ than person 1 is in $\bar{u}$. This information together with the fact that person 1 is better-off in $\bar{u}$ than person 2 ($\bar{u}_1 > \bar{u}_2$) allows us to state the following: $\bar{u}_2 < u_2 < u_1 < \bar{u}_1$. Since utility vectors $u$ and $\bar{u}$ stand for the utility values of persons one and two under two social states, let's call them $y$ and $z$, we also have $u(z, 2) < u(y, 2) < u(y, 1) < u(z, 1)$. The reader should note that such a constellation lies at the basis of both the equity axiom $EQ$ and the inequity axiom $INEQ$.

What can be said about other points in region VIII when we make use of the informational requirement $OMCL$? Let us relate vector $a$ to $\bar{u}$ and vector $b$ to $\bar{u}$. Clearly, $\bar{u}_2 < a_2 < a_1 < \bar{u}_1$ and $\bar{u}_2 < b_2 < b_1 < \bar{u}_1$. Condition $OMCL$ allows us to use a strictly increasing transformation, common to both individuals, to map $\bar{u}$ into itself and to map $a$ into $b$ (see figure 7.2). Therefore, due to this informational requirement together with $IU$, the ranking of $a$ versus $\bar{u}$ must be the same as the ranking of $b$ against $\bar{u}$.

Since an ordering over $n$-tuples of utility values exists, utility vectors $u$ in region VIII must (a) either be preferred to $\bar{u}$ or (b) be indifferent to $\bar{u}$ or (c) must be dispreferred to $\bar{u}$. The case of indifference, however, can be deleted because otherwise, transitivity together with the Pareto condition would lead to contradictions between utility vectors in region VIII. Note that anonymity requires that utility vectors in region IX must be ranked the same way in relation to $\bar{u}$ as vectors in region VIII. Thus, two cases remain. Either

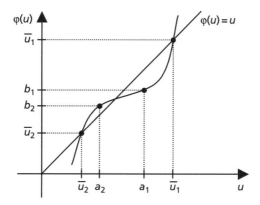

**Figure 7.2.**

points in VIII and IX are preferred to $\bar{u}$ or $\bar{u}$ is preferred to any points in these regions.

An argument analogous to the one given two paragraphs above shows that all utility vectors in region X and, by anonymity, all vectors in region IV are ranked identically in relation to $\bar{u}$. An argument similar to the one in the diagrammatic proof of Arrow's theorem shows that if utility vectors in regions VIII and IX are preferred to $\bar{u}$, then $\bar{u}$ is preferred to points in region X (such as $\hat{u}$) and region IV. We only have to find a common strictly increasing transformation that maps points in VIII (such as $u$) into $\bar{u}$ and $\bar{u}$ into points in X (such as $\hat{u}$). And the opposite direction of preference holds if points in region X such as $\hat{u}$ and in region IV are preferred to $\bar{u}$. Finally, if two adjacent regions have the same ranking in relation to $\bar{u}$, points on the common boundary have the same ranking with respect to $\bar{u}$ as well. Assume that points in region X are preferred to $\bar{u}$. Take $\hat{u}$, for example, and choose a vector perpendicular to $\hat{u}$ on the dashed line. According to strict Pareto, this point is preferred to $\hat{u}$. Then, by transitivity, this point is also ranked better than $\bar{u}$.

Let us step back again and see what we have shown. Obviously there are two basic constellations. These are depicted in figure 7.3(a) and (b). Everything depends on specifying the ranking of points in region VIII (and region IX) versus $\bar{u}$ (and this can be any $\bar{u}$ in the two-dimensional space). If points in region VIII are preferred to $\bar{u}$, we obtain figure 7.3(a) where $b$ stands for points better than $\bar{u}$ and $w$ stands for vectors worse than $\bar{u}$. On the other hand, if points in VIII are ranked worse than $\bar{u}$, we arrive at figure 7.3(b).

Let us go back to the utility vectors $u$ and $\bar{u}$ in figure 7.1 and let us consider vector $\hat{u}$ as well. Earlier on, we had said that $u$ and $\bar{u}$ represent the utility values of persons 1 and 2 under states $y$ and $z$. Suppose that vector $\hat{u}$ specifies the utilities under state $x$. From figure 7.1 we can infer (we have done this before) that $u(z, 2) < u(y, 2) < u(y, 1) < u(z, 1)$. With respect to $\hat{u}$, we can add

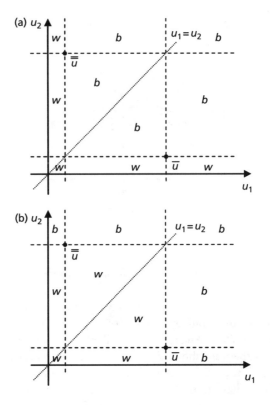

**Figure 7.3.**

$u(x, 2) < u(z, 2) < u(z, 1) < u(x, 1)$. If we now assume that points in region VIII are strictly preferred to $\bar{\bar{u}}$ and $\bar{u}$ is ranked strictly higher than points in region X, then, obviously, the equity axiom *EQ* is satisfied (for our case of two individuals). In terms of social states, $y$ is socially preferred to $z$ and $z$ is socially preferred to $x$. If, however, the converse case holds, the inequity axiom *INEQ* is fulfilled. And this is the assertion of theorem 7.1 above.

One final point. We had stated at the beginning of the diagrammatic proof that Blackorby et al. were using the weak Pareto principle, while theorem 7.1 uses the strong version. The strong Pareto principle, together with separability (for the case of more than two persons), leads to a lexicographic positional dictatorship, either 'leximin' or 'leximax'. For example, all points on the dotted line perpendicular and north of $\bar{\bar{u}}$ in figure 7.1 and all points on the dotted line horizontal and east of $\bar{u}$ would be socially preferred to $\bar{\bar{u}}$ and $\bar{u}$, respectively. The worse-off in our two-person situation is equally worse-off along the dotted line so that it is the other person's say. But this already relates to theorem 7.2 while our interest was to depict and understand the contents of theorem 7.1.

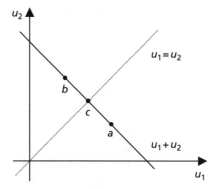

**Figure 7.4.**

Utilitarianism focuses on the sum of utility values. It does not pay special attention to any particular utility level or rank within the sum. The version which was defined in section 7.2 attaches the same weight to every individual in society. Blackorby et al. (1984) provide a simple geometric proof, again for the case of two persons (see figure 7.4).

We know that conditions $IU$ and $SP$ permit us to consider vectors of utilities alone. The informational requirement $CMCU$ allows us to form utility differences and to compare them across individuals. Thus, welfare gains and losses for society can be formed. Consider point $c$ on the ray of equality through the origin. Let $a$ be another point in $\mathbb{R}_+^2$ yielding the same sum of utilities for persons 1 and 2. Point $a$ must lie on a straight line through $c$, forming a right angle to the line $u_1 = u_2$. The latter property follows from the assumption of equal weights in the utility function. Due to anonymity, $a$ must be equivalent to $b$ which is a permutation of $a$. Suppose that utility vector $c$ is preferred to $a$. By adding $(c - a)$ to both $a$ and $c$, point $a$ is mapped into $c$ and $c$ is mapped into $b$. Note that this is a permissible transformation under condition $CMCU$. Therefore, since $c$ is preferred to $a$, $b$ must be preferred to $c$ and, by transitivity, $b$ is preferred to $a$, yielding a contradiction. Similarly, the hypothesis that $a$ is preferred to $c$ would lead to the same type of contradiction. Therefore, $a$ is indifferent to $c$ and the line through $a$ and $b$ represents a line of socially equivalent points. Point $a$ was, of course, chosen arbitrarily along the line with slope '$-1$'. Strong Pareto then determines the directions of social improvements in the sense of increasing the sum of utilities, and this is utilitarianism as defined in connection with theorem 7.4.

If we drop the requirement of anonymity, we obtain generalized utilitarian rules in the sense that for all $x, y \in X$, $x R_U y$ iff $\sum_i^n \alpha_i u(x, i) \geq \sum_i^n \alpha_i u(y, i)$, where $\alpha_i \geq 0$ for all $i$ and $\alpha_j > 0$ for at least one $j$. The focus is again on the sum of utilities, but now it is possible to discriminate among the members of society. Some individuals may be given more weight than others in the social decision.

## 7.5. **Harsanyi's utilitarianism**

Harsanyi (1975) was very critical towards Rawls's *Theory of Justice*, the difference principle or maximin rule as decision rule in particular. For Harsanyi, the choice of the maximin rule 'cannot fail to have highly paradoxical implications' (1975, p. 595). In his criticism, Harsanyi was in particular referring to an attitude of extreme risk aversion that he saw behind this rule. Harsanyi's own attempt over several decades was to develop and establish a utilitarian approach based on the Bayesian concept of rationality. For Harsanyi, 'the Bayesian rationality postulates are absolutely inescapable criteria of rationality for policy decisions' (1978, p. 223) entailing, together with a Pareto condition, '*utilitarian ethics* as a matter of mathematical necessity' (1978, p. 223).

Harsanyi argued that choices will be made over sure outcomes (as in much of social choice theory) as well as over probability distributions of outcomes. Furthermore, individuals and society should act rationally not only under certainty but also in situations of risk and uncertainty. This, however, means that they should follow the so-called von Neumann–Morgenstern axioms.

Let us assume that there is a finite number of pure prospects or outcomes $x_1, x_2, \ldots, x_m, m \geq 1$. A lottery $\mathbf{p} := (p_1, \ldots, p_m)$ offers the pure prospect $x_i$ as the outcome with probability $p_i$. The set of all lotteries $L$ can be defined as $L = \{\mathbf{p} \in \mathbb{R}^m | p_i \geq 0 \text{ for all } i \text{ and } \sum_{i=1}^{m} p_i = 1\}$. According to the Bayesian theory, a rational decision-maker will assess the utility of any lottery as being equal to its expected utility. Thus, for $\mathbf{p} \in L$ and $U_j$ being the cardinal utility function of person $j$, $U_j(\mathbf{p}) = \sum_{i=1}^{m} p_i U_j(e_i)$, where $U_j(e_i)$ is the utility of person $j$, when event $e_i$ occurs and $p_i$ is the associated probability. A rational decision-maker under risk and under uncertainty will maximize his or her expected utility.

Harsanyi actually offered two models of utilitarian ethics. The first model which is sometimes called Harsanyi's aggregation theorem (see, e.g. Weymark (1991)) says the following: Let the individuals' preferences and the social preference relation satisfy the axioms of expected utility and let $U_j, j \in \{1, \ldots, n\}$, and $U$ be the von Neumann–Morgenstern utility representations of the individuals' preferences and the social preference relation, respectively. Then, given that Pareto indifference is satisfied (which was defined in section 2.4 and is now applied to lotteries), there exist numbers $a_j, j \in \{1, \ldots, n\}$, and $b$ such that for all elements $\mathbf{p}$ from the set of lotteries $L$, $U(\mathbf{p}) = \sum_{j=1}^{n} a_j U_j(\mathbf{p}) + b$, where $U_j(\mathbf{p})$ is person $j$'s cardinal utility function as defined above (Harsanyi, 1955). This formula says that social utility or social welfare of any lottery $\mathbf{p} \in L$ must be a weighted linear combination of the individual utilities.

From an interpretative point of view, it is important to note that Harsanyi's result does not say that the weights or coefficients $a_j$ must be positive or at least non-negative (if coefficient $a_k$ of person $k$, let's say, were negative or zero, this would be tantamount to saying that person $k$'s utility would contribute negatively or not contribute at all to social welfare). Nor does the theorem say that the vector of coefficients $(a_1, \ldots, a_n; b)$ is unique. Furthermore, this mathematical representation theorem does not assume that utility comparisons across individuals are possible. This is in stark contrast to what, at the end of the last section, we called a generalized utilitarian rule. A weighted sum of individual utilities was considered, embedded in a framework of cardinally measurable unit-comparable utilities. Though Harsanyi believed in the possibility of making interpersonal utility comparisons, the above linear aggregation rule does not presuppose this possibility. In his 1978 paper, Harsanyi laconically remarks that if such comparisons are ruled out, then the weights $a_j$ will have to be based completely on the personal value judgments of the evaluator. Harsanyi adds that if at least interpersonal comparisons of utility differences are admissible (since the individuals' utility functions are expressed in equal utility units), the introduction of an anonymity axiom would assign equal weights to these individual utility functions. This formulation then comes close to the definition of a utilitarian rule given in the preceding section (except that we did not consider lotteries but sure prospects).

The vector of coefficients $(a_1, \ldots, a_n)$ can be rendered strictly positive by replacing Pareto indifference by the strong Pareto principle. The vector $(a_1, \ldots, a_n; b)$ becomes unique when a further requirement is introduced that Harsanyi had not made explicitly. It is the axiom of 'Independent Prospects' which says that for each individual one can find two lotteries between which this person is not indifferent while everyone else in society is.

Harsanyi's second model, his equiprobability model of the impartial observer (1953, 1955), presupposed the possibility of interpersonal comparisons of utility. This is done in the way that an impartial observer who is sympathetic to the interests of each member of society, makes moral value judgments for this society. More explicitly, the observer is to imagine himself being person $i$, $i \in \{1, \ldots, n\}$, under different social situations $x, y, \ldots$ which can be sure prospects or lotteries as before. In making this sympathetic identification with individual $i$, the observer not only considers himself with person $i$'s objective circumstances under $x, y, \ldots$, he is also supposed to imagine himself with $i$'s subjective characteristics, $i$'s preference ordering in particular. In order to be impartial, the observer has to enter a thought experiment in which he is imagining that he has an equal chance of being any person in society, complete with that person's objective and subjective circumstances. In this way, an equal consideration is given to each person's interests. In making moral value judgments, the impartial observer is to evaluate each social outcome in terms of the average utility level that the $n$ members of society would enjoy in this situation. Technically, the observer's choice among alternative social outcomes is a choice among alternative risky prospects. Therefore, in order to render his choice rational, he must maximize his expected utility. Any social alternative $x$ now yields the expected utility or social welfare $W(x) = (1/n) \sum_j^n U_j(x)$. The impartial observer can be any person among the members of society.

Various scholars have critically examined Harsanyi's second model. Mongin (2001) asserts that 'the impartial observer theorem is surrounded with conceptual difficulties' (p. 173). One of these relates to the requirement that the observer makes extended preference comparisons. When reading Harsanyi's 1953 and 1955 articles, one gets the impression that he wants the welfare judgments to be observer-independent. Mongin argues that given the chosen primitives and premises in Harsanyi's model, 'there is no way out of observer-dependence' (p. 175), and, moreover, the individuals or members of society generally have non-uniform weights. This, however, collides with Harsanyi's arithmetic mean formula given above.

## 7.6. A short summary

Enlarging the informational basis can be done in several ways. In Chapter 6, we looked at positional information within profiles. In the current chapter, we have increased the available utility information. Remember that in Arrow's world of ordinal utility, there is absolutely no possibility to compare utilities across persons. In the Rawlsian framework where the focus is on the worst-off group in society, a comparison of levels of utilities is inevitable. Therefore, at least ordinal level comparability has to be required. The well-known utilitarian rule needs the cardinal utility concept and demands that utility differences can be compared across individuals.

Various characterizations of the Rawlsian maxim and the utilitarian principle exist in the literature. It is interesting to note that, axiomatically speaking, both philosophies have various properties in common. Apart from the different types of utility information that the two approaches need, it is the principle of summing utilities across persons in the case of utilitarianism and an equity axiom in the case of Rawlsianism that separate the two principles. The equity axiom shows the concern for the worst-off very clearly. The lexicographic extension of the Rawlsian maximin rule provides a compatibility with the strict Pareto principle. If the worst-off groups under two policies $a$ and $b$, let's say, are equally badly off, one looks for welfare differences between those groups that are second worst-off. Harsanyi's modern version of utilitarianism is based on the Bayesian theory of rationality. Harsanyi actually proposed two models, one based on the utility observations of an outside evaluator, the other done by an impartial observer who has an equal chance of being any person in society himself. The weighted sum of individual utilities in both models has been the object of much controversy.

## □ RECOMMENDED READING

Blackorby, Ch., Donaldson, D. and Weymark, J. A. (1984). 'Social Choice with Interpersonal Utility Comparisons: A Diagrammatic Introduction'. *International Economic Review*, 25: 327–356.

Sen, A. K. (1970b). *Collective Choice and Social Welfare*, chapter 9. San Francisco, Cambridge: Holden-Day.

## □ HISTORICAL SOURCES

Harsanyi, J. C. (1953). 'Cardinal Utility in Welfare Economics and in the Theory of Risk-Taking'. *Journal of Political Economy*, 61: 434–435.

Harsanyi, J. C. (1955). 'Cardinal Welfare, Individualistic Ethics, and Interpersonal Comparisons of Utility'. *Journal of Political Economy*, 63: 309–321.

Rawls, J. (1971). *A Theory of Justice*. Cambridge, Mass.: Harvard University Press.

## □ MORE ADVANCED

D'Aspremont, C. and Gevers, L. (1977). 'Equity and the Informational Basis of Collective Choice'. *Review of Economic Studies*, 44: 199–209.

Hammond, P. J. (1976). 'Equity, Arrow's Conditions, and Rawls' Difference Principle'. *Econometrica*, 44: 793–804.

Roemer, J. E. (1996). *Theories of Distributive Justice*, chapters 4–5. Cambridge, Ma.: Harvard University Press.

Weymark, J. (1991). 'A Reconsideration of the Harsanyi–Sen Debate on Utilitarianism', in J. Elster and J. E. Roemer (eds.), *Interpersonal Comparisons of Well-Being*, 255–320. Cambridge: Cambridge University Press.

# 8 Cooperative bargaining

## 8.1. The bargaining problem

Bargaining situations are ubiquitous in our times, both in the Western and the Eastern hemisphere. Wage negotiations between a group of employers and a trade union, trade agreements between single countries (e.g. the US and Mexico) or between larger associations (the European Union and the US) or, in the political sphere, disarmament talks between East and West during the Cold War era, and, last but not least, environmental negotiations among developed nations and between developed and less developed countries, are only some examples of bargaining that have received considerable attention over the years. The problem is one of a choice of a feasible alternative by a group of people or nations or associations with often conflicting preferences in a framework of cooperation. As Kalai (1985, p. 77) writes, this 'may be viewed as a theory of consensus, because when it is applied it is often assumed that a final choice can be made if and only if every member of the group supports this choice'. Kalai continues saying that 'because this theory deals with the aggregation of peoples' preferences over a set of feasible alternatives, it bears close similarities to theories of social choice and the design of social welfare functions'. The final outcome that the individuals (or groups) involved strive for may be attained by the parties themselves. Sometimes, however, the final result will be reached via the mediation of an outside person, an arbitrator.

There is one feature that distinguishes the bargaining problem fundamentally from almost all the other social choice approaches. It is the existence of a threat or disagreement outcome which comes about when the people involved in bargaining fail to reach an agreement. Consequently, the gains that the bargainers (may) achieve are evaluated or measured with reference to the disagreement point.

A particularly vivid and perspicuous situation was discussed by Braithwaite (1955). Luke and Matthew occupy two flats in a house. There is no third party around. Unfortunately, the acoustics in this house are such that each of the two men can hear everything louder than a conversation that takes place in the other person's flat. Luke likes to play classical music on the piano, Matthew likes to improvise jazz on the trumpet. It just happens to be the case that each of the two men has only the hour from 9 to 10 in the evening for recreation, i.e. to play music, and that it is impossible for either to change to another time. Suppose that the satisfaction of each man from playing his instrument for the hour is affected by whether or not the other is also playing. More explicitly, Luke, the pianist, prefers most that he play alone, next that Matthew play alone, third that neither play, and finally that both play. Matthew, the trumpeter, prefers most that he play alone, then that Luke play alone, third that they both play at the same time, and last that neither play.

The solution that Braithwaite suggests for this conflict situation allocates substantially more time (in terms of number of evenings per month, let's say, though the author's analysis is in utility values) to the jazz trumpeter than to the classical pianist. The reason for this lies in the diverging preferences of the two men. Matthew has a threat advantage before there is a contract since he prefers that both of them play at the same time to neither of them playing while Luke's preferences on these two outcomes are just the opposite.

There is another feature that distinguishes bargaining theory from much of social choice theory. It is the fact that in bargaining problems physical outcomes or objects that are to be distributed (such as commodity bundles and/or amounts of labour to be provided) are almost entirely ignored. What matters are the utility combinations of the agents, more precisely their net gains over the starting point or status quo. Any two bargaining situations are considered the same whenever they are described by the same set of feasible utility vectors. This comes very close to the diagrammatic analysis in section 7.4 where, as the reader will remember, only utility allocations mattered. We called this approach welfaristic. Bargaining theory also evolves in a welfaristic framework.

## 8.2. Nash's bargaining solution

We shall start by introducing a certain amount of formalism that will be valid throughout this chapter. Let $N = \{1, 2, \ldots, n\}$ be a finite set of agents or players and let $X = \{x_1, x_2, \ldots, x_m\}$ be a finite set of physical objects or social outcomes. In section 7.5, we called the latter pure prospects and we introduced the notion of a lottery $\mathbf{p} = (p_1, \ldots, p_m)$ that offers the pure prospect $x_i$ with probability $p_i$. We shall do exactly the same here and define the set of all lotteries $L$ as $L = \{\mathbf{p} \in \mathbb{R}^m | p_i \geq 0$ for all $i$ and $\sum_{i=1}^{m} p_i = 1\}$. So if there are two prizes in case of a lottery, a weekend in a nice hotel (occurring with probability $p$) and 300 euros in cash (occurring with probability $1 - p$), an increase or decrease of $p$ is tantamount to saying that the weekend becomes more or less likely as the final outcome of this lottery. A second example of such convex combinations is further away from the notion of a lottery and closer to the concept of a 'mixed alternative'. If in case of a legacy, there is a house in the city ($x_i$) and a flat at the sea ($x_j$), two children who inherited these two indivisible objects from their deceased parents could decide that each gets $px_i + (1 - p)x_j$ with $p = 1/2$, which means that each child obtains the right to spend half a year in the house in the city and half a year in the flat at the sea. By varying $p$, all points along the straight line between $x_i$ and $x_j$ become feasible. The formal consequence of permitting probability combinations among any number of discrete objects is that a convex space is obtained. In other words, the space of all lotteries or mixed alternatives is convex. This fact is of importance for the analysis that follows. Furthermore, we wish to assume that the space of lotteries is compact which means that this space is closed and bounded.

Also in the current chapter (as in section 7.5), it is postulated that all agents possess a von Neumann–Morgenstern utility function. Each player will assess the utility of any lottery $\mathbf{p} \in L$ in terms of expected utility. If $u_k$ is agent $k$'s cardinal utility function on the space of lotteries and agent $k$ obtains the mixed alternative or option $[px_i, (1 - p)x_j]$, then the utility of this mixed alternative according to expected utility theory is $u_k([px_i, (1 - p)x_j]) = p \cdot u_k(x_i) + (1 - p) \cdot u_k(x_j)$.

Given the set $X$ of social states and the convex space of lotteries $L$, we still have to introduce $x_0 \in L$, the status quo or threat point in case of disagreement. It could, for example, be a historically given point before bargaining starts and/or a point to which the agents revert in case there will be no bargaining agreement. Next, we use the set of individual von Neumann–Morgenstern utility functions, one utility function for each of the $n$ individuals where each function is determined only up to some positive affine transformation (this is the case of cardinal measurability without interpersonal comparability, abbreviated by *CMN* in section 7.2 on the informational structure of utility representations). Applying these utility functions, we map the space $L$ together with the threat point $x_0$ into a feasible set $S$ of utility vectors and the corresponding disagreement point $d$. Since $L$ was assumed to be convex and compact, the feasible set $S$ will inherit these properties, given the $n$ von Neumann–Morgenstern utility functions. Let us now consider the following two definitions.

**Definition 8.1.** A pair $(S, d)$ with $S \subseteq \mathbb{R}^n$ and $d \in S$ is called a bargaining situation for $n$ persons, if $S$ is convex and compact and there is at least one $s \in S$ with $s > d$.

The last requirement $s > d$ means that for each of the $n$ individuals, there is a genuine incentive to reach an agreement. It is individually rational for each person to reach and support such an agreement.

Let $B^n$ be the set of all bargaining situations with $n$ agents.

**Definition 8.2.** A function $f: B^n \to \mathbb{R}^n$ such that for every $(S, d) \in B^n, f(S, d) \in S$ is a bargaining solution. The coordinates of the solution are $f_1(S, d), \ldots, f_n(S, d)$.

Figure 8.1 illustrates the two definitions in two-dimensional utility space.

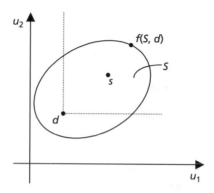

**Figure 8.1.**

Nash (1950) had a unique solution to the bargaining problem in mind. It should be a 'fair bargain' in a situation where the individuals are highly rational, are equal in bargaining skill and 'each has full knowledge of the tastes and preferences of the other' (1950, p. 155). Nash formulated four requirements to be satisfied by $f(S, d)$.

**Axiom 1 (Invariance with respect to utility transformations).** Given a bargaining situation $(S, d) \in B^n$ and $2n$ numbers $a_1 > 0, \ldots, a_n > 0$ and $b_1, \ldots, b_n$, let the bargaining situation $(S', d')$ be defined by $S' = \{y \in \mathbb{R}^n | \exists x \in S : y_i = a_i x_i + b_i\}$, $d'_i = a_i d_i + b_i$ for all $i \in \{1, \ldots, n\}$. Then $f_i(S', d') = a_i f_i(S, d) + b_i$.

This means that if the agents transform their utility scales independently, the $n$ coordinates of the solution will change by the same utility transformations. Let us consider the following example in $\mathbb{R}^2_+$ (figure 8.2(a)). There is the status quo point $d = (0, 0)$, point $\bar{u} = (0, \bar{u}_2)$, point $\bar{\bar{u}} = (\bar{\bar{u}}_1, 0)$, moreover all utility allocations as convex combinations between $d$ and $\bar{u}$, $d$ and $\bar{\bar{u}}$ and between $\bar{u}$ and $\bar{\bar{u}}$, and all points in the interior of this triangle. All these points together constitute bargaining situation $(S, d)$ in $\mathbb{R}^2_+$. Let the solution $f(S, d)$ be the point halfway on the hypotenuse of this triangle. We now choose the following transformations of the two utility functions: $u'_1(\cdot) = a_1 u_1(\cdot) + b_1$, $u'_2(\cdot) = a_2 u_2(\cdot) + b_2$. Let $a_1 = 2$ and $a_2 = \frac{1}{2}$. Then $d = (0, 0)$ is transformed into $d' = (b_1, b_2)$, $\bar{u}$ is transformed into $\bar{u}' = (b_1, \frac{1}{2}\bar{u}_2 + b_2)$, and $\bar{\bar{u}}$ is transformed into $\bar{\bar{u}}' = (2\bar{\bar{u}}_1 + b_1, b_2)$. If the solution point $f(S', d')$ of the transformed bargaining situation lies halfway on the line between $\bar{u}'$ and $\bar{\bar{u}}'$, i.e. $f(S', d') = (\bar{\bar{u}}_1 + b_1, \frac{1}{4}\bar{u}_2 + b_2)$, then this is exactly what axiom 1 requires (see figure 8.2(b)). The independent utility transformations must not change 'the character' of the solution point $f(S, d)$.

**Axiom 2 (Weak Pareto efficiency).** If $x \in S$ and there exists another point $y \in S$ such that $y > x$ (i.e. $y_i > x_i$ for all $i$), then $x \neq f(S, d)$.

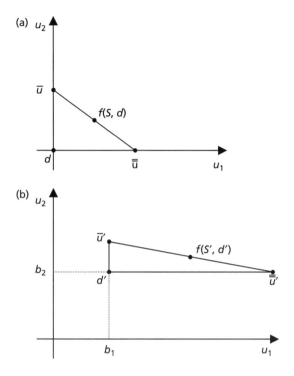

**Figure 8.2.**

The solution point $f(S, d)$ always lies on the boundary of the convex set $S$ in the north-east direction.

**Axiom 3 (Symmetry).**   Let $(S, d)$ be a symmetric bargaining situation in $B^n$, i.e. $d_1 = d_2 = \cdots = d_n$, and for each $x \in S$, every permutation of $x$ is also in $S$. Then, $f_1(S, d) = f_2(S, d) = \cdots = f_n(S, d)$.

This condition requires that if the persons involved in a bargaining situation are indistinguishable both with respect to their status quo point and their possible utility allocations, the solution will have to be equal for all players. The bargaining situation $(S, d)$ in figure 8.3(a) is symmetric, the one in figure 8.3(b) is not.

In figure 8.3(a), the solution $f(S, d)$, according to axioms 2 and 3, will lie at the point where the 45° line through the origin and the hypotenuse of the triangle intersect.

Axiom 3 documents the welfaristic character of bargaining theory very clearly. The only information that counts is the information contained in the pair $(S, d)$. The labelling of the agents and the underlying allocations in the outcome space do not count at all. It can, for example, be the case that in the outcome space, the allocations are not 'symmetric' but that they

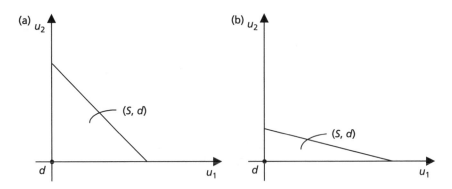

**Figure 8.3.**

become symmetric in utility space because of the individually independent utility assessments.

Note that in all cases in which set $S$ is triangular, the solution can be determined via a combination of axioms 3 and 1, together with weak Pareto efficiency.

**Axiom 4 (Independence of irrelevant alternatives or contraction consistency).** If $(S, d)$ and $(T, d)$ are bargaining situations in $B^n$ with $S \subset T$ and if, in addition, $f(T, d) \in S$, then $f(S, d) = f(T, d)$.

This fourth condition is very important for the Nash bargaining solution and therefore requires a couple of extra comments. Axiom 4 looks at any two bargaining situations with an identical status quo point $d$. Both situations differ in so far as certain points which are feasible in $T$ are no longer possible when the set shrinks from $T$ to $S$. The axiom requires that the solution for $T$ should also be the solution for $S$, if $f(T, d)$ is a point in $S$. The fact that certain utility vectors are no longer possible should not matter in such cases. Nash's fourth requirement can be interpreted as a rationality condition under set contraction. In the social choice literature, this axiom is known as property $\alpha$ (though Nash's requirement is confined to the choice of unique points). It was defined and discussed in Chapter 1. Figure 8.4 depicts the consistency issue.

Axiom 4 can also be viewed in a different, though analogous way. Starting with a feasible set $S$ and its solution $f(S, d)$, the choice from the larger set $T$ when some new alternatives are added should either be $f(S, d)$, the 'old' choice, or one of the new alternatives. The choice of the name 'independence of irrelevant alternatives' which was not given by Nash himself but by Luce and Raiffa (1957) and others, was very unfortunate indeed because of Arrow's condition of the same name. At the beginning, quite a few scholars thought that Arrow's and Nash's condition meant the same. As the reader who studied chapter 2 above, of course, knows, this conjecture is totally false.

We can now formulate Nash's theorem for bargaining situations.

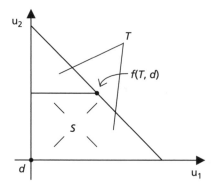

**Figure 8.4.**

**Theorem 8.1.**    There is exactly one bargaining solution on $B^n$ that satisfies axioms 1–4. It is the function $F$ with $F(S, d) = x$ such that $x > d$ and $\prod_{i=1}^{n}(x_i - d_i) > \prod_{i=1}^{n}(y_i - d_i)$ for all $y \in S$ with $y > d$ and $y \neq x$.

$F$ is called the cooperative Nash solution. $F$ maximizes, in the individually rational region of $S(s_i \geq d_i$ for all $i)$, the product of utility gains over the status quo point $d$.

In what follows, we shall present a proof of this result in $\mathbb{R}^2$. Proofs have been given at various places in the literature. First of all, there is Nash's (1950) original proof. Similar proofs can be found in Luce and Raiffa (1957, Chapter 6.5), Harsanyi (1977, Chapter 8.3), Roemer (1996, Chapter 2.2) and others.

*Proof.*    It is easily seen that $F$ satisfies the four axioms. Let us consider the other direction. We begin with any bargaining situation $(S, d)$ and denote by $x$ the point selected by the Nash formula on $S$. Such a point will always exist because of compactness of $S$, and since $S$ is convex, this point will also be unique. We now apply axiom 1 and transform $(S, d)$ into $(S', d')$ such that $ad + b = d' = (0, 0)$ and $ax + b = (1, 1)$, where $a_1 > 0$, $a_2 > 0$ and $b_1, b_2 \in \mathbb{R}$.

We next show that $(1, 1)$ is the solution of $(S', (0, 0))$. The Nash formula took its maximum value on $S$ at point $x$; this property is preserved under positive affine transformations. In other words, $(1, 1)$ maximizes the product $s_1' \cdot s_2'$ in $S'$. The point $(1, 1)$ clearly lies on the line $s_1' + s_2' = 2$. This line which has the character of a hyperplane separates the rectangular hyperbola $s_1' \cdot s_2'$ from the convex set $S'$ at the point $(1, 1)$. This is shown in figure 8.5. We now construct a triangle $ABC$ containing $d' = (0, 0)$ which is symmetric with respect to the $45°$ line between $d'$ and $(1, 1)$. We call this bargaining situation $(T, (0, 0))$. It fully contains set $S'$. By axioms 2 and 3, since $T$ is symmetric, the solution must be $(1, 1)$. Consequently, by axiom 4, the point $(1, 1)$ must also be the solution

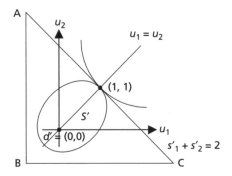

**Figure 8.5.**

for $(S', d')$, i.e. $f(S', d') = (1, 1)$. But then, by invariance axiom 1, $f(S, d) = x$ for the original bargaining situation, which completes the proof.

For a two-person society (as in our proof above), the Nash solution can be illustrated in the following geometrical way. Compare the areas of all rectangles which have as their common 'south-west' corner point $d$ and each of them has as its 'north-east' corner a point on the boundary of $S$. Look for that point on the boundary of $S$ where the area of the corresponding rectangle is maximal or where the product of coordinates among the Pareto efficient points is a maximum. The coordinates of this point represent the Nash bargaining solution. Rectangles in geometry represent extensions in two dimensions. Here, the dimensions are the utilities of two persons.

Various objections have been raised against Nash's bargaining solution and the underlying axioms. One criticism deals with the fact that Nash's approach does not allow for interpersonal comparisons of utility. Since in the *CMN* set-up, utility scales and origins can be chosen and varied independently among agents, there is no hope for any 'degree' of interpersonal comparability. Does this then imply that such a framework is totally inappropriate for questions of distributive justice?

Another objection refers to the fact that Nash's solution crucially depends on the position of the status quo point. A favourable coordinate as well as a not-so-favourable coordinate in the vector of status quo utilities are well reflected in the final bargaining solution à la Nash. Since the status quo indicates the threat potentials or the strength of the different agents involved in the bargaining procedure, the question arises whether the Nash approach can generate a solution that is ethically appealing. Rawls's (1971) answer to this question is clear. Rawls's two principles of justice were the object of a collective agreement under a veil of ignorance. Gauthier, another philosopher, saw this point differently. Natural differences such as talents should not be viewed as arbitrary. They should count and enter into the description of a status quo.

Society should not redress them (Gauthier, 1978). Rawls deliberately prevented certain types of information from entering an agreement over basic principles for society. 'To each according to his or her threat advantage' would be an unacceptable principle of justice for him.

The argument that the Nash approach only considers utility allocations and ignores the underlying economic environment, i.e. the physical objects to be distributed, has been mentioned before. This objection will apply to the other models of bargaining presented in this chapter as well.

A lot of criticism has been levelled against Nash's independence condition. This criticism actually led to an alternative proposal, to be discussed in the fourth section of this chapter, where Nash's independence axiom is replaced by an axiom of monotonicity. In order to understand and appreciate the criticism against independence, we can go back to figure 8.4 above. Imagine that 'at the beginning', there is the triangular set $T$ of utility allocations for players 1 and 2. According to the Nash formula, $f(T, d)$ is the solution. Now imagine that the utility possibilities of person 2 shrink so that the new set is the trapezoid $S$. According to Nash, the solution is exactly the same as before. Is this reasonable? Agent 2 lost some of his or her potential, but apparently, the solution does not reflect this. Agent 2 even gets the maximum possible utility under the new situation. Luce and Raiffa (1957, p. 133) raise the question whether this can be considered as 'fair'. The two authors reverse the procedure, i.e. they start with $S$ and then go to $T$. Does agent 2 now deserve more? Luce and Raiffa argue that 'the status quo serves to point out that certain aspirations are merely empty dreams' (p. 133), admitting that they have changed their mind on this question in the course of time. We shall revert to this issue in section 8.4 below.

## 8.3. **Zeuthen's principle of alternating concessions**

Zeuthen (1930) proposed a bargaining procedure in which agents make alternating offers. Harsanyi (1977, chapter 8) has shown that the equilibrium of Zeuthen's approach, though quite different in character from that of Nash himself, constitutes the Nash bargaining solution. In this way, elements of non-cooperative games are introduced that may render the Nash bargaining solution as the predicted outcome of self-interested players more convincing. Here are the details of Harsanyi's analysis.

Zeuthen described collective bargaining on the labour market. Offers were made in terms of monetary units (wages) but without loss of generality, these can be expressed as units of utility. Remember that in the case of Nash's bargaining solution, we started from a set $X$ of social states and the corresponding space of lotteries $L$ and then mapped the latter into a set $S$ of utility vectors. Let there be two agents or players 1 and 2. At a certain point in time, both players propose a Pareto-efficient agreement. Let us assume that agent 1 proposes $x = (x_1, x_2)$ and agent 2 proposes $y = (y_1, y_2)$, where the first component always refers to player 1. If the agents fail to reach an agreement, a conflict situation arises which gives, in terms of utilities, $u_1(x_{01})$ to agent 1 and $u_2(x_{02})$ to agent 2, where $x_0 = (x_{01}, x_{02})$ is the conflict or status quo situation. We assume that $u_1(x_{01}) < u_1(y_1) < u_1(x_1)$ and $u_2(x_{02}) < u_2(x_2) < u_2(y_2)$. In other words, player 1(2) prefers their own proposal to the offer made by player 2(1) but prefers either proposal to the conflict or status quo situation $x_0$.

What will now happen? If one of the two players accepts the other's proposal, an agreement is reached. If this is not the case, neither for agent 1 nor for agent 2, the conflict situation may arise. Or, at least one of the players comes up with a new proposal (for example, player 1 with a new proposal $x' = (x_1', x_2')$) that is more favourable to the other player than the last proposal but less favourable than the other player's own last offer. In other words, any new proposal $x'$ by player 1 will satisfy $u_2(x_2) < u_2(x_2') < u_2(y_2)$.

At this point, Zeuthen's idea of a concession comes in. If player 1 accepts the offer $y$ made by player 2, the concession of player 1 is $u_1(x_1) - u_1(y_1)$. If player 2 agrees to the proposal $x$ of player 1, the concession of player 2 is $u_2(y_2) - u_2(x_2)$. Zeuthen then asks, given that at a certain stage of mutual offers, an agreement has not yet been reached: 'Which player will (have to) make the next concession?' His answer is that the next concession must always come from the player less willing to face the risk of a conflict, in other words face the point $(x_{01}, x_{02})$.

How can one measure a given agent's willingness to risk a conflict rather than accept the opponent's terms? Zeuthen proposes that each of the two players basically has two options, viz. to stick to his or her last offer or to accept the opponent's terms. Let player 1's last offer be $x$ and the opponent's last offer be $y$. If both agents are Bayesian expected-utility maximizers, they assign subjective probabilities to the two possible choices that the other agent can make. Let $p_{12}$ be the subjective probability that 1 assigns to the hypothesis that 2 will stick to his or her last offer, and $(1 - p_{12})$ be the subjective probability that 1 assigns to the hypothesis that player 2 will accept player 1's last offer.

If player 1 accepts the opponent's last offer, player 1 will obtain $u_1(y_1)$. If 1 simply sticks to his or her last proposal, player 1 may obtain $u_1(x_1) > u_1(y_1)$ with probability $(1 - p_{12})$, but player 1 may also obtain the lower utility $u_1(x_{01}) < u_1(y_1)$ with probability $p_{12}$. Consequently, if player 1 maximizes the own expected utility, he or she will stick to their own last offer $x$ only if $(1 - p_{12}) \cdot u_1(x_1) + p_{12} \cdot u_1(x_{01}) \geq u_1(y_1)$. This expression is equivalent to

$$p_{12} \leq \frac{u_1(x_1) - u_1(y_1)}{u_1(x_1) - u_1(x_{01})}.$$

The latter ratio is called player 1's risk limit $r_1$, since it stands for the highest risk (the highest subjective probability of ending in a conflict situation) that player 1 would be willing to face in order to achieve a settlement according to their own proposal $x$ rather than on the opponent's terms $y$. With probability $p_{12}$, player 1 must expect a conflict to occur if he or she sticks to their last own offer. According to the formula above, the highest value of probability $p_{12}$ that 1 can accept without consenting to the opponent's last offer is $p_{12} = r_1$ (note that $0 \leq r_i \leq 1$ for $i \in \{1, 2\}$).

The quantity $r_i$ is the ratio of two utility differences. The numerator, for example $u_1(x_1) - u_1(y_1)$ for agent 1, has already been interpreted as the concession of this player. In Harsanyi's words, it is 'the *cost* to player $i$ *of reaching an agreement on the opponent's terms* instead of an agreement on player $i$'s own terms' (p. 151, the italics are Harsanyi's). The denominator is the cost to agent $i$ if there is no agreement with the opponent. The ratio $r_i$ is 'a measure of the strength of player $i$'s incentives for insisting on his own last offer rather than accepting his opponent's last offer' (p. 151).

As already stated above, the quantity $r_i$ measures the highest risk that agent $i$ is prepared to take rather than to accept his or her opponent's terms. If $r_i < r_j$, player $i$ is less willing than player $j$ is to risk a conflict and therefore has weaker incentives to do so. This information is known to both players. Therefore, there will be a strong incentive for player $i$ to make the next concession. Thus, Zeuthen proposes the following decision rule which Harsanyi calls 'Zeuthen's principle':

(a) If $r_1 > r_2$, then player 2 has to make the next concession.
(b) If $r_1 < r_2$, then player 1 has to make the next concession.
(c) If $r_1 = r_2$, then both players have to make some concessions.

The player who has to make a concession along the rule above is free to make a quite small concession. However, it should not be smaller than some minimum size ensuring that the agents' alternating offers will converge to some agreement after a finite number of bargaining rounds. This alternating offer bargaining process will eventually reach an agreement that corresponds to the Nash bargaining solution. This will now be shown.

Let us assume that person 1 proposes $x = (x_1, x_2)$, while person 2 proposes $y = (y_1, y_2)$ with

$$r_1 = \frac{u_1(x_1) - u_1(y_1)}{u_1(x_1) - u_1(x_{01})} \leq \frac{u_2(y_2) - u_2(x_2)}{u_2(y_2) - u_2(x_{02})} = r_2. \qquad \text{(a)}$$

According to the Zeuthen principle, agent 1 has to make the next concession. Let us specify this as $x' = (x_1', x_2')$ such that

$$r_1' = \frac{u_1(x_1') - u_1(y_1)}{u_1(x_1') - u_1(x_{01})} \geq \frac{u_2(y_2) - u_2(x_2')}{u_2(y_2) - u_2(x_{02})} = r_2'. \qquad \text{(b)}$$

Expression (a) can be shown to be equivalent to

$$(u_1(x_1) - u_1(x_{01})) \cdot (u_2(x_2) - u_2(x_{02}))$$
$$\leq (u_1(y_1) - u_1(x_{01})) \cdot (u_2(y_2) - u_2(x_{02})). \tag{a$'$}$$

Expression (b) can be shown to be equivalent to

$$(u_1(y_1) - u_1(x_{01})) \cdot (u_2(y_2) - u_2(x_{02}))$$
$$\leq (u_1(x_1') - u_1(x_{01})) \cdot (u_2(x_2') - u_2(x_{02})). \tag{b$'$}$$

Expression (a$'$) says that the Nash product according to player 1's first offer is smaller or equal to the Nash product according to player 2's first offer. Expression (b$'$) says that the latter is smaller or equal to the revised proposal of the first player. Because of relation (b) and Zeuthen's principle, the next proposal should be made by player 2, and it is easy to see that it will yield an even higher Nash product. In other words, in each round the offer corresponding to the smaller value of the Nash product will be eliminated, while the offer corresponding to the larger Nash product will be retained until the next round. This alternating procedure will continue until one of the two players makes a proposal that corresponds to the largest possible value of the Nash product. Since no further improvement will be possible from there, both players will accept this offer. In other words, the final point in Zeuthen's alternating sequence will be the point where the Nash product is maximal, and this is, as we know from the last section, the Nash solution point. There are various other models with alternating offers within a non-cooperative set-up that eventually lead to the Nash bargaining solution (see, e.g. Rubinstein et al. (1992)).

## 8.4. The Kalai–Smorodinsky bargaining solution

At the end of section 8.2, we discussed an objection against Nash's independence condition that is related to the situation in figure 8.4, but we also mentioned Luce and Raiffa's change of mind on this issue. Should a player receive more when the set of feasible utility vectors expands in a direction that is favourable to this person?

Let us look at the following situation which is taken from Kalai and Smorodinsky (1975) and is depicted in figure 8.6. We assume that there are two bargaining situations $(S^1, 0)$ and $(S^2, 0)$ in $\mathbb{R}^2$ with the following characteristics:

$$S^1 = \text{convex hull } \{(0, 1), (1, 0), (3/4, 3/4)\},$$
$$S^2 = \text{convex hull } \{(0, 1), (1, 0), (0.99, 0.7)\},$$

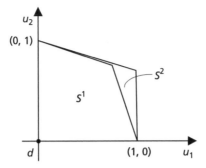

**Figure 8.6.**

For any given value of $u_1$ such that $0 < u_1 < \max u_1$, there is a value of $u_2$ such that $(u_1, u_2) \in (S^2, 0)$ and this utility level for player 2 is strictly higher than the corresponding maximally possible utility value attainable in $(S^1, 0)$. Kalai and Smorodinsky (1975, p. 515) argue that 'based on these facts', player 2 has good reason to demand that he get more under $(S^2, 0)$ than he does under $(S^1, 0)$. However, the Nash solution which in each of the two bargaining situations lies on the kink does not satisfy player 2's demand.

Kalai and Smorodinsky propose to replace Nash's independence condition by an axiom of monotonicity. In order to describe their solution concept, we have to introduce the concept of an 'ideal point'.

**Definition 8.3.**    Given any bargaining solution $(S, d) \in B^2$, the vector $\bar{x}(S, d) = (\bar{x}_1, \bar{x}_2)$ with $\bar{x}_i = \max_{(S,d)} \{s_i | (s_1, s_2) \geq d\}$ for $i \in \{1, 2\}$ is called the ideal point of $(S, d)$.

The ideal point of $(S, d)$ has as its components the maximally possible utility value of each player. In figure 8.6, the maximally possible utility value of player 1 is $\bar{x}_1 = 1$, for player 2 it is $\bar{x}_2 = 1$ so that $\bar{x}(S, d) = (1, 1)$. The reader should note that very often, the ideal point lies outside the feasible set.

**Axiom 5 (Monotonicity).**    If $(S^1, d)$ and $(S^2, d)$ are two bargaining situations in $B^2$ such that $S^1 \subseteq S^2$ and $\bar{x}_1(S^1, d) = \bar{x}_1(S^2, d)$, then $f_2(S^1, d) \leq f_2(S^2, d)$. Similarly, if $\bar{x}_2(S^1, d) = \bar{x}_2(S^2, d)$, then $f_1(S^1, d) \leq f_1(S^2, d)$.

This axiom uses the intuition from figure 8.6 and states that if there is a set expansion from $S^1$ to $S^2$ with a fixed status quo $d$, while the maximally possible utility level for player 1 remains unchanged, player 2's utility level according to $f(S, d)$ should not go down but weakly increase (and analogously, when players 1 and 2 are interchanged).

We have reached some kind of a bifurcation. Axioms 1–3 from section 8.2 together with axiom 4 yield the Nash solution; axioms 1–3 together with axiom 5 above yield the Kalai–Smorodinsky solution.

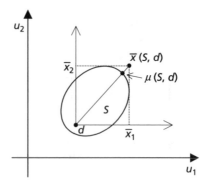

**Figure 8.7.**

**Theorem 8.2.** There is one and only one solution, $\mu$, on $B^2$ satisfying axioms 1–3 and the axiom of monotonicity. The solution $\mu$ has the following representation. For $(S, d) \in B^2$, construct the line from $d$ to $\bar{x}(S, d)$. The maximal element of $S$ on this line is $\mu(S, d)$.

Note first that this theorem is formulated for bargaining situations in $B^2$. We shall say more about this point after the proof of this result. Secondly, the solution point on the ray from $d$ to $\bar{x}(S, d)$ can be nicely interpreted in a geometrical way. The Kalai–Smorodinsky solution is the maximal point $\mu(S, d) = x$ in the set of individually rational points such that

$$\frac{x_1 - d_1}{\bar{x}_1 - d_1} = \frac{x_2 - d_2}{\bar{x}_2 - d_2}.$$

If $(x_i - d_i)/(\bar{x}_i - d_i)$ is interpreted as a relative utility gain of person $i$, the Kalai–Smorodinsky solution leads to an equalization of relative utility gains of the two players. This equalization holds for every point along the ray between $d$ and $\bar{x}(S, d)$. Again, we obtain a unique bargaining solution (see figure 8.7).

*Proof.* The proof follows Thomson (1994c) and Roemer (1996). It is clear that the Kalai–Smorodinsky solution $\mu$ satisfies the four conditions in the theorem. Conversely, let there be an arbitrary bargaining situation $(S, d)$ in the plane. Due to axiom 1, it is possible to transform $(S, d)$ into $(S', d')$ such that $d' = (0, 0)$ and $\bar{x}(S, d)$ is mapped into $(1, 1)$. We call the new bargaining situation $(S', 0)$. Under invariance axiom 1, the solution under $f$ on $(S, d)$ maps into the solution on $(S', 0)$. The solution $\mu(S', 0)$ on $(S', 0)$ is a point that has equal coordinates because the ray connecting the threat point $(0, 0)$ to the point $\bar{x}(S', 0) = (1, 1)$ has slope one. Let us call this solution point $(a, a)$.

Now construct $S''$ inside $S'$ in the following way. Connect point $(a, a)$ to the points $(1, 0)$ and $(0, 1)$. $S''$ will be a four-sided convex set where two sides are segments along the axes and the other two sides are the lines between $(1, 0)$ and

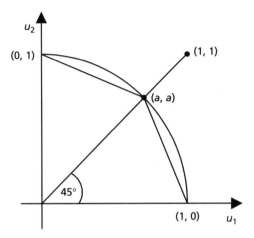

**Figure 8.8.**

$(a, a)$, and between $(a, a)$ and $(0, 1)$ – see figure 8.8. The bargaining situation $(S'', 0)$ is symmetric. Therefore, due to the Pareto condition and the symmetry axiom, $f(S'', 0) = (a, a)$. Note that $(S'', 0)$ and $(S', 0)$ are related to each other in the way spelled out in the antecedent of axiom 5, i.e. $\bar{x}_1(S'', 0) = \bar{x}_1(S', 0)$ and $\bar{x}_2(S'', 0) = \bar{x}_2(S', 0)$. Therefore, from this axiom, $f_i(S', 0) \geq f_i(S'', 0)$ for $i \in \{1, 2\}$. Thus, $f(S', 0) \geq (a, a)$ and since $(a, a)$ is Pareto-optimal on $S'$, $f(S', 0) = (a, a)$. Notice that $(a, a)$ is the Kalai–Smorodinsky solution on $(S', 0)$. So $f(S', 0) = \mu(S', 0)$. But then, by invariance axiom 1, it follows that $f(S, d) = \mu(S, d)$ for the original bargaining situation, which completes the proof.

The Kalai–Smorodinsky solution is well defined for situations with any finite number of participants. However, this solution does not necessarily satisfy the Pareto efficiency condition for bargaining situations with more than two players. Actually, Roth (1979) has shown that for bargaining situations with three or more participants, no solution exists that fulfils the conditions of Pareto efficiency and symmetry together with monotonicity.

In order to illustrate Roth's negative result, we give the following example which is also due to Roth (1979). Consider a three-person bargaining situation whose disagreement point is equal to the origin. Let the feasible set $S$ be equal to the convex hull of $d = (0, 0, 0)$ and the two points $(1, 0, 1)$ and $(0, 1, 1)$. Clearly, the set of Pareto-efficient points in $S$ is the line segment joining $(1, 0, 1)$ and $(0, 1, 1)$. Any solution $f(S, d)$ that is to satisfy Pareto efficiency has to allocate one unit of utility to person 3. The ideal point of this game is $\bar{x}(S, d) = (1, 1, 1)$. For this set (see figure 8.9), the Kalai–Smorodinsky solution is $\mu(S, d) = (0, 0, 0)$ which collides heavily with Pareto efficiency. This solution is in fact dominated by all other points of $S$.

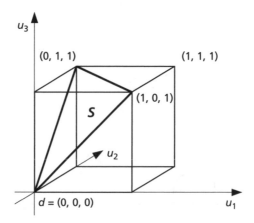

**Figure 8.9.**

The problem just depicted vanishes if one is willing to accept the assumption of free disposal of utility. This means that if $x \in S$ and $d \leq y \leq x$, then $y \in S$. Reductions of utilities lead to points in $S$, whenever the point from which the reduction originates is weakly individual rational (i.e. for all $x \in S, x \geq d$). Under free disposal of utility, the Kalai–Smorodinsky solution is the unique weakly Pareto optimal point with equal relative utility gains for all players. However, this solution is not always strongly Pareto-optimal. If one additionally accepts the availability of small utility transfers, then this problem disappears, too. One of the approaches that generalize the axiomatic characterization of the Kalai–Smorodinsky solution to the case of $n$ persons is due to Imai (1983). He replaces Nash's independence axiom by two axioms, an axiom of individual monotonicity together with an axiom of independence of irrelevant alternatives other than the ideal point. The latter is a weakened version of Nash's independence condition, where situations which are being compared have identical status quo points and identical ideal points. Imai's set of axioms uniquely characterizes a lexicographic maximin solution in relative utility gains.

## 8.5. **A philosopher's view**

The ideal point plays a central role in the Kalai–Smorodinsky solution. Each coordinate in $\bar{x}(S, d)$ is such that the particular agent considered is assumed to get his or her maximal utility, while all the other players realize some individually rational feasible utility value. What importance does the ideal point have? Is it a legal or historical claim that agents can make? This is not clear at all and furthermore remember that in many cases, $\bar{x}(S, d)$ lies outside the set of feasible utility vectors.

The philosopher Gauthier views the Kalai–Smorodinsky solution as the outcome of a non-cooperative bargaining process where players have to make concessions but start, as an initial claim, from their maximally possible utility levels. The process that Gauthier considers is somewhat similar to the Zeuthen procedure of alternating concessions that led to the Nash solution, as we saw in section 8.3. From a conceptual point of view, Gauthier's theory is much broader than Zeuthen's proposal. Gauthier's approach has to be considered as a bargaining model of moral choice where social values are to be distributed.

Gauthier argues that a just principle for determining social values has to be based on the agreement of all individuals in a given society. The only such principle upon which rational individuals will agree, is one which is achieved through bargaining. The existence of such an agreement is necessitated by the possibility of a 'market failure', or, using Smith's metaphor, 'where the invisible hand fails to direct each person, mindful only of her own gain, to promote the benefit of all, cooperation provides a visible hand' (Gauthier, 1986, p. 113). Thus, in situations in which strategic rationality leads to inefficiency, Gauthier's theory suggests that rational individuals will cooperate in order to exploit common utility gains. Gauthier (1986, p. 128) writes that 'cooperation arises from the failure of market interaction to bring about an optimal outcome because of the presence of externalities. We may then think of cooperative interaction as a visible hand which supplants the invisible hand, in order to realize the same ideal as the market provides under conditions of perfect competition'. In cooperating, each agent accepts some restrictions on his or her aim of maximizing utility. That is, each person must agree to constrain her behaviour, provided others similarly agree. Only where each person takes the interests of all others into account, can every individual achieve a utility value which is greater than his or her utility value without cooperation. Subsequently, we wish to give some more details of Gauthier's approach.

Let each bargainer $i$ propose that the ideal payoff $\bar{x}_i$ be allocated to him or her. We know that in most cases the vector of ideal payoffs is no solution since it lies outside the feasible set. Consider any feasible outcome $x$ which is individually rational. The concession required by person $i$ if she agrees to $x$ is, according to the Zeuthen formula, $(\bar{x}_i - x_i)/(\bar{x}_i - d_i)$. As explained earlier, this expression determines the ratio between the payoff person $i$ forgoes if $x$ is accepted in comparison to the ideal payoff and her ideal gain over the disagreement payoff. In other words, Gauthier applies Zeuthen's formula to utility differences between ideal utility values and proposed utility values and between ideal utility values and the status quo. Gauthier argues, 'Each bargainer looks upon the utility, to him, of the status quo as a minimum, and evaluates other social states in relation to that minimum' (1978, p. 246). The second modification of Zeuthen's procedure is that every concession of player $i$ during the bargaining process is measured in relation to $\bar{x}_i - d_i$, while in Zeuthen's formula the denominator changes. This underlines the importance of the ideal point not only for the first proposals of the bargainers but also for the whole procedure.

Naturally, a person is the less willing to make a concession the larger this concession is. Therefore, consider the largest concession required for each of the possible bargaining outcomes. For any $x$ in the set of individually rational utility vectors, the maximum concession is $\max_i(\bar{x}_i - x_i)/(\bar{x}_i - d_i)$. Since the maximum concession will obviously elicit the maximum degree of resistance to agreement, we are looking for an outcome with the least maximum degree of resistance to agreement. For Gauthier it is rational that such an outcome will be accepted. 'The person required to make the maximum concession needed to yield this outcome is more willing to concede than any person required to make the maximum concession needed to yield any other outcome' (Gauthier, 1985, p. 37). Thus, the bargaining solution is the outcome with the least maximum concession. However, as Gauthier shows, the requirement that the maximum concession be minimized is equivalent to the demand that the minimum proportion of possible utility gain be maximized. The minimum proportion of possible utility gain is, of course, $\min_i(x_i - d_i)/(\bar{x}_i - d_i)$ so that according to Gauthier, given an $n$-person bargaining situation $(S, d)$, $x \in S$ is the solution if and only if

$$\min_{i\in N} \frac{x_i - d_i}{\bar{x}_i - d_i} > \min_{j\in N} \frac{y_j - d_j}{\bar{x}_j - d_j}$$

for all $y(y \neq x)$ that are individually rational.

Notice that the comparisons which are made with respect to proportionate gains or concessions do not presuppose any degree of interpersonal comparability of individual utilities. The Gauthier solution shares this characteristic with all the other solutions we have discussed so far. Notice also that for only two individuals, the Gauthier solution and the solution à la Kalai–Smorodinsky are identical. This is due to the fact that in the case of two agents, maximizing the minimum proportion of possible utility gains leads to an equalization of the two ratios. Unfortunately, for more than two players, Gauthier's solution concept runs into similar problems as the Kalai–Smorodinsky solution. It is not well defined. For three agents, for example, the above (strict) inequality has to be changed into a weak inequality. Additionally, strong Pareto optimality has to be required. Only then is a unique solution point achieved (for details, see Klemisch-Ahlert (1992, pp. 87–91)). For the general case of $n$ players, this author proposed a characterization of the Gauthier solution as well (Klemisch-Ahlert, 1992, chapter 4). In this characterization, a generalized equity axiom in relative utility gains is formulated that is reminiscent of the equity requirement used in section 7.3.

## 8.6. **Kalai's egalitarian solution**

In his survey on cooperative models of bargaining, Thomson (1994c) writes that 'three solutions play the central role in the theory as it appears today' (p. 1242). Therefore, let us have a brief look at the third approach, whose main distinguishing feature from Nash's solution and the Kalai–Smorodinsky solution is that it requires interpersonal comparisons of utility. Kalai (1985) discusses in greater detail an example of two bargainers 1 and 2 who are confronted with four possible allocations of money, viz. ($0, $0), ($10, $0), ($0, $10) and ($0, $1000). It is assumed that both bargainers have utility functions that increase monotonically in money. Kalai sets $u_i(\$0) = 0$ and $u_i(\$10) = 1$ for $i = 1, 2$. Now consider two bargaining situations $A$ and $B$ with the common status quo point $d = (0, 0)$. In $A$, the feasible set consists of all the lotteries among the three outcomes ($0, $0), ($10, $0) and ($0, $10). In $B$, the feasible set consists of all the lotteries between the outcomes ($0, $0), ($10, $0) and ($0, $1000). In utility space, situation $A$ is mapped into $\hat{A}$ = convex hull $\{(0,0), (1,0), (0,1)\}$, situation $B$ is mapped into $\hat{B}$ = convex hull $\{(0,0), (1,0), (0, u_2(\$1000))\}$. Under the informational set-up $CMN$, agent 2's utility scale can be changed such that $u_2$ is transformed into $v_2 = u_2/u_2(\$1000)$. Then situation $\hat{B}$ can be described by $\hat{\hat{B}}$ = convex hull $\{(0,0), (1,0), (0,1)\}$, which in terms of utility values becomes identical to $\hat{A}$.

Kalai now argues convincingly that $\hat{A}$ and $\hat{\hat{B}}$ are not identical in the sense that they should yield the same outcome. 'Player 2 stands to lose significantly more that player 1, if . . . negotiations break off. Both players are aware of this fact, and it seems like a threat of player 1 to break the negotiation would have significant credibility behind it' (p. 89).

Therefore, in this section we assume that the utility scales of all individuals are comparable so that the solution should be invariant only for cases when *all* individuals' utility scales are changed linearly by the same factor.

The egalitarian solution proposed by Kalai (1977) is defined by setting, for all $(S, d) \in B^n$, $E(S, d)$ to be the maximal point of $S$ of equal coordinates, i.e. for all $i, j \in N, E_i(S, d) - d_i = E_j(S, d) - d_j$. Figure 8.10(a) illustrates the solution for the case that $d = (0, 0)$ in $\mathbb{R}^2$. The egalitarian solution satisfies a monotonicity condition that is strong, since no restriction is imposed on the expansion of utility possibilities that take some $S$ into $S'$. In other words, all players should benefit from any expansion of opportunities, irrespective of whether the expansion is biased in favour of one of them.

**Axiom 6 (Strong monotonicity).**   If $(S^1, d)$ and $(S^2, d)$ are any two bargaining situations in $B^n$ such that $S^1 \subseteq S^2$, then $f(S^1, d) \leq f(S^2, d)$.

The following characterization result is closely related to a theorem developed in Kalai (1977).

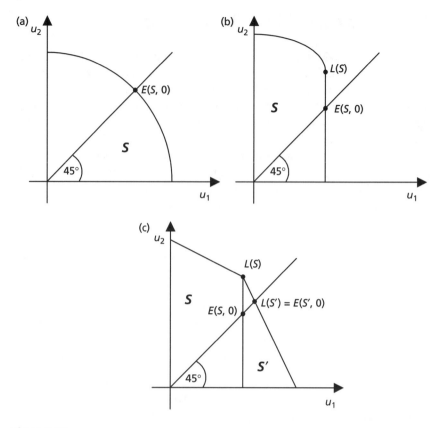

**Figure 8.10.**

**Theorem 8.3.** A solution on $B^n$ satisfies weak Pareto efficiency, symmetry and strong monotonicity iff it is the egalitarian solution $(E(S, d))$.

The proof is easy. Therefore, we shall abstain from giving it here (see, however, Thomson (1994c) or Thomson and Lensberg (1989)).

Figure 8.10(b) shows that weak Pareto efficiency in theorem 8.3 cannot be strengthened to strict Pareto. However, there is a natural extension of solution $E(S, d)$ that is obtained by a lexicographic operation. Given $w \in \mathbb{R}^n$, let $\tilde{w} \in \mathbb{R}^n$ denote the vector obtained from $w$ by writing its coordinates in increasing order. Given two utility vectors $x, y \in \mathbb{R}^n$, $x$ is lexicographically larger than $y$ if $\tilde{x}_1 > \tilde{y}_1$ or $[\tilde{x}_1 = \tilde{y}_1$, and $\tilde{x}_2 > \tilde{y}_2]$, or, more generally, for some $l \in \{1, \ldots, n-1\}$, $[\tilde{x}_1 = \tilde{y}_1, \ldots, \tilde{x}_l = \tilde{y}_l$, and $\tilde{x}_{l+1} > \tilde{y}_{l+1}]$. For $(S, d) \in B^n$, the lexicographic egalitarian solution $L(S)$ is the point of $S$ that is lexicographically maximal (see Figure 8.10(b) again for the case of two persons). The lexicographic extension $L(S)$, however, does not fulfil the axiom of strong monotonicity, as can be seen from Figure 8.10(c). In this situation, $S \subset S'$, but person 2 receives less utility under $L(S')$ than under $L(S)$.

Kalai (1977) shows that the egalitarian solution satisfies what he calls 'the step-by-step negotiation' condition. This means that bargaining can be done in stages without affecting the final outcome. Let $(S, d)$ and $(T, d)$ be two bargaining pairs with $S \subseteq T$. The bargaining agents could divide the process into two stages. In the first stage, they would agree on an outcome in $(S, d)$, which they then use as a disagreement point for a second round of negotiations where they may agree on a new alternative in $T \backslash S$. So the egalitarian solution satisfies the property that $f(T, d) = f(S, d) + f(R)$, where $R$ is a bargaining situation with threat point 0 and all those individually rational points that remain after agreeing upon $f(S, d)$ in the first round.

The egalitarian solution, in spite of allowing for interpersonal utility comparisons, clearly has the following welfaristic feature that the other two major solution concepts also exhibit: if two problems set up in an economic environment lead to the same set of utility possibilities, then the solution mechanism must assign solution points for the two problems which are indistinguishable in terms of utility. We shall come back to this point in the next chapter and shall discuss it from a somewhat different angle.

## 8.7. A short summary

The bargaining approach differs from the typical social choice approach in several respects; the existence of a status quo or disagreement point is perhaps the most significant. The analysis is entirely done in utility space, based on von Neumann–Morgenstern utility functions. We discussed the Nash solution and the solution concept by Kalai–Smorodinsky in greater detail. Both approaches provide a unique solution point. Also, both proposals have three axioms in common. A bifurcation occurs when Nash requires a consistency condition with respect to set contraction and Kalai and Smorodinsky postulate a monotonicity condition instead. The argument behind the latter is that a solution should appropriately reflect changes in the utility possibilities of the players.

It has been shown by Harsanyi that the Nash solution of maximizing the product of utility gains over the status quo can be explained by a process of alternating concessions among the agents involved in bargaining. This idea which goes back to Zeuthen introduces elements of non-cooperative games. The Kalai–Smorodinsky solution is such that the relative utility gains of the agents are equalized. Gauthier picked up Zeuthen's idea of successive concessions and proposed a solution where the maximum concession that one of the players is required to make in order to achieve a common solution is minimal.

This implies that any other bargaining outcome proposed would require a larger concession from one of the agents.

All these approaches do without any form of interpersonal comparability of utilities. Kalai's egalitarian solution presupposes that the utility scales of all persons be comparable.

## ☐ RECOMMENDED READING

Kalai, E. (1985). 'Solutions to the Bargaining Problem', in L. Hurwicz, D. Schmeidler and H. Sonnenschein (eds.), *Social Goals and Social Organization. Essays in Memory of Elisha Pazner.* Cambridge: Cambridge University Press.

Roemer, J. E. (1996). *Theories of Distributive Justice,* chapter 2. Cambridge, Mass.: Harvard University Press.

## ☐ HISTORICAL SOURCES

Luce, R. D. and Raiffa, H. (1957). *Games and Decisions.* New York: John Wiley.

Nash, J. F. (1950). 'The Bargaining Problem'. *Econometrica*, 18: 155–162.

Nash, J. F. (1953). 'Two-Person Cooperative Games'. *Econometrica*, 21: 128–140.

von Neumann, J. and Morgenstern, O. (1944). *Theory of Games and Economic Behavior.* Princeton: Princeton University Press.

## ☐ MORE ADVANCED

Thomson, W. (1994c). 'Cooperative Models of Bargaining', chapter 35 in R. J. Aumann and S. Hart (eds.), *Handbook of Game Theory*, vol. 2. Amsterdam: North-Holland.

# 9 Empirical social choice

## 9.1. Theory and opinions of the general public

There is no such thing as *the* theory of justice, neither in jurisprudence nor in philosophy nor in the sphere of economics where we often use the term 'distributive justice' in order to indicate that here, the issue of justice is frequently linked up with a problem of redistribution. Consider a fixed amount of well-defined, quantitatively measurable and perfectly divisible entities that is to be divided among a certain number of individuals. Or consider a government that thinks about changing its tax policy such that some of its citizens will suffer losses while others will benefit. According to which rules should the distribution in the first problem be carried out? Which criteria should decide in the second case whether to introduce a new policy or leave things as they are?

In Chapter 7, we discussed two major approaches to distributive justice, viz. Rawlsianism and utilitarianism, the former being means-oriented, the latter being outcome-oriented and consequentialist. In Chapter 8, we described bargaining solutions where everyday examples range from wage negotiations between employers and employees to the 'simple' task of cutting a cake at a children's birthday party. Which rules should govern these distribution problems such that 'in the end', all parties involved agree to a solution and don't resort to the status quo? Here, we focused in particular on the cooperative Nash solution and the proposal by Kalai and Smorodinsky.

All these different approaches to distributive justice should not be seen as *l'art pour l'art* exercises of a theoretical mind who indulges in abstract reasoning by throwing in different combinations of axioms. On the contrary. Our claim is that all these approaches have very much to do with real-world problems about which many people care and what is more, on which quite a few people have strong views.

Yaari and Bar-Hillel (1984) have used a flow-chart diagram to depict a process of deliberation, i.e. an iterative process of self-correction and revision that starts from a basic list of axioms. These axioms yield a distribution mechanism. In the next step, one attempts to characterize all mechanisms that in fact satisfy this list of axioms. Then the issue of tenability is raised which may lead back to the collection of axioms from which one started, if the distribution mechanisms that were generated possess some undesirable features or yield prescriptions that are deemed unacceptable.

At the end of this iterative process, there should be a state where no further revisions should be justified. Yaari and Bar-Hillel call such a situation a state of equilibrium and refer to Rawls's (1971) notion of 'reflective equilibrium'. The two authors argue that 'the notion of reflective equilibrium hinges crucially on what is meant by "tenability"' (1984, p. 3). And they ask what the test is to which a theory of distributive justice is to be submitted. The authors assert that a theory of distributive justice, like any other theory, has to be tested in order to see how well it performs when confronted with evidence. However, in this particular case, evidence cannot come from statistical data and econometric modelling. It has to come from '*observed ethical judgements or moral intuitions*' (p. 3, the italics are theirs).

The general public has an opinion on issues of distributive justice. This opinion may sometimes be very vague, it may depend on the particular context into which the actual problem is embedded; it may also be culture-dependent and may vary over time. But it exists and should be taken into consideration in a political democracy. Schokkaert (1999) is very clear on this. He argues that an essential prerequisite and element of a theory of justice in a democratic society is that it can be explained to the citizens. Justice and fairness is about the basic structure of society, as Rawls (1971) put it, and the general public should have its say about these basic institutions. If normative economics wants its analysis to have real influence on the decisions taken within a political system, Schokkaert continues, it has to consider the opinions and preferences of its citizens. These determine the social context. Public support for a particular policy proposal is crucial to its feasibility. Empirical research can provide information on the acceptance of concepts of justice by different social groups that live in different cultural and geographical environments. Of course, public opinion is sometimes uninformed or even incoherent. However, some notion of fairness and a special concern for the poor, at least under certain circumstances, seem to be widely spread among the general public. We shall say more about this in due course.

## 9.2. Needs vs. tastes – the approach by Yaari and Bar-Hillel

Let us resume the idea of what above was called a process of deliberation. We start with the issue of axiomatizable mechanisms. Yaari and Bar-Hillel (1984) have, among others, examined the following distribution mechanisms:

(a)  Bargaining from equal split.
Two distribution mechanisms are considered, viz. the Nash bargaining solution and the approach by Kalai and Smorodinsky. Bargaining from equal split

means that in case of failure to reach an agreement, each individual or party engaged in the bargaining should get, in case of $n$ parties involved, $1/n$ of the total bundle to be distributed.

(b)  Bargaining from zero.
Again the Nash bargaining solution and the Kalai–Smorodinsky mechanism are considered, this time, however, under the threat that failure to reach an agreement would lead to a situation where everybody receives nothing.

(c)  Bargaining over the strong Pareto set.
Here, the authors require that bargaining be limited only to those areas where a genuine conflict of interest arises. In other words, bargaining takes place under the rule 'that, in case of failure to reach agreement, each agent is awarded that part of the bundle being distributed, if any, which can in no way benefit any other agent' (1984, p. 5). Again, bargaining is performed according to Nash and according to Kalai–Smorodinsky, respectively.

(d)  Maximin.
The division of a bundle of goods has to be such that after the division, the position of the least advantaged individual or party has to be as high as possible.

(e)  Utilitarianism.
The division of a given bundle has to be such that after the division the resulting sum of utilities of the persons involved has to be at least as large as the sum under any other division of the same bundle.

The reader will recollect that both the Nash bargaining approach and the Kalai–Smorodinsky solution required a symmetry axiom saying that if individuals are indistinguishable in terms of utility information, their allocation in utility space should be the same. This may be interpreted as an equal treatment of equals.

A departure from equal division requires a justification. Yaari and Bar-Hillel consider, among other criteria, differences in needs and differences in tastes. They also discuss the aspect of beliefs. In the following, we shall, however, just concentrate on the first two criteria. We shall start with the aspect of needs and invite the reader to study the following situation which is quoted word for word (for good reasons) from the original text (1984, pp. 8–9).

Q1:  A shipment containing 12 grapefruit and 12 avocados is to be distributed between Jones and Smith. The following information is given, and is known also to the two recipients:

- Doctors have determined that Jones's metabolism is such that his body derives 100 milligrammes of vitamin F from each grapefruit consumed, while it derives no vitamin F whatsoever from avocado.

- Doctors have also determined that Smith's metabolism is such that his body derives 50 milligrammes of vitamin F from each grapefruit consumed and also from each avocado consumed.

- Both persons, Jones and Smith, are interested in the consumption of grapefruit and/or avocados only insofar as such consumption provides vitamin F, and the more the better. All the other traits of the two fruits (such as taste, calorie content, etc.) are of no consequence to them.

- No trades can be made after the division takes place.

How should the fruits be divided between Jones and Smith, if the division is to be just?

This problem of dividing grapefruit and avocados can be expressed more succinctly or more technically in the following way. Let $\omega$ be the bundle of fruits to be divided between Jones and Smith so that we have $\omega = (12, 12)$. Jones and Smith have different abilities to metabolize the fruits into vitamins. Therefore, we shall write $u_J(x, y) = 100x$ for Jones and $u_S(x, y) = 50x + 50y$ for Smith, with $x$ and $y$ being quantities of grapefruit and avocados, respectively. The functions $u_J$ and $u_S$ can be interpreted purely technically. We shall, however, view them as utility functions of the two persons. Moreover, these functions can be interpreted as cardinal utility functions with the property that the units of measurement (milligrammes of vitamin) are comparable across the individuals.

Let us come back to the distribution mechanisms listed above. How would these divide the given bundle of 12 grapefruit and 12 avocados between Jones and Smith? Table 9.1 answers this question where ($J$: 9,0; $S$: 3,12), for example, means that Jones gets 9 grapefruit and no avocados, while Smith receives 3 grapefruit and 12 avocados. Note that we have added the equal-split division as a reference point.

**Table 9.1.**

| Mechanism | Prescribed distribution |
|---|---|
| Equal split | J: 6,6; S: 6,6 |
| Bargaining from equal split (Nash) | J: 9,0; S: 3,12 |
| Bargaining from equal split (Kalai–Smorodinsky) | J: 9,0; S: 3,12 |
| Bargaining from zero (Nash) | J: 12,0; S: 0,12 |
| Bargaining from zero (Kalai–Smorodinsky) | J: 8,0; S: 4,12 |
| Bargaining over the strong Pareto set (Nash) | J: 6,0; S: 6,12 |
| Bargaining over the strong Pareto set (Kalai–Smorodinsky) | J: 6,0; S: 6,12 |
| Utilitarianism | J: 12,0; S: 0,12 |
| Maximin | J: 8,0; S: 4,12 |

**Table 9.2.** Q1: $n = 163$.

| Distribution | % of respondents |
|---|---|
| J: 6,6; S: 6,6 | 8 |
| J: 6,0; S: 6,12 | 0 |
| J: 8,0; S: 4,12 | 82 |
| J: 9,0; S: 3,12 | 8 |
| J: 12,0; S: 0,12 | 2 |

Which distribution is the appropriate one? Yaari and Bar-Hillel presented the five different distributions (not the underlying models, of course) to young male and female applicants for admission to the Hebrew University of Jerusalem in the years 1978–1980. The respondents were confronted with two versions of question Q1. One version asked the respondents to mark which of the five distributions *they* considered as the most just. The other version asked the respondents to assess how Jones and Smith would divide the shipment, 'on the assumption that both recipients are committed to looking for a just division' (1984, p. 10, footnote 10). The authors report that differences between the distributions of responses to these two versions were negligible.

The answers are listed in table 9.2.

We now come to the issue of what Yaari and Bar-Hillel have called tenability. The wording of the authors is extremely cautious as the reader will see. 'We are prepared to interpret the numbers ... as saying, for example, that the distribution (J: 8,0; S: 4,12) is much more in agreement with moral intuition than, say, the distribution (J: 12,0; S: 0,12). ... Indeed, it would be hard to make a case for a distribution mechanism that picks the distribution (J: 12,0; S: 0,12) ... without explaining why this distribution should fare so badly in an experimental setting designed to trace out prevailing moral intuitions' (1984, p. 10).

Table 9.1 informs us that distribution (J: 8,0; S: 4,12) can be achieved by mechanisms as diverse as maximin and bargaining from zero according to Kalai and Smorodinsky. We know from our discussion in Chapters 7 and 8 that these two mechanisms are indeed very different as far as their underlying philosophy is concerned. Both mechanisms happened to resolve the given distribution problem in the same way but does this mean that they shared the same degree of popularity among the respondents? To answer this question, Yaari and Bar-Hillel modified the original situation Q1 in the following way.

Replace the third paragraph in Q1 by

Q2:

- Doctors have also determined that Smith's metabolism is such that his body derives 20 milligrammes of vitamin F from each grapefruit consumed and also from each avocado consumed.

**Table 9.3.** Q2: $n = 146$.

| Distribution | % of respondents |
|---|---|
| J: 6,6; S: 6,6 | 4 |
| J: 4,0; S: 8,12 | 82 |
| J: 6,0; S: 6,12 | 4 |
| J: 8,0; S: 4,12 | 7 |
| J: 12,0; S: 0,12 | 3 |

The 'only' change from Q1 is that Smith's metabolism is less effective than originally. In technical terms, the problem now reads:

$$\omega = (12, 12);$$
$$u_J(x, y) = 100x;$$
$$u_S(x, y) = 20x + 20y.$$

The authors note, and this is important, that for all mechanisms but one listed in table 9.1, the distribution being proposed is the same as the one that was proposed in the original situation. Maximin, in contrast, selected $(J: 8,0; S: 4,12)$ in Q1 and now advocates $(J: 4,0; S: 8,12)$. Yaari and Bar-Hillel note that maximin is the only mechanism from table 9.1 that compensates Smith for the deterioration in his metabolism. The results for Q2 are listed in table 9.3 (the respondents were, of course, different from the ones who had answered Q1).

The students' 'vote' in favour of maximin is really amazing, both in absolute terms and in relation to the other mechanisms. Yaari and Bar-Hillel remark that one might, perhaps, have expected this, given the fact that obviously, the problem presented to the students can be viewed as an issue of needs, where in addition, needs are readily quantifiable.

A question that now arises is the following: 'How long' or to what extent would the respondents be willing to compensate Smith for any further deterioration in his metabolism, all the more because, simultaneously, Jones's share of the fruits is 'mercilessly' (Yaari and Bar-Hillel, p. 11) cut down? Sooner or later, the issue of tenability would render further compensations questionable. Therefore, the authors conceived yet another variant of the same distribution problem, named Q3. Everything is again the same as in Q1, except that the third paragraph now reads:

Q3:

- Doctors have also determined that Smith's metabolism is such that his body derives 9.1 milligrammes of vitamin F from each grapefruit and also from each avocado consumed.

**Table 9.4.**  Q3: $n = 52$.

| Distribution | % of respondents |
|---|---|
| J: 6,6; S: 6,6 | 17 |
| J: 2,0; S: 10,12 | 38 |
| J: 6,0; S: 6,12 | 27 |
| J: 8,0; S: 4,12 | 6 |
| J: 12,0; S: 0,12 | 12 |

In technical terms, the situation now looks as follows:

$$\omega = (12, 12);$$
$$u_J(x, y) = 100x;$$
$$u_S(x, y) = 9.1x + 9.1y.$$

The answers are listed in table 9.4.

Maximin proposes the distribution ($J$: 2,0; $S$: 10,12) where the vitamin intake of the two persons is equalized. Table 9.4 shows that maximin has now lost much of its former attractiveness. It still receives the largest number of responses but other proposals such as bargaining over the strong Pareto set ($J$: 6,0; $S$: 6,12) and even equal split which is totally insensitive to 'the story behind' gain much more support than before. Would maximin be abandoned altogether if Smith's metabolic deficiency were enhanced even further? We do not know. Yaari and Bar-Hillel's investigation, however, indicates that the criterion of equalizing the satisfaction of needs which maximin requires in the present case, may at some point collide with moral intuition.

What happens when the underlying issue is not needs but tastes? Yaari and Bar-Hillel have rewritten situation 1 such that Jones and Smith now differ in their tastes for grapefruit and avocados. Consider the following situation:

Q4: A shipment containing 12 grapefruit and 12 avocados is to be distributed between Jones and Smith. The following information is given, and is known also to the two recipients:

- Jones likes grapefruit very much, and is willing to buy any number of them, provided that the price does not exceed $1.00 per pound. He detests avocados, so he never buys them.
- Smith likes grapefruit and avocados equally well, and is willing to buy both grapefruit and avocado in any number, provided that the price does not exceed $0.50 per pound.
- Jones and Smith are in the same income-tax bracket.
- No trades can be made after the division takes place.

How should the fruits be divided between Jones and Smith, if the division is to be just?

This situation can be described technically in the following way:

$$\omega = (12, 12);$$

$$u_J(x, y) = 100x;$$

$$u_S(x, y) = 50x + 50y,$$

where the two functions $u_J$ and $u_S$ now describe the willingness to pay of the two individuals who are in the same income-tax bracket. It is important to note that the present formalization and the one given at the outset (for Q1) are *exactly* the same. The information, however, that is conveyed now is information about the tastes of Jones and Smith, while previously, the two functions contained information about the respective needs of the two individuals. From the standpoint of welfarism, these differences should only matter if they resulted in different utility information. Other information such as the interpretation of the individuals' utilities should be irrelevant. The reader will remember that this point was mentioned at various instances in earlier chapters, in Chapter 8 in particular. Since the utility information is identical in situations Q1 and Q4, as we have just seen, a 'welfarist respondent' should take the same decision in both cases. Table 9.5 shows that the Israeli students did not react this way. It obviously mattered a lot to them whether the underlying issue referred to needs or to tastes.

It should be noted that all the distribution mechanisms given in table 9.1 advocate the same distribution for Q4 as they had proposed for Q1. Clearly, due to the given utility information, these mechanisms are not able to treat the two given distribution problems differently. When we now compare table 9.5 with table 9.2, we see that the distributions of answers to the two problems are quite different from each other (the authors mention that under a chi-squared test, the difference between the distributions is significant at the 1% level). The distribution ($J$: 8,0; $S$: 4,12) still receives a relatively high percentage of support (much less, however, than under Q1), but it is surpassed by ($J$: 12,0; $S$: 0,12) which is supported, for example, by utilitarianism.

**Table 9.5.** Q4: $n = 122$.

| Distribution | % of respondents |
| --- | --- |
| J: 6,6; S: 6,6 | 9 |
| J: 6,0; S: 6,12 | 4 |
| J: 8,0; S: 4,12 | 28 |
| J: 9,0; S: 3,12 | 24 |
| J: 12,0; S: 0,12 | 35 |

**Table 9.6.** Q5: $n = 102$.

| Distribution | % of respondents |
|---|---|
| J: 6,6; S: 6,6 | 12 |
| J: 4,0; S: 8,12 | 6 |
| J: 6,0; S: 6,12 | 7 |
| J: 8,0; S: 4,12 | 28 |
| J: 12,0; S: 0,12 | 47 |

Let us now alter Smith's willingness to pay in such a way that the technical description becomes identical to the one in problem Q2. Yaari and Bar-Hillel change the text of Q4 so that the third paragraph now reads:

Q5:
- Smith likes grapefruit and avocado equally well, and is willing to buy both grapefruit and avocado in any number, provided that the price does not exceed $0.20 per pound.

As just indicated, the formalization is now given by

$$\omega = (12, 12);$$
$$u_J(x, y) = 100x;$$
$$u_S(x, y) = 20x + 20y.$$

The results are depicted in table 9.6.

This outcome is very interesting. While a very large number of students wanted to compensate Smith for the setback in his metabolism in situation Q2 (and cutting Jones's share simultaneously), nothing of this kind happened in the case of tastes. The considerable decline in responses consistent with maximin (from 28% in Q4 to 6% in Q5) and the clear increase in answers consistent with utilitarianism (from 35% in Q4 to 47% in Q5) appear to penalize Smith for a drop in his willingness to pay.

It seems as if the Israeli students had a distinct liking for the maximin criterion in cases of needs but tended toward utilitarianism in situations where the focus was on tastes without, of course, knowing details about either distribution rule.

## 9.3. Rawls's equity axiom – how does it fare?

We saw in section 7.3 that an equity axiom is fundamental for Rawls's second principle of justice, the so-called difference principle which requires that economic and social inequalities are to be arranged such that they are to the greatest benefit of the least advantaged members of society. The reader will remember that the equity axiom makes a particular demand for a society of only two individuals or, more generally, for a society where only two individuals are affected by a change from one policy to another. Just to refresh our memories, let there be two policies $x$ and $y$. We postulate that person 1 prefers $x$ to $y$, person 2 prefers $y$ to $x$, and independently of whether $x$ or $y$ will eventually be the social outcome, person 2 is always better off than person 1. We know that in such a situation, the equity axiom requires $x$ to be socially preferred to $y$.

Is there a possibility to check whether individuals follow the Rawlsian difference principle in their judgments (check in an indirect way, of course; to ask people directly would be rather naive)? The question we wish to discuss is twofold. First of all, we would like to know whether people's evaluations satisfy the demands of the equity principle. In a second step, we will ask whether those who fulfil this axiom would follow it unconditionally, i.e. focus always exclusively on the worst-off members of society. How can this possibly be done?

In Gaertner (1992), we made the following suggestion. Let us consider the subsequent two-person profile of so-called extended orderings $\tilde{R}_i$, $i \in \{1, 2\}$, that we shall denote by $E^1$:

$$\tilde{R}_1 : (y, 2)(x, 2)(x, 1)(y, 1);$$

$$\tilde{R}_2 : (y, 2)(x, 2)(x, 1)(y, 1).$$

These lines should be read as follows. Both individuals agree that it is best to be person 2 under policy $y$. This is deemed better than being person 2 under policy $x$. This, again, is better than being person 1 under $x$ which is better than being person 1 under $y$. The reader should verify that this two-person profile reflects the structure of the equity axiom from section 7.3. Both persons diverge in their evaluations of policies $x$ and $y$ as far as *their own position* is concerned, but they agree that it is person 2 who is always better off.

According to the equity axiom, $x$ will be declared as preferable to $y$. We shall now enlarge this basic profile by adding the extended orderings of persons 3, 4, ... , thereby preserving the structure of $E^1$. $E^2$, for example, is:

$$\tilde{R}_1 : (y, 3)(x, 3)(y, 2)(x, 2)(x, 1)(y, 1),$$
$$\tilde{R}_2 : (y, 3)(x, 3)(y, 2)(x, 2)(x, 1)(y, 1),$$
$$\tilde{R}_3 : (y, 3)(x, 3)(y, 2)(x, 2)(x, 1)(y, 1).$$

We then ask all members of society how they would wish to resolve the situations $E^1, E^2, \ldots$ All those individuals who accept the equity axiom will, of course, say that for $E^1$ alternative $x$ should be the preferred state. For the moment, let us focus on just one member of the society. Will he or she find $x$

also preferable in situation $E^2$? If 'yes', will the same verdict hold in $E^3, E^4, \ldots$? It is very well possible that at some point in this successive questioning the individual wishes to switch from '$x$ preferable to $y$' to 'now $y$ should be preferred to $x$ socially'. It could, however, also be the case that given the size of the society, the evaluating member of society would always want $x$ to be socially preferred to $y$ and thus decide in the spirit of the equity axiom unconditionally.

The situation that we shall present and discuss now can be found on the internet[1] together with several other cases. The structure of all situations is similar to the one in our $E^1, E^2, \ldots$ profiles above. There is always one (group of) person(s) who is worst-off under both alternatives $x$ and $y$. That person is better-off under $x$ than under $y$ whereas all the other (groups of) individuals who are introduced successively are better off under $y$ than under $x$. This situation as well as the others was presented to classes of undergraduate students at the University of Osnabrück between 1989 and 2002 as well as to students in the three Baltic states during 1997–1998 and to students in Israel in 1999. All students were enrolled in economics or business administration. At the time of the investigation the students had not yet had a course on welfare economics and theories of distributive justice, such as utilitarianism, Rawlsianism and game theoretical solutions.

Here is the situation we wish to focus on:

(o)  A small society has received a certain amount of money which can be used either to provide some help and assistance for a handicapped person or to further the education of an intelligent child. The child could receive a good education in languages and in natural sciences, let's say. Let the handicapped person be person 1; if the sum of money were used for her support (alternative $x$), she would be able to learn some very basic things, so that at least in certain areas of daily life she would no longer be totally dependent on the assistance from other people. Let the intelligent child be person 2; the investment into its education represents alternative $y$. The interpersonal welfare ranking reads:

$$(y, 2)(x, 2)(x, 1)(y, 1).$$

Which alternative should be realized in your view, $x$ or $y$?

(a)  Imagine that the sum of money which could be used to help the handicapped person is so large that, on the other hand, this amount would suffice

[1] The internet address is http://nts4.oec.uni-osnabrueck.de/mikro/darp.pdf. All in all, we had given six different situations to the students. All these situations are fully reproduced in Gaertner and Jungeilges (2002). We should mention that in Osnabrück, we had two versions of our questionnaire, a technical and a non-technical version (the technical version is reproduced here and on the internet). The non-technical version did not use the specification in terms of extended orderings but provided a somewhat lengthier verbal description of the same 'facts' instead. Of course, each student only saw one version. Since in Israel and the Baltics, we used the non-technical version, table 9.7 gives the results from this version only. The Osnabrück results for the two versions did not show any difference on the basis of a two-sample non-parametric test, given an error probability of 5%.

for the education of not only person 2 but also a second child (person 3) who is even somewhat more intelligent than person 2. Person 3 would, therefore, benefit even a bit more from the education so that the following interpersonal welfare ranking can be assumed:

$$(y, 3)(y, 2)(x, 3)(x, 2)(x, 1)(y, 1).$$

Would you choose $x$ or $y$ under these conditions?

(b) Imagine that if the money were used to finance alternative $y$ it would be possible to educate still another child (person 4). The reason may simply be 'economies of scale' or the fact that a talented teacher will be able to provide a good education for several children simultaneously. Let us assume that all the other characteristics of the situation remain as before. The interpersonal welfare ranking now reads:

$$(y, 4)(y, 3)(y, 2)(x, 4)(x, 3)(x, 2)(x, 1)(y, 1).$$

Which alternative should be picked in your view, $x$ or $y$?

(c) Add another child to the situation (person 5), who could also receive an instruction in languages and the natural sciences out of the given budget. Everything else remains the same and the interpersonal welfare ranking reads:

$$(y, 5)(y, 4)(y, 3)(y, 2)(x, 5)(x, 4)(x, 3)(x, 2)(x, 1)(y, 1).$$

Would you want $x$ or $y$ to be realized?

The underlying issue apparently is to allocate a certain amount of money to provide some help for a handicapped person (alternative $x$) or to teach one (or several) intelligent child(ren). Clearly, the intelligent child(ren) is (are) always better off than the handicapped person whatever decision will be taken. When we compare the current situation with the various cases presented by Yaari and Bar-Hillel, we can with some justification argue that the present situation reflects the needs aspect. But it also contains an aspect of efficiency, since an investment in human capital usually leads to an increase in efficiency.

Our students most likely played the role of an external judge. In other words, their identification with the position and the circumstances of a particular person was only of an indirect nature. On second thought, however, this need not necessarily have been the case. Imagine that a student himself (herself) turned out to be handicapped or that one member within his (her) family or a close friend suffered from a handicap. We do not know this, of course, but had it been the case, it would certainly have mattered.

In table 9.7, we first give the results for the Osnabrück students during the period 1989–2002. Explaining the digits and numbers in table 9.7, 0 always represents the choice of alternative $x$, 1 stands for the choice of alternative $y$.

**Table 9.7.**

| Sequence | Year of investigation | | | | |
|---|---|---|---|---|---|
| | 1989 $n = 65$ | 1990 $n = 93$ | 1993 $n = 81$ | 1994 $n = 63$ | 2002 $n = 86$ |
| 0 0 0 0 | 0.723 | 0.581 | 0.494 | 0.603 | 0.407 |
| 0 0 0 1 | 0.046 | 0.086 | 0.062 | 0.016 | 0.035 |
| 0 0 1 0 | 0.0 | 0.0 | 0.0 | 0.0 | 0.0 |
| 0 0 1 1 | 0.077 | 0.151 | 0.148 | 0.095 | 0.174 |
| 0 1 0 0 | 0.0 | 0.0 | 0.0 | 0.0 | 0.0 |
| 0 1 0 1 | 0.0 | 0.0 | 0.0 | 0.0 | 0.0 |
| 0 1 1 0 | 0.0 | 0.0 | 0.0 | 0.0 | 0.012 |
| 0 1 1 1 | 0.077 | 0.086 | 0.173 | 0.143 | 0.233 |
| 1 0 0 0 | 0.0 | 0.0 | 0.0 | 0.0 | 0.0 |
| 1 0 0 1 | 0.0 | 0.0 | 0.0 | 0.0 | 0.0 |
| 1 0 1 0 | 0.0 | 0.0 | 0.0 | 0.0 | 0.0 |
| 1 0 1 1 | 0.0 | 0.0 | 0.0 | 0.0 | 0.0 |
| 1 1 0 0 | 0.0 | 0.011 | 0.0 | 0.0 | 0.0 |
| 1 1 0 1 | 0.0 | 0.0 | 0.0 | 0.0 | 0.0 |
| 1 1 1 0 | 0.0 | 0.0 | 0.0 | 0.0 | 0.0 |
| 1 1 1 1 | 0.077 | 0.086 | 0.123 | 0.143 | 0.140 |
| % of switch | 19.8 | 32.1 | 38.3 | 25.4 | 44.2 |
| % fulfilment of equity axiom | 92.3 | 90.3 | 87.7 | 85.7 | 86.0 |

In order to be more explicit, the sequence 0000, for example, refers to those students who took a decision in favour of $x$ in all cases, i.e. in the basic situation and in all of its variants. 0001, 0011, and 0111 represent the verdicts of those respondents who decided at one point to revise their original judgment. The numbers in the columns give the percentages of answers within each of the cohorts of undergraduates. Relative frequencies of a revision or 'switch' are contained in the lower part of the table. All those sequences which begin with 0 represent students who satisfied the equity axiom. Correspondingly, all those sequences which start with 1 hint at a violation of the equity axiom. The percentages of students who satisfied the equity axiom are given at the bottom of each table.

Let us try to interpret our findings. We start with the year 1989. The decision to give the money to the handicapped person in all cases, i.e. unconditionally, was very strong indeed (72.3%). Only 7.7% of the respondents wanted the amount of money to go into the education of the intelligent child(ren) right away. Those who wished to revise their original decision which, at the outset, was in favour of helping the handicapped were 19.8% of the students. The percentages of those who wanted to revise their decision after the first or second 'round' were equally high (7.7%). All in all, the equity axiom was fulfilled by 92.3% of the respondents.

When we now examine the following years, we have to state that the percentages for the unconditional support of the handicapped have more or less continually gone down. At the same time, the unconditional support for the education of the child(ren) as well as the desire to switch already after the first round (the latter from 7.7% in 1989 to 23.3% in 2002) experienced a steady increase over the years. All these developments are reflected in a steady decline of the fulfilment of the equity axiom and in a considerable increase of the desire to revise an originally made decision (the latter from 19.8% in 1989 to 44.2% in 2002).

These tendencies or differences, rather, that evolved over time were checked statistically by using a chi-squared test with the $H_0$-hypothesis of an identical distribution of the responses between any two cohorts (years). The results of these tests are such that the $H_0$-hypothesis was rejected at the 5% significance level between the cohorts of 1989 and 1993 and between 1989 and 2002. Furthermore, the $H_0$-hypothesis was rejected at the 10% level between the years 1994 and 2002. So the statistical analysis confirms what has become apparent from a purely descriptive comparison: the respondents to a considerable degree turned away from the unconditional support of the worse-off and developed a greater concern for the better-off.

Does the cultural, political or social background matter in a situation such as the one given above? This is a question we have not examined so far. One could turn this question around and assert that it would be surprising if the social, political or historical context would not matter at all. This issue is quite complex and an answer can only be given with utmost caution. We invite the reader to look at the results that we gained from investigations in Israel in 1999 and in the Baltics in 1997–98 (table 9.8).

Table 9.8 contains two surprises. One surprise is that the Israeli results from 1999 are very close to the Osnabrück results from 1989–1990. The other surprise are the drastically different results from the Baltics. We have to admit that the student samples in the present case are quite small, but in 2001 we were able to repeat the investigation in the Baltics, this time only in Lithuania, with almost exactly the same results as in the years 1997–1998. Without exaggerating too much, one can assert that the results in Osnabrück around 1989 and 1990 and the ones from Israel in 1999 are 'worlds apart' from those in the Baltic countries. What could be the reasons? One reason most probably is the particular historical and political situation of the Baltics after the collapse of the Soviet Union. Since the education of talented children stands for a gain in efficiency, an emphasis on reconstruction and economic growth may explain the evaluations of the Baltic respondents. And it should not be overlooked that the more recent figures from the Osnabrück students document a certain departure from unconditional support of the worst-off in society and, at the same time, a greater emphasis on the aspect of efficiency.

**Table 9.8.**

| Sequence | Israel 1999 $n = 46$ | The Baltics 1997/98 $n = 67$ |
|---|---|---|
| 0  0  0  0 | 0.609 | 0.030 |
| 0  0  0  1 | 0.0 | 0.0 |
| 0  0  1  0 | 0.021 | 0.045 |
| 0  0  1  1 | 0.174 | 0.179 |
| 0  1  0  0 | 0.0 | 0.0 |
| 0  1  0  1 | 0.021 | 0.015 |
| 0  1  1  0 | 0.0 | 0.045 |
| 0  1  1  1 | 0.109 | 0.343 |
| 1  0  0  0 | 0.0 | 0.015 |
| 1  0  0  1 | 0.0 | 0.015 |
| 1  0  1  0 | 0.0 | 0.015 |
| 1  0  1  1 | 0.0 | 0.030 |
| 1  1  0  0 | 0.0 | 0.015 |
| 1  1  0  1 | 0.0 | 0.015 |
| 1  1  1  0 | 0.0 | 0.0 |
| 1  1  1  1 | 0.065 | 0.239 |
| % of switch | 28.3 | 52.2 |
| % fulfilment of equity axiom | 93.5 | 65.7 |

## 9.4. **From here to where?**

The reader most likely gathered from the previous pages that the author of this primer considers empirical social choice as an important addendum to abstract social choice theory. Reasons for this view were presented at the outset of this chapter. But are the situations given to the students in various countries perhaps too naive, too simplistic? Yaari and Bar-Hillel said at the end of their own investigations that 'the only general conclusion which we are prepared to draw from our work so far is that a satisfactory theory of distributive justice would have to be endowed with considerable detail and finesse' (1984, p. 22). And they continued asserting that 'sweeping solutions and world-embracing theories are not likely to be adequate for dealing with the intricacies inherent in the problem of How to Distribute' (p. 22).

   We should mention that we presented situations more complex than the one discussed above to students for evaluation (see Gaertner (1992, 1994), Gaertner et al. (2001, 2002). One case, for example, considered either giving money to various countries in Subsaharan Africa to alleviate famine in these regions or financing environmental programmes in the home country. Another situation focused on a relatively poor country that considered either to buy badly needed dialysis machines on the world market or import vitamins and fresh fruit for pregnant women and small children. Since these cases, admittedly, are more complex than the situations described in sections 9.2

and 9.3 (one characteristic of these other cases, for example, is that the number of people affected by the different programmes remains largely unspecified), the outcome in terms of observed ethical judgments was more diffuse. All in all, we still witness a strong concern for the worse-off members of society, but other aspects such as productivity and efficiency considerations – in part directed towards future generations – enter as competing arguments.

During the last two decades, empirical social choice has gathered momentum. There are many aspects that are worth looking at. For example, do individuals when they are involved in a particular distribution problem follow the principle of Pareto efficiency widely cherished in economics? To what extent are people interested in fair solutions? Will effort and higher productivity be rewarded? Do people follow the Pigou–Dalton principle of transfers in their evaluations when income or wealth are redistributed?

Beckmann et al. (2002) have shown that envy and malice are powerful motivations to block Pareto improvement. Malice hereby refers to a situation where the evaluating person opposes a Pareto gain when the recipient occupies a lower income position than the evaluator; envy refers to the case of opposition to Pareto gains when the recipient is above the evaluating person. Opposition to Pareto improvement diminishes when gains are spread more widely over the individuals. The findings of Beckmann et al. interestingly refer to different cultures.

Konow (2001) examined, among other aspects, the accountability principle. A person's entitlement depends on the perceived output of an allocable variable and the person's perceived input to the production of this variable. In the question of how to reach a just allocation of output, so-called discretionary variables are distinguished from exogenous variables. The former affect production and can be influenced by a person (his or her work effort, for example); the latter cannot reasonably be influenced by a person but may nevertheless have an impact on production. Konow's findings show that an allocation according to a person's contribution of effort is considered fair, while an unequal allocation due to an explicit exogenous difference is deemed unfair.

The Pigou–Dalton principle of transfers states that a transfer from a richer person to a poorer person always reduces inequality. This principle is one of the fundamental axioms in inequality analysis. Will it be satisfied by the general public on a larger scale? Amiel and Cowell (1999) ran an extensive international questionnaire experiment over several years using student respondents. Their findings are that consistency with the transfer principle across various income situations involving transfers between differing groups is no more than roughly 20%. The percentage is, of course, higher in situations where the transfer occurs between extremes, from 'rich' to 'poor', so to speak.

The issues to which we have just been referring constitute only a fraction of questions that were recently investigated in empirical social choice (see Konow (2003) for further details).

## 9.5. **A short summary**

Chapter 7 dealt with issues of distributive justice and proposed different solution concepts. Chapter 8 discussed various approaches to cooperative bargaining. At the beginning of this chapter, we quoted Bar-Hillel and Yaari who said that a theory of distributive justice, like any other theory in economics, has to be tested in order to see how well it performs when confronted with evidence. However, evidence in this context does not come from econometric analysis but will have to be based on observed ethical judgments or moral intuition. Bar-Hillel and Yaari probably were the first to systematically investigate whether 'the public' intuitively follows fundamental principles of justice and fairness. Game theory has been doing experimental analysis for several decades; empirical social choice is a relatively recent phenomenon.

Yaari and Bar-Hillel found that the same distributive problem would be solved quite differently for a case where needs were the prevalent characteristic as compared to a situation where tastes were the dominating aspect. In situations of need, for example, the answers or choices of the respondents could largely be explained by the Rawlsian maximin principle.

The latter principle also was at the centre of several investigations run by the author of this primer. Most of the questions in this study started from a situation where money or some other desirable commodity could be given either to a badly-off person or to a better-off individual. The question was whether the valuables would be allocated to the worse-off person *unconditionally*, which would be in conformity with the Rawlsian maximin postulate. In other words, would the allocative decision be made independently of the number of better-off persons who would also benefit if the valuable items were given to them, or would the decision indeed hinge on the number or the collective benefit of those positively affected? Not surprisingly, it was found that contexts matter but the cultural and political background also influences the judgment of the evaluating individuals.

☐ **RECOMMENDED READING**

Gaertner, W. and Jungeilges, J. (2002). 'Evaluation via Extended Orderings: Empirical Findings from Western and Eastern Europe'. *Social Choice and Welfare*, 19: 29–55.

Konow, J. (2003). 'Which Is the Fairest One of All? A Positive Analysis of Justice Theories'. *Journal of Economic Literature*, 41: 1188–1239.

Schokkaert, E. (1999). 'Tout-le-monde est "post-welfariste". Opinions sur la justice redistributive'. *Revue économique*, 50: 811–831. Available in English as: 'Mr. Fairmind

Is Post-Welfarist. Opinions on Distributive Justice'. *Discussion Paper DPS 98.09.* Catholic University of Leuven, Department of Economics.

Yaari, M. E. and Bar-Hillel, M. (1984). 'On Dividing Justly'. *Social Choice and Welfare,* 1: 1–24.

## ☐ HISTORICAL SOURCE

Yaari, M. E. and Bar-Hillel, M. (1984). 'On Dividing Justly'. See above.

# 10     A few steps beyond

In this last chapter, we want to go a little beyond a primer in social choice theory. Going beyond means that the issues discussed on the following pages perhaps do not belong to the 'core' of social choice theory, though they tackle interesting and important problems and each of them has been witnessing, without any doubt, a very involved discussion over the last 15–20 years. Going beyond also means that in at least one of the three items that we wish to cover, the formal analysis gets quite involved if done properly. We shall start with an analysis of aggregation rules in continuous space and shall encounter another impossibility result. Then, we shall consider the problem of allocating an infinitely divisible commodity among a group of individuals who have single-peaked preferences. Finally, we shall look at the issue of freedom of choice, an aspect that really goes beyond social choice proper.

## 10.1. Social choice rules in continuous space

In most of the previous chapters, we considered a finite set of alternatives and looked for adequate aggregation procedures under different circumstances. The exception was Chapter 8 where we discussed various bargaining solutions in utility space, i.e. in $n$-dimensional Euclidean space. But also in that chapter, we started from a finite set of physical objects or social outcomes. Only via the introduction of lotteries did we eventually obtain a convex space in $\mathbb{R}^n$. In the present section, our starting point is a multidimensional choice space. The reader probably knows this kind of space from a course in general equilibrium theory. In this area, one is, among other things, interested in conditions under which there is an equalization of demand and supply on markets. Supply and demand functions are either assumed to be continuous from the outset or axioms are introduced such that these functions become continuous. Continuity means, loosely speaking, that a 'small' change in the domain of a function does not yield a 'big' change in the range of the function (for example, a small change in relative prices leads to a small change in the demand for a particular commodity, let's say). Applied to the present context of aggregation rules, continuity implies that small changes in a given preference profile of society yield a small change in the aggregate outcome.

This is definitely not so for well-known aggregation rules in the Arrovian framework with a finite set of discrete alternatives. Consider the following profile of strict preferences for four individuals:

| 1 | 2 | 3 | 4 |
|---|---|---|---|
| $x$ | $y$ | $z$ | $v$ |
| $y$ | $z$ | $v$ | $x$ |
| $z$ | $v$ | $x$ | $y$ |
| $v$ | $x$ | $y$ | $z$ |

In this situation, there is no Condorcet winner, and the Borda rule would declare all four alternatives as equally desirable socially. When we change the second individual's ranking 'slightly' by inverting alternatives $x$ and $v$ so that we get $2'$ : $yzxv$, we now obtain the existence of a Condorcet winner, viz. option $x$, and the same result is achieved via the Borda method. We see that a relatively small change in the latter half of agent 2's ordering yields a *unique* winner which is quite different from the result before the change.

Or consider the following profile for five individuals:

| 1 | 2 | 3 | 4 | 5 |
|---|---|---|---|---|
| $x$ | $y$ | $z$ | $x$ | $z$ |
| $y$ | $v$ | $v$ | $v$ | $x$ |
| $z$ | $x$ | $y$ | $z$ | $v$ |
| $v$ | $z$ | $x$ | $y$ | $y$ |

In this situation, $x$ is the Condorcet winner and $x$ also wins according to the Borda rule. Now invert $x$ and $z$ in the preference ranking of person 2. Then $z$ becomes the Condorcet winner and also the Borda scheme chooses alternative $z$.

In section 6.3 we mentioned that Dodgson's proposal for cases that no Condorcet winner exists can be interpreted as a kind of distance minimization procedure. We then introduced the Kemeny metric which defines a distance between two binary relations. Kemeny's procedure looked for a ranking to be viewed as a unanimous social ranking that is closest to a given preference profile of society. In the finite framework, it is not possible to speak of continuity but for this Arrovian set-up, Baigent (1987b) and others have introduced the notion of proximity preservation. This concept which is based on a metric on preferences, requires that small changes in the individuals' preferences only lead to small changes in the resulting social preference. Does this property hold in the finite framework? We shall come back to this question once we have discussed the issue of continuous aggregation functions in $n$-dimensional Euclidean space.

Chichilnisky (1980, 1982) was interested in the existence of continuous aggregation rules. The author argued that continuity of such rules would not only be a natural property, it would also be desirable for the aggregation rule to be relatively insensitive to small variations in individuals' preferences. She explained that 'this makes mistakes in identifying preferences less crucial. It also permits one to approximate social preferences on the basis of a sample of individual preferences' (1982, p. 337). Making mistakes, or rather, avoiding mistakes is a valid argument in a set-up where a social planner, let's say, registers the individuals' preferences and then determines the social outcome.

In order to present Chichilnisky's findings, we have to become more formal. We consider a choice space $X$ which is contained in the positive orthant of the $n$-dimensional Euclidean space $\mathbb{R}_+^n$. Let $X$ be a cube in $\mathbb{R}_+^n$. Each individual preference $p_i$ is a $C^1$ locally integrable vector field over the space of alternatives. This means that to each alternative $x$ in $X$, one attaches a vector $p_i(x)$ in a continuously differentiable fashion which indicates the direction of the largest increase of utility. This direction is that of the normal to the tangent plane of the indifference surface through $x$. Since ordinal preferences are considered, it is the direction of the vectors rather than the length which is important. Therefore, all vectors are assumed to be of length 1. Since all preferences are assumed to be continuously differentiable and locally integrable, they can be represented locally by a smooth utility function. The space of preferences $P$ is defined as the set of all $C^1$ integrable unit vector fields defined on the choice space $X$. An important subspace of $P$ is the set $Q$ of all linear preference orderings. These are constant vector fields on $X$. Such preferences can be represented by a linear utility function and their indifference surfaces are hyperplanes, i.e. straight lines in $\mathbb{R}^2$, for example.

There are $n$ individuals in society. A social aggregation rule for individual preferences is a function that assigns to each $n$-tuple of individual preferences, i.e. to each profile $(p_1, \ldots, p_n) \in P^n$, a social preference in $P$. If $\Phi$ stands for a social aggregation rule, we obtain

$$\Phi : \underbrace{P \times \cdots \times P}_{n\text{-times}} \to P$$

Following Chichilnisky (1980, 1982), the rule $\Phi$ is required to fulfil the following three properties. First of all, the social preference has to define at each choice a most desirable direction in a continuous manner. The continuity of $\Phi$ is defined in terms of convergence in the space of preferences which implies that proximity of preferences in $P$ is equivalent to the proximity of their indifference surfaces. What is meant here will become clearer when we study figures 10.1(a)–(c) a bit further on. Secondly, the choice rule $\Phi$ is assumed to satisfy the condition of anonymity, i.e. $\Phi(p_1, \ldots, p_n) = \Phi(p_{\sigma(1)}, \ldots, p_{\sigma(n)})$, where $\sigma(1), \ldots, \sigma(n)$ denotes any permutation of the set of integers $\{1, \ldots, n\}$. Thirdly, the aggregation rule $\Phi$ is required to respect unanimity, i.e. $\Phi(p, \ldots, p) = p$ for all $p \in P$.

Note that respect for unanimity, as defined here, is a condition that is weaker than the weak Pareto principle, since it makes a requirement only in the case where all preferences within a profile are the same. The condition of anonymity is stronger than Arrow's non-dictatorship condition, because it demands an equal treatment of the agents' preferences, while Arrow's condition only forbids an extreme unevenness of treatment. Chichilnisky (1980, 1982) arrived at the following impossibility result.

**Theorem 10.1 (Impossibility of continuous aggregation).**  Any continuous social aggregation rule $\Phi : P^n \to P$ cannot simultaneously satisfy anonymity and unanimity.

A proof of this result goes well beyond the present chapter. However, a reader who is interested in details should either consult the original source or go to sections 2 and 6 in Baigent (2002). Chichilnisky (1982) gave a nice geometrical illustration underlying her impossibility result. Saari (1997) and Baigent (2002, section 2) picked this up and turned it into a beach-party problem: There is a circular lake and the question is to determine a location at the edge of this lake to have a party for several individuals. All agents have preferences for the possible locations around the lake. The group choice should continuously depend on the individuals' preferences.

More abstractly, let the choice space $X$ be two-dimensional, a unit cube denoted $I^2$. Furthermore, let the space of preferences consist of linear preferences only. This space is denoted by $Q$. Now let $o$ be the centre of $X$. Then each preference $Q$ can be uniquely identified by a point on the circle $S^1$. Let us be somewhat more explicit. Figures 10.1(a)–(c) will show what is going on here. We assume that there are only two individuals. Figure 10.1(a) depicts the linear indifference surface of person 1's preferences where the arrow indicates the most desirable direction of these preferences. Figure 10.1(b) does the same for person 2 with the most desirable direction going elsewhere. In this special case, each linear preference can be uniquely identified by one vector $p$ of unit length, i.e. by a point on the circle $S^1$. For this special case, the theorem states that there exists no continuous map $\psi$ assigning to each pair $(p_1, p_2)$ in $S^1$ a third point $p$ in $S^1$ (the social preference), such that

$$\psi(p_1, p_2) = \psi(p_2, p_1), \quad \text{and}$$
$$\psi(p_1, p_2) = p_1 = p_2, \quad \text{if } p_1 = p_2 \quad \text{(unanimity)}.$$

Chichilnisky illustrated her impossibility result by means of an aggregation rule which is some kind of an averaging rule. Let $p_1$ and $p_2$ be two vectors in $S^1$ and let $\psi(p_1, p_2)$ be the unit vector in a direction that is determined by half the angular distance between $p_1$ and $p_2$ in the clockwise direction. Now let $p_1$ rotate clockwise around the unit circle $S^1$. Then as $p_1 \to p_2, \psi(p_1, p_2)$ must converge to $p_3$. On the other hand, due to unanimity, $\psi(p_1, p_2)$ must

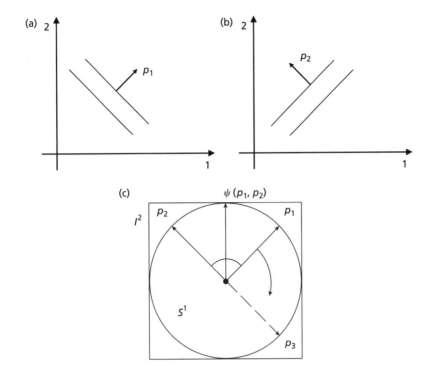

**Figure 10.1.**

also converge to $p_2$, as $p_1$ converges to $p_2$. Thus, this anonymous choice rule suggests a clash between continuity and unanimity. If the rule had been to assign half the larger angular distance between $p_1$ and $p_2$, the group choice $\psi(p_1, p_2)$ would have jumped discontinuously from a location left of $p_3$ to a position right of $p_3$, a similar problem.

Can Chichilnisky's impossibility theorem be turned into a possibility result? Yes, it can by introducing a topological domain restriction. In the beach-party problem, such a restriction would require that one location on the circle $S^1$ be unavailable for the party. The topological condition is called contractibility. Its introduction into social choice theory is due to Chichilnisky and Heal (1983). Roughly speaking, a contractible space is one that has no holes in it and can, therefore, be contracted continuously through itself into one of its points. The unit disk is, for example, contractible since it has no holes. Any convex space is contractible. Consider a convex space $X$, take an $n$-tuple of points $(x_1, \ldots, x_n)$, each of which is in $X$, and assign to them another point $y$ in $X$ which is their aggregate. In mathematical terms, a map $g$ from the $n$-fold product of $X$ with itself into $X$ has to be constructed, i.e. $g : X \times \cdots \times X \to X$. Let $g$ satisfy continuity. Under convexity of $X$, the following continuous aggregation rule is possible: $g(x) = \frac{1}{n} \sum_{i=1}^{n} x_i$, which is convex addition.

Coming back to the circle in $\mathbb{R}^2$, this geometrical figure is not contractible. The same holds for the boundary of a square or a triangle. However, in the case of the circle, if there is a convex cone of directions, no matter how small, which no agent will have as his or her most preferred directions, the space of preferences becomes contractible. Chichilnisky and Heal (1983) proved that if and only if the space of preferences $P$ is contractible, there exists a social choice rule from $P^n$ to $P$ which is continuous, anonymous and respects unanimity. We hasten to add that Chichilnisky and Heal required space $P$ to satisfy certain extra technical conditions, i.e. topological requirements.

Let us finally come back to the issue of proximity preservation in the finite framework. The idea and illustration we use in order to show an impossibility result in this framework go back to Baigent (1987b). Let $\mathcal{E}$ stand for the set of all preference orderings on $X$, a finite set of alternatives. $R$, $R'$, and $R''$ are typical elements of $\mathcal{E}$. In the sequel, we shall consider profiles of preference orderings such as $\bar{R} = (R_1, \ldots, R_n)$, $\bar{R}' = (R'_1, \ldots, R'_n)$, etc. representing the orderings of $n$ individuals. Similar to section 6.3, we introduce a distance function on $\mathcal{E}$, viz. $d : \mathcal{E}^2 \to \mathbb{R}_+$. We define a metric on $\mathcal{E}$ as a distance function $d$, defined on pairs of preference orderings, having the three properties specified in section 6.3.

If $d$ is any metric on $\mathcal{E}$, then the metric on profiles will be defined as follows. For any two profiles $\bar{R}$ and $\bar{R}'$, we define $\Delta_d(\bar{R}, \bar{R}') = \sum_{i \in N} d(R_i, R'_i)$. We can now define what it means for a social welfare function $f$ to preserve proximity (Baigent, 1987b).

**Proximity preservation.**  A social welfare function $f$ preserves proximity if there exists any metric $d$ on $\mathcal{E}$ such that, for any profiles $\bar{R}$, $\bar{R}'$, and $\bar{R}''$,

$$\Delta_d(\bar{R}, \bar{R}') < \Delta_d(\bar{R}, \bar{R}'') \quad \text{implies that}$$
$$d(f(\bar{R}), f(\bar{R}')) \leq d(f(\bar{R}), f(\bar{R}'')).$$

The properties of unanimity and anonymity were defined above, though in the context of continuous aggregation. Therefore, there is no need to define them again in the present finite framework. Baigent's (1987b) result was

**Theorem 10.2.**  There is no social welfare function that is anonymous, respects unanimity, and preserves proximity.

We shall not give a proof of this theorem but shall provide a simple illustration of this result for the case of two individuals and two alternatives, which is also due to Baigent (1987b).

Let there be two alternatives $a$ and $b$ and let us assume that the two persons only have strict preferences. Then only two preferences are possible over $a$ and $b$, either $aPb$ or $bPa$. We define $\bar{R} = (aP_1b, aP_2b)$, $\bar{R}' = (bP'_1a, bP'_2a)$, $\bar{R}'' = (bP''_1a, aP''_2b)$, and $\bar{R}''' = (aP'''_1b, bP'''_2a)$. For any metric $d$ on $\mathcal{E}$, the distance between profiles $\bar{R}''$ and $\bar{R}$ can be expressed as follows:

$$\Delta_d(\bar{R}'', \bar{R}) = d(bP_1'' a, aP_1 b) + d(aP_2'' b, aP_2 b)$$
$$= d(bP_1'' a, aP_1 b) > 0,$$

due to the specified properties of a metric on $\mathcal{E}$.

Similarly, the distance between profiles $\bar{R}''$ and $\bar{R}'''$ can be expressed by

$$\Delta_d(\bar{R}'', \bar{R}''') = d(bP_1'' a, aP_1''' b) + d(aP_2'' b, bP_2''' a)$$
$$= 2\Delta_d(\bar{R}'', \bar{R}).$$

Therefore, $\Delta_d(\bar{R}'', \bar{R}) < \Delta_d(\bar{R}'', \bar{R}''')$. In other words, profile $\bar{R}''$ is closer to $\bar{R}$ than it is to $\bar{R}'''$.

We now have to check whether this proximity relation also holds for the social preferences $f(\bar{R}''), f(\bar{R})$ and $f(\bar{R}''')$. If the social welfare function $f$ respects unanimity, then $f(\bar{R})$ yields $aPb$ which is unequal to $f(\bar{R}')$ which yields $bPa$. Therefore, either $f(\bar{R}'') \neq f(\bar{R})$ or $f(\bar{R}'') \neq f(\bar{R}')$. Assume that $f(\bar{R}'') \neq f(\bar{R})$ which implies that $d(f(\bar{R}''), f(\bar{R})) > 0$. If $f$ is anonymous, $f(\bar{R}'') = f(\bar{R}''')$ must hold. This implies that $d(f(\bar{R}''), f(\bar{R}''')) = 0 < d(f(\bar{R}''), f(\bar{R}))$. Therefore, even though $\bar{R}''$ is nearer to $\bar{R}$ than it is to $\bar{R}'''$, $f(\bar{R}'')$ is farther from $f(\bar{R})$ than it is from $f(\bar{R}''')$.

If $f(\bar{R}'') = f(\bar{R})$, then $f(\bar{R}'') \neq f(\bar{R}')$. In this case, an analogous argument holds, i.e. $d(f(\bar{R}''), f(\bar{R}''')) < d(f(\bar{R}''), f(\bar{R}'))$, whereas the distance between profiles $\bar{R}''$ and $\bar{R}'''$ is larger than the distance between $\bar{R}''$ and $\bar{R}'$. This shows that the social welfare function does not fulfil the requirement of proximity preservation. It is interesting to note that the transitivity property was neither used in relation to the individual preferences nor in relation to the social preferences. This suggests that the problem just depicted is not restricted to social welfare functions. Baigent showed that the problem also arises for social choice functions.

## 10.2. **The uniform rule**

The second topic in this chapter discusses the issue of allocating an infinitely divisible commodity, a consumption good of some quantity $M$, let's say, among a group of individuals who have single-peaked preferences. We know from Chapters 3 and 5 that the latter means that each person has a most preferred level of the commodity. In general, there will be different preferred levels of consumption for different individuals. The further an individual moves away from the peak, in either direction, the worse-off the individual is. Are there methods of 'fair' division, i.e. are there rules or solutions that are able to perform well on this task?

The easiest situation is the case where the amount to allocate to the agents is exactly equal to the sum of the preferred consumption levels. Then, every individual will get his or her preferred level of consumption. What happens in the cases where the amount to divide is either less than the sum of the preferred levels or more than the sum of the preferred levels?

If the amount to divide is some consumption good, the reader might wonder why in the latter case, 'the rest' is not disposed of. Free disposal is not permitted in this analysis. Consider the following situation where free disposal would make no sense at all. It is a case where a certain amount of work has to be done in some production process. Sprumont (1991) gave such an example: a group of agents participates in some production. Each person is to contribute some amount of a homogeneous labour input to this production. The total amount of work required is fixed. All agents agreed that they would be compensated in terms of output proportional to their work effort. Sprumont argues that in such a setting, preferences over the levels of participation would be single-peaked: 'each agent has an optimal share around which his utility decreases monotonically' (1991, p. 509) The optimal shares of the agents will only accidentally add up to the total amount of work needed. They may add up to less or more than this amount. How should everyone's share in the production process be determined?

Quantity rationing at disequilibrium prices is another example. Imagine a two-good economy where prices got stuck, for one reason or another, at disequilibrium. Distribution nevertheless must take place and, therefore, a rationing scheme has to be designed. If the preference relations of the agents over the two-dimensional space are strictly convex, then these preferences, when restricted to the budget lines, are single-peaked.

In order to be more precise in what follows, we have to introduce some notation. Let $M \in \mathbb{R}_+$ be the fixed amount of some infinitely divisible commodity to be allocated among a set $N = \{1, \ldots, n\}$ of individuals. Each person $i$ is assumed to possess a continuous preference relation $R_i$ defined over $\mathbb{R}_+$. $P_i$ and $I_i$ are the strict preference relation and the indifference relation associated with $R_i$. These preference relations are assumed to be single-peaked. For each $R_i$, there exists a number $p(R_i) \in \mathbb{R}_+$ such that for all $x_i, x_i' \in \mathbb{R}_+$, if $x_i' < x_i \le p(R_i)$, or $p(R_i) \le x_i < x_i'$, $x_i P_i x_i'$ holds. We shall call $p(R_i)$ the preferred level or peak of $R_i$. Let $\mathcal{R}$ be the class of all such preference relations and let $\bar{R} = (R_1, \ldots, R_n)$ be a profile of $n$ continuous preferences relations defined over $\mathbb{R}_+$ which, henceforth, will be restricted to the interval $[0, M]$. Given $\bar{R} \in \mathcal{R}^n, p(\bar{R}) = (p(R_1), \ldots, p(R_n))$ is the profile of preferred consumption levels.

Following Thomson (1994a, b), a single-peaked preference relation $R_i \in \mathcal{R}$ can be described in terms of the function $r_i \colon [0, M] \to [0, M]$ defined as follows: $r_i(x_i)$ is the amount of consumption on the other side of person $i$'s preferred consumption level that is indifferent for her to $x_i$, if such a consumption exists. If there is none, $r_i(x_i)$ is the end-point of the interval $[0, M]$ on the other side of her preferred consumption. More formally, given $x_i \leq p(R_i), r_i(x_i) \geq p(R_i)$, and $x_i I_i r_i(x_i)$ if such a number exists, and $r_i(x_i) = M$ otherwise. Analogously, given $x_i \geq p(R_i), r_i(x_i) \leq p(R_i)$, and $x_i I_i r_i(x_i)$ if such a number exists, and $r_i(x_i) = 0$ otherwise.

An economy is a pair $(\bar{R}, M) \in \mathcal{R}^n \times \mathbb{R}_+$. A feasible allocation for $(\bar{R}, M) \in \mathcal{R}^n \times \mathbb{R}_+$ is a vector $x = (x_1, \ldots, x_n) \in \mathbb{R}_+^n$ such that $\sum_{i \in N} x_i = M$. Let $X(M)$ be the set of feasible allocations of $(\bar{R}, M)$. A solution to the problem or an allocation rule is a mapping $\varphi : \mathcal{R}^n \times \mathbb{R}_+ \to \mathbb{R}_+^n$, which associates with each economy $(\bar{R}, M) \in \mathcal{R}^n \times \mathbb{R}_+$ a non-empty subset of $X(M)$. In the following, we will almost entirely focus on single-valuedness of the mapping $\varphi$. We let $\varphi_i$ denote the share going to person $i$.

What kind of properties should an allocation rule fulfil? Sprumont (1991) proposed two sets of conditions. We start with the first one: a solution should be Pareto-efficient, anonymous and strategy-proof. All three conditions are well known to the reader. The definition of efficiency is somewhat different in the present context. Therefore, we state all three properties again for the reader's convenience.

**Efficiency.** For all $\bar{R} \in \mathcal{R}^n$,

$$\left\{ \sum_{i \in N} p(R_i) \leq M \right\} \quad \to \quad \{\varphi_i(\bar{R}, M) \geq p(R_i) \quad \text{for all } i \in N\},$$

$$\left\{ \sum_{i \in N} p(R_i) \geq M \right\} \quad \to \quad \{\varphi_i(\bar{R}, M) \leq p(R_i) \quad \text{for all } i \in N\}.$$

We now consider all permutations on set $N$ with typical element $\sigma$, so that $\bar{R}^\sigma = (R_{\sigma(1)}, \ldots, R_{\sigma(n)})$. Remember that in connection with the majority rule, we had argued that a renumbering of individuals, i.e. changing their name-tags, should not matter.

**Anonymity.** For all permutations $\sigma$ on $N$, all $\bar{R} \in \mathcal{R}^n$, $\varphi_i(\bar{R}^\sigma, M) = \varphi_{\sigma(i)}(\bar{R}, M)$, where $\bar{R}^\sigma = (R_{\sigma(1)}, \ldots, R_{\sigma(n)})$.

**Strategy-proofness.** For all $i \in N$, all $\bar{R} \in \mathcal{R}^n$ and all $R_i' \in \mathcal{R}$, $\varphi_i(R_i, R_{-i}; M) R_i \varphi_i(R_i', R_{-i}; M)$, where $R_{-i} = (R_1, \ldots, R_{i-1}, R_{i+1}, \ldots, R_n)$.

These three axioms characterize a unique rule, the so-called uniform allocation rule which is known from the fixed-price literature (Benassy 1982). It is a single-valued mapping with domain $\mathcal{R}^n \times [0, M]$ and range $[0, M]^n$, where the individual shares $\varphi_i$ add up to $M$.

**Definition 10.1 (Uniform allocation rule).** The uniform allocation rule $\hat{\varphi} : \mathcal{R}^n \times [0, M] \to [0, M]^n$ is such that for all $i \in N$,

$$\hat{\varphi}_i(\bar{R}, M) = \begin{cases} \min\{p(R_i), \lambda(\bar{R})\} & \text{if } \sum_{i \in N} p(R_i) \geq M, \\[2em] \max\{p(R_i), \mu(\bar{R})\} & \text{if } \sum_{i \in N} p(R_i) < M, \end{cases}$$

where $\lambda(\bar{R})$ solves $\sum \min\{p(R_i), \lambda(\bar{R})\} = M$ and $\mu(\bar{R})$ solves $\sum \max\{p(R_i), \mu(\bar{R})\} = M$.

Let us explain what this rule does. If $M$ is small, all agents receive the same amount, viz. $\lambda(\bar{R})$. This holds until all persons have received an amount equal to the smallest peak. Then, any further increase in $M$ is divided equally among the remaining agents, with the agent having the smallest preferred consumption remaining at his or her peak. This process continues until each of the remaining agents has received an amount equal to the second smallest preferred consumption . . . and so on until each person has received her preferred level.

As an illustration, consider the following example where there are three agents with $p(R_1) = 2, p(R_2) = 4$, and $p(R_3) = 6$. For $M = 1.5, \lambda(\bar{R}) = 0.5$ so that $\hat{\varphi}_1 = \hat{\varphi}_2 = \hat{\varphi}_3 = 0.5$; for $M = 3, \lambda(\bar{R}) = 1$ and $\hat{\varphi}_1 = \hat{\varphi}_2 = \hat{\varphi}_3 = 1$. For $M = 6, \hat{\varphi}_1 = p(R_1) = 2, \hat{\varphi}_2 = \hat{\varphi}_3 = 2$. For $M = 9, \hat{\varphi}_1 = p(R_1) = 2, \hat{\varphi}_2 = \hat{\varphi}_3 = 3.5$. For $M = 10, \hat{\varphi}_1 = p(R_1) = 2, \hat{\varphi}_2 = p(R_2) = 4$ and $\hat{\varphi}_3 = 4$. For $M = 12, \hat{\varphi}_1 = p(R_1) = 2, \hat{\varphi}_2 = p(R_2) = 4$ and $\hat{\varphi}_3 = p(R_3) = 6$. All agents have achieved their preferred level. Finally, for $\sum p(R_i) > M$, for example $M = 14, \hat{\varphi}_1 = \hat{\varphi}_2 = 4$ and $\hat{\varphi}_3 = 6$. And now Sprumont's (1991) result.

**Theorem 10.3 (Characterization of the uniform rule).** The allocation rule $\varphi : \mathcal{R}^n \times [0, M] \to [0, M]^n$ is efficient, anonymous and strategy-proof if and only if $\varphi = \hat{\varphi}$.

The second set of conditions that Sprumont examined comprises efficiency, strategy-proofness and a new condition called envy-freeness going back to Foley (1967) and Kolm (1971).

**Envy-freeness.** For all $\bar{R} \in \mathcal{R}^n$ and all $i, j \in N$,

$$\varphi_i(\bar{R}, M) R_i \varphi_j(\bar{R}, M).$$

This means that there is no envy in the economy whenever every person $i$ finds his or her share $\varphi_i$ at least as good as everybody else's share $\varphi_j$.

We obtain

**Theorem 10.3'.** The uniform allocation rule is characterized by the following three conditions: efficiency, strategy-proofness and envy-freeness.

The uniform rule seems to be a rather unique rule. Consider other allocation rules. The egalitarian rule $\varphi_i^e(\bar{R}, M) = \frac{1}{n} \cdot M$ for all $i$ is strategy-proof and anonymous but not efficient. Trivially, it is envy-free. The proportional rule $\varphi_i^{pr}(\bar{R}, M) = p(R_i)/\sum_j p(R_j)$ is anonymous and efficient, but not strategy-proof. That it also does not satisfy envy-freeness is shown in the following example (Thomson, 1994a). Let $N = \{1, 2\}$ and $\bar{R} \in \mathcal{R}^2$ be such that $p(\bar{R}) = (2, 4)$ and $1.5 I_1 4$, i.e. $r_1(1.5) = 4$. Let $M = 4.5$. Then $\varphi^{pr}(\bar{R}, M) = (1.5, 3)$. Since agent 1 prefers share 3 to share 1.5, there is envy. Thomson also showed that the proportional rule does not necessarily pick allocations that are 'individually rational from equal division'. The latter means that for each $i \in N$, the following should hold: $\varphi_i R_i(M/n)$. Let $N = \{1, 2\}$ again and $\bar{R} \in \mathcal{R}^2$ be such that $p(\bar{R}) = (3, 6)$ and let $M = 6$. Then $\varphi^{pr}(\bar{R}, M) = (2, 4)$. Since $M/2 = 3$ and $3 P_1 2$, the proportional solution violates individual rationality from equal split. From the construction of the uniform rule, it is clear that this rule satisfies the latter condition.

It is well known that the Walrasian equilibrium allocation from equal division is efficient and envy-free. That it also satisfies individual rationality from equal split is trivial. Note, however, that the Walrasian mechanism requires that the individual preferences be monotonic everywhere, which does not hold for single-peaked preferences, of course.

What happens in cases where the amount to divide changes? If all individuals had monotone preferences and all agents were treated similarly, an increase in the amount to divide would effect all persons positively. In the case of single-peaked preferences, having more of a commodity may not be socially desirable. Therefore, a condition seems natural where all individuals lose together or all gain together when the amount to divide increases or decreases. This is what Thomson (1994a) called resource monotonicity. However, the author showed that both the concept of individual rationality from equal division and the requirement of no-envy are incompatible with resource monotonicity. Therefore, he proposed a weakening of this condition which only applies to cases where for all $M, M' \in \mathbb{R}_+$, either $M \le \sum p(R_i)$ and $M' \le \sum p(R_i)$ or $\sum p(R_i) \le M$ and $\sum p(R_i) \le M'$. In other words, if both before and after the change of the amount to divide there either is not enough in relation to $\sum p(R_i)$ or there is too much in relation to $\sum p(R_i)$, it is required that agents be similarly affected. Thomson called this condition 'one-sided resource monotonicity'.

Several solution concepts satisfy this condition, among them the proportional solution, but as outlined above, the proportional solution has problems with envy-freeness. Again, the uniform rule stands out (Thomson, 1994a).

When we discussed single-peakedness in Chapter 3, we did not mention that this property can be generalized in several directions. One possibility is to allow the set of best elements, the preferred level, which in the case of single-peaked preferences is a singleton, to be a non-degenerate interval in the set of positive real numbers. In other words, 'a plateau on top' is possible. For the domain of single-plateaued preferences, Ching (1992) showed that the uniform rule is the only allocation rule that satisfies Pareto efficiency, Pareto indifference, strategy-proofness and envy-freeness. Pareto indifference was defined in section 2.4. In the present case, this condition says that if there are two allocations $x$ and $y$, let's say, such that for all $i \in N$, $x_i I_i y_i$, then $x$ is a solution if and only if $y$ is a solution. We now see that Ching's allocation rule actually is a correspondence, a multivalued function. This follows quite naturally from the author's assumption to consider plateaus.

## 10.3. **Freedom of choice**

We now come to the last issue in this chapter and to the final topic in this primer. The issue is called 'freedom of choice'. What does it have to do with the problem of social choice? If the latter concept isn't interpreted very narrowly, there actually are a lot of interrelations. Sen (1988) argues that 'given the importance of the quality of life of the members of the society in judging the success of economic policies, it is easy to see the centrality of freedom of choice to economic evaluation and assessment'. And Sen continues saying that 'such basic economic notions as individual well-being, social welfare, living standard, consistent choice and rational behaviour can all be fruitfully reexamined by paying more adequate attention to the perspective of freedom' (1988, pp. 269–70).

One can distinguish between a purely consequentialist or instrumentalist view of the value of freedom of choice and an intrinsic view. The long and intensive discussion on free markets has taught us that an unhindered exchange on markets is instrumental in achieving higher levels of utilities for the individuals acting on these markets. So far so good, but let us now assume the following two variants. In variant 1, a particular market allocation $\hat{x}$ has been reached through free contracting where each person achieves her utility-maximizing commodity bundle given her individual budget set. In variant 2, a central planning bureau establishes allocation $\hat{x}$ by command and each agent $i$ is ordered to consume bundle $\hat{x}_i$, exactly the same bundle that she would have materialized under free exchange. Is there any difference in terms of social welfare between the two situations?

There isn't any if the social welfare judgments are solely based on the utilities the agents achieve under allocation $\hat{x}$. Clearly, each person's set of opportunities

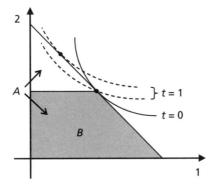

**Figure 10.2.**

(her budget set) is 'very large' in variant 1 and has shrunk to a single point in variant 2. However, the final outcome is exactly the same in both situations. If the latter is all that should count eventually, giving up a set of opportunities, in other words, losing freedom of choice would not matter.

But wait a minute. Consider an intertemporal context where there is uncertainty about future tastes (Kreps, 1979). Couldn't a shrinkage of the opportunity set be detrimental to the person concerned, even if the shrinkage were not as extreme as in variant 2 above, where the only opportunity left is a single point? Consider figure 10.2. Here a shrinkage occurs from set $A$ to subset $B$. At time $t = 0$, there is no utility loss for the individual considered, when the set of opportunities shrinks from $A$ to $B$. But imagine that at time $t = 1$, there is a chance that the person's indifference contours would be given by the dotted curves. Then, a shrinkage from $A$ to $B$ matters utility-wise. Note, however, that the argumentation in terms of richer choices or a higher degree of flexibility under $A$ than under $B$ is still entirely instrumental since again, only achievements in terms of utilities are considered, though within the intertemporal context the perspective is, admittedly, substantially widened. Freedom is now instrumental for attaining a better uncertain prospect. The instrumental aspect holds in many different circumstances. A broader education at the college level yields a larger set of options as far as successful future job search is concerned. More mundanely, booking a table at a restaurant with an international menu for next Saturday evening makes you worry less about what your and your friends' tastes will be like on that particular night.

Given all this, there is what Sen (1988) and others call the intrinsic value of freedom. There exists a long-standing libertarian tradition which believes that freedom is a value per se apart from whatever higher level of utility it may enable human beings to achieve. Pattanaik and Xu (1998) quote Nozick (1974, p. 50) who related the intrinsic value of freedom of choice to the idea of long-term life plans and to the notion of leading a meaningful life. 'A person's shaping his life in accordance with some overall plan is his way of giving meaning to his life; only a being with the capacity to so shape his life can have or strive for meaningful life'.

How can alternative situations be evaluated in terms of freedom of choice when the emphasis is on the intrinsic value of such freedom? Pattanaik and Xu (1990) offered a very simple, yet rather debatable first approach where judgments about the degree of freedom in different situations are reduced to counting the number of options available in those choice situations.

Let us become somewhat more formal. Let $X$ be the set of feasible alternatives, which is assumed to be finite. The elements of $X$ can be commodity bundles or bundles of material characteristics (Lancaster, 1966) or bundles of functionings (Sen, 1985). Let $K$ be the set of all non-empty subsets of $X$. The individual considered will be faced with the problem to evaluate the elements of $K$. Let $\succsim$ be a reflexive and transitive binary relation (not necessarily complete) defined over $K$. We hitherto want to say, for all $A, B \in K$, that $A \succsim B$ means that the degree of freedom offered by the feasible set $A$ is at least as great as the degree of freedom offered by set $B$. The asymmetric and symmetric parts of $\succsim$, i.e. $\succ$ and $\sim$, will be interpreted accordingly. Pattanaik and Xu (1990) introduce three properties that the relation $\succsim$ should satisfy.

**Indifference between no-choice situations ($INS$).** The relation $\succsim$ satisfies $INS$, if and only if, for all $x, y \in X, \{x\} \sim \{y\}$.

**Strict monotonicity ($SM$).** The relation $\succsim$ satisfies $SM$, if and only if for all distinct $x, y \in X, \{x, y\} \succ \{x\}$.

**Independence ($IND$).** The relation $\succsim$ satisfies $IND$, if and only if for all $A, B \in K$, and for all $x \in X - (A \cup B), [A \succsim B$ iff $A \cup \{x\} \succsim B \cup \{x\}]$.

Pattanaik and Xu take great care to point out the limitations of this axiom system. Property $INS$ requires that two singleton sets be considered as equivalent in terms of freedom of choice. Neither set grants any degree of freedom to the choosing individual. Note that this verdict is totally independent of whether, from the individual's point of view, $x$ is highly desirable and $y$ is very unpleasant, or vice versa. The only aspect that matters is the aspect of freedom of choice. No vestige of any concept of preference is involved here.

Property $SM$ says that a situation where there is some choice, is to be considered as being better in terms of freedom of choice than a situation where there is no choice at all. Again, the desirability of the additional alternative $y$ is not an issue here. Finally, condition $IND$ requires that the ranking between $A$ and $B$ in terms of freedom of choice is upheld if to both $A$ and $B$ any alternative $x$ is added that lies outside of $A \cup B$. Possible complementarity or substitutability relations between $x$ and elements in $A$ and $B$, respectively, are not considered.

Pattanaik and Xu define the following ranking rule which is cardinality-based.

**Definition 10.2.** The binary relation $\succsim$ will be called a simple cardinality-based ordering if and only if, for all $A, B \in K$, $A \succsim B$ iff $|A| \geq |B|$, where $|A|$ and $|B|$ denote the cardinality of set $A$ and set $B$, respectively.

Pattanaik and Xu (1990) obtain the following result.

**Theorem 10.4 (Freedom of choice in terms of cardinality).** The relation $\succsim$ is the simple cardinality-based ordering if and only if $\succsim$ satisfies properties *INS*, *SM* and *IND*.

Given the three axioms above, this result will not come as a total surprise. On the one hand, this is a very neat result – the principle of just counting elements is very simple. On the other hand, this principle is extremely limiting since the underlying axioms are very restrictive. Why, for example, does the addition of another alternative, no matter how terrible this alternative may be, improve the situation in terms of freedom of choice? Pattanaik and Xu raise an argument against their third requirement, the independence axiom. Suppose that alternative modes of transportation are the options to choose from. Let us assume that a train ride and a ride in a blue car express the same degree of freedom of choice (as is required by axiom *INS* above). However, it is very plausible to view the option set {train, red car} as providing a higher degree of freedom of choice than the option set {blue car, red car}, contrary to property *IND*. The issue behind this example is the similarity or closeness between objects. A red car and a blue car are almost the same, whereas a train and a car, no matter which colour, are different modes of transportation.

While closeness or distance is the issue here, the absence of any concept of personal preference as an evaluating device was the issue in the earlier argumentation. Clearly, if evaluative aspects or personal preferences are totally ignored, one cannot speak of 'terrible' options. One can only say that there is or is not an additional alternative.

Sen (1993) raised strong criticism against the cardinal approach by Pattanaik and Xu. 'The evaluation of the freedom I enjoy from a certain menu of achievements must depend to a crucial extent on how I value the elements included in that menu. The "size" of a set, or the "extent" of freedom enjoyed by a person, cannot, except in very special cases, be judged without reference to the person's values and preferences' (1993, p. 528). In relation to the cardinality approach, Sen asks whether it is possible that three alternative achievements which are seen as 'bad', 'terrible' and 'disastrous' can possibly render as much freedom of choice as three alternative achievements which are viewed as 'good', 'terrific' and 'wonderful'. 'If the latter set is seen as giving us more freedom to achieve – giving us more opportunity to live the way we would choose to live – then this is precisely because our preferences are important in the evaluation of freedom' (Sen, 1993, p. 529).

The question then is which preferences are to count: the present preferences of an individual, his or her future preferences, 'reasonable' or, perhaps, 'serious' preferences, however defined? On the next few pages, we shall discuss a follow-up paper by Pattanaik and Xu (1998) in which the authors argued that consideration of preferences is important in assessing the intrinsic value of freedom of choice. However, crucial in such an assessment 'are not the preferences that the agent actually has, nor the preference orderings that have positive probabilities of emerging as his future preference ordering, but the preference orderings that a reasonable person in the agent's situation can possibly have' (1998, p. 180).

Let $\mathcal{P}$ be the set of all possible orderings that a reasonable person can have in the agent's situation. We denote by $\mathcal{P} = \{R_1, \ldots, R_n\}$ the reference set of preferences over $X$, the universal and finite set of alternatives. $K$ is again the set of all non-empty subsets of $X$. For all $R \in \mathcal{P}$ and for all $A \in K$, we let max $(A)$ stand for the set of all $a \in A$ such that $a$ is an $R$-greatest element in $A$ for some $R \in \mathcal{P}$. Thus, max $(A)$ is the set of all alternatives $x$ in $A$ such that $x$ is a best alternative in $A$ for some preference ordering in $\mathcal{P}$. The reader realizes that Pattanaik and Xu have taken Sen's sharp criticism to heart. Alternatives are 'scrutinized' from the viewpoint of a reasonable person in the agent's situation. This will become even more obvious when the reader has gone through the following definitions.

The authors define, for all $x \in X$ and all $A \in K$,

$x[I]A$ iff max $(A \cup \{x\}) = A \cup \{x\}$;
$x[P]A$ iff $\{x\} = $ max $(A \cup \{x\})$;
$A[P]x$ iff $x \notin$ max $(A \cup \{x\})$.

The first expression, i.e. $x[I]A$ holds if and only if every alternative in $A \cup \{x\}$ is a best alternative in $A \cup \{x\}$ in terms of a reference ordering of a reasonable person in the agent's situation. The second expression $x[P]A$ means that $x$ is ranked strictly above all alternatives in $A - \{x\}$ in terms of every ordering that a reasonable person in the agent's situation may possibly have. And $A[P]x$ if and only if, for every ordering that a reasonable person may have under the agent's circumstances, some alternative in $A$ is ranked strictly higher than $x$. The 'suitability' of these relationships will become clearer as we proceed.

In the following, we shall restrict ourselves to discussing one of the preference-based results of Pattanaik and Xu (1998), viz. a theorem that on the one hand is 'close' to their earlier result but on the other hand demonstrates how preferences can be 'reasonably' integrated into the analysis.

The first condition on the binary relation $\succsim$ over $K$ that the authors consider is property *INS* from above, i.e. indifference between no-choice situations. This property is taken over without any change. The second axiom is

[*I*]-**Monotonicity (*IM*).** The relation $\succsim$ over $K$ satisfies *IM*, if and only if, for all $A, B \in K$ and all $x \in X - A$, $(x[I]A$ and $A \succsim B)$ implies $[A \cup \{x\} \succ B]$.

This axiom has some resemblance with property *SM* from above, but it is different. It is a response to Sen's (1993) criticism that adding an alternative to a given set does not necessarily mean that the freedom of choice has increased. Sen's example was such that the option of 'being beheaded at dawn' was added to a given set of alternatives. Does such an option increase the freedom of choice? Most probably not, given 'normal' preferences. But don't be too rash.

What does *IM* now claim? One has to look very carefully in order to see what it requires. Axiom *IM* says that if set $A$ offers at least as much freedom as set $B$ and if one adds to $A$ an alternative $x \in X - A$ such that, for every alternative $a$ in $A \cup \{x\}$, $a$ can be a best alternative in $A \cup \{x\}$ for a reasonable person, then $A \cup \{x\}$ offers strictly more freedom than $B$. Note that axiom *IM* requires that every alternative in $A \cup \{x\}$ is best in $A \cup \{x\}$ in terms of some ordering in $\mathcal{P}$.

Coming back to Sen's example, assume that the opportunity set of a particular person contains just one option, viz. spending the rest of her life in a solitary cell. Now add the additional option of being beheaded at dawn. Does this increase the person's freedom? Perhaps *yes*, if a reasonable person can consider being beheaded at dawn to be at least as good as spending the rest of the life in solitary custody and if a reasonable person can consider spending the rest of her life in a solitary cell to be at least as good as being beheaded at dawn. If this is the case, and the reader will realize the subtlety of the formulation, then axiom *IM* will declare that the expanded set of options offers strictly more freedom than the original set.

The next axiom considers the case that an 'uninteresting' alternative is added to an opportunity set.

**Irrelevance of dominated alternatives (*IDA*).** The binary relation $\succsim$ over $K$ satisfies *IDA*, if and only if, for all $A, B \in K$ and all $x \in X$, if $A[P]x$, then $[A \succsim B$ iff $A \cup \{x\} \succsim B]$ and $[B \succsim A$ iff $B \succsim A \cup \{x\}]$.

This property requires that if an option $x$ is such that, for every possible preference ordering of a reasonable person, at least one alternative in $A$ is ranked strictly higher than $x$, then the ranking of $A \cup \{x\}$ and $B$ must be exactly the same as the ranking of $A$ and $B$, and the ranking of $B$ and $A \cup \{x\}$ must be exactly the same as the ranking of $B$ and $A$. In other words, if in terms of every possible ordering of a reasonable person, at least one alternative in an existing opportunity set $A$ is strictly better than the new option $x$, then the addition of $x$ to set $A$ does not increase the degree of freedom of the agent.

Finally, consider the following requirement which is related to the earlier independence axiom *IND*.

**Composition (*COM*).**  The binary relation $\succsim$ over $K$ satisfies *COM* if and only if, for all $A, B, C, D \in K$ such that $A \cap C = B \cap D = \emptyset$ and max $(A \cup C) = A \cup C$ and max $(B \cup D) = B \cup D$,

[$A \succsim B$ and $C \succsim D$] implies [$A \cup C \succsim B \cup D$], and
[$A \succsim B$ and $C \succ D$] implies [$A \cup C \succ B \cup D$].

Note that the applicability of this axiom is restricted in several ways. First of all, the restriction that $A \cap C = \emptyset$ and $B \cap D = \emptyset$ excludes situations, where $A$ and $C$ would have a lot of elements in common whereas $B$ and $D$ would not, so that adding the elements of $D$ to $B$ would increase the person's number of options substantially, whereas adding the elements of $C$ to $A$ would not increase the person's freedom of choice much. Such a conceptual difficulty is removed altogether. Secondly, every alternative in $A \cup C$ can be considered by a reasonable person to be at least as good as all alternatives in $A \cup C$, and the same is assumed to hold for $B \cup D$. Pattanaik and Xu (1998) obtain the following result.

**Theorem 10.5 (Refined cardinality).**  The relation $\succsim$ satisfies properties *INS*, *IM*, *IDA* and *COM* if and only if, for all $A, B \in K$,

$$A \succsim B \text{ iff } | \max(A)| \geq | \max(B)|,$$

where $| \max(A)|$ is the cardinality of the set of all alternatives $x$ in $A$ such that $x$ is a best alternative in $A$ for some ordering in $\mathcal{P}$ (with an analogous interpretation for $| \max(B)|$).

The present ranking rule in terms of freedom of choice ranks opportunity sets on the basis of the number of $R$-greatest elements in the sets for some $R \in \mathcal{P}$. In other words, the cardinality refers to the number of elements in each set which are considered best by a reasonable person. Note that if $\mathcal{P}$ comprises the set of all possible preference orderings over $X$, in other words, every possible preference ordering could be held by a reasonable person, the above ranking rule based on refined cardinality reduces to Pattanaik and Xu's earlier rule of simple cardinality.

In our discussion earlier on in this section of whether preferences should count – and we presented several arguments *why* preferences should be considered in an analysis of freedom of choice – we posed the question which preferences should be taken into consideration. This question cannot be answered 'once for all'. There are good arguments for several approaches. Pattanaik and Xu argued in favour of the preference orderings of a reasonable person in the agent's situation. There would be a good argument for choosing preferences behind the veil of ignorance, at least under certain circumstances when societal aspects come to the fore. Puppe (1996) evaded this issue to some degree by postulating that for every non-empty set of options

$A \in K$, there exists one alternative $x \in A$ such that $A$ is strictly ranked above $A - \{x\}$. Such an alternative $x$ can be called valuable or essential for a decision maker. Puppe rightly pointed out that such an assumption is much weaker than what is implied by the first approach proposed by Pattanaik and Xu (1990) where there is indiscriminate number counting. The latter approach clearly implies that $A$ is ranked strictly above $A - \{x\}$ for *every* $x \in A$. In other words, every alternative is, at least to some degree, valuable to the decision maker. Puppe (1996) worked with the set of essential alternatives $E(A) = \{x \in A : A \succ A - \{x\}\}$ and obtained various characterizations. This approach would, of course, not be applicable in cases where there are only non-essential or dreadful alternatives, but fortunately, such situations will be rare in general. Or is this view too optimistic?

To conclude this final part of the book, the focus on the intrinsic importance of freedom of choice has led to valuable new insights into the theories of individual choice and collective decisions. We say this without wishing to belittle the instrumental relevance of freedom which is most often evoked in discussions on democracy and free markets.

## 10.4. **An epilogue instead of a summary**

It is not true that social choice theory started with Arrow's impossibility theorem but it is perhaps correct to say that the beginning of precise formal analysis in collective choice can largely be attributed to the appearance of Arrow's famous book on *Social Choice and Individual Values* in 1951. There were indeed important forerunners, among them above all Condorcet and Borda around the time of the French Revolution. And again, there were scholars well before the latter who should not be forgotten. We have, in particular, mentioned Lull and Cusanus in our brief look into history at the very beginning of this primer. Ten-to-fifteen years before Arrow, the so-called new welfare economists, of course, pursued strict formal analysis, but Hicks, Kaldor and others, unfortunately, ran into problems of consistency in their attempt to go beyond the Pareto relation by introducing the idea of hypothetical compensation.

This book has tried to cover a wide spectrum of themes. We looked at institutional devices such as the majority rule as well as closely or only loosely related types of voting mechanisms, dealt with the aspect of rights-exercising and personal autonomy within collective choice and discussed at greater length various principles of distributive justice and schemes of cooperation in bargaining environments. All these processes are quite distinct from each other, focusing on different aspects and using different types and different amounts of information.

The majority rule can be seen as the appropriate device of aggregating individual views in an institutional setting. In such an environment, requirements such as an equal treatment of individuals (anonymity) and an equal treatment of alternatives or issues (neutrality) make a lot of sense. But not necessarily always. A society may require different kinds of majorities for issues of different degrees of importance. The decision on admitting new members to a club may be based on a simple majority outcome. On the other hand, the re-introduction of the death penalty or the declaration of war against another nation should, with good reasons, be based on very large majorities. The application of the simple majority rule also looks inadequate when it comes to achieving an equitable state. Though alternatives can be described quite comprehensively, a simple count of pros and cons may be informationally too 'thin'. The majority rule can be terribly rude to minorities. In certain decisions, one may want to use more 'data and facts' understandably which are largely based on non-utility information. Legal rights and historical claims, information on wealth or on the degree of impoverishment of certain layers of society may be highly relevant in such a context. But as always, both in science proper and in real life, such views are not uncontroversial. For example, on the issue of distributive justice, Rawls was against considering the status quo or disagreement point while Gauthier argued in favour of natural differences of those who seek an agreement. That controversies exist, is a good sign for science in general and for social choice theory in particular.

We said above that we have tried to discuss a wide spectrum of topics in this primer, but we are well aware of the fact that there are many more interesting themes that were not covered. Fortunately, they can be found in other existing publications.

# ☐ REFERENCES

Amiel, Y. and Cowell, F. A. (1999). *Thinking about Inequality. Personal Judgment and Income Distributions.* Cambridge: Cambridge University Press.

Arrow, K. J. (1951, 1963). *Social Choice and Individual Values,* 2nd edn. New York: John Wiley.

—— (1959). 'Rational Choice Functions and Orderings'. *Economica,* 26: 121–127.

Baigent, N. (1987a). 'Metric Rationalization of Social Choice Functions According to Principles of Social Choice'. *Mathematical Social Sciences,* 13: 51–65.

—— (1987b). 'Preference Proximity and Anonymous Social Choice'. *The Quarterly Journal of Economics,* 102: 161–169.

—— (2002). 'Topological Theories of Social Choice', Manuscript. To appear in K. J. Arrow, A. K. Sen, and K. Suzumura (eds.), *Handbook of Social Choice and Welfare,* Vol. 2. Amsterdam: Elsevier.

—— and Klamler, Ch. (2004). 'Transitive Closure, Proximity and Intransitivities'. *Economic Theory,* 23: 175–181.

Barberà, S. (2001). 'An Introduction to Strategy-Proof Social Choice Functions'. *Social Choice and Welfare,* 18: 619–653.

——, Gul, F., and Stacchetti, E. (1993). 'Generalized Median Voter Schemes and Committees'. *Journal of Economic Theory,* 61: 262–289.

——, Sonnenschein, H., and Zhou, L. (1991). 'Voting by Committees'. *Econometrica,* 59: 595–609.

Beckmann, S. R., Formby, J. P., Smith, W. J., and Zheng, B. (2002). 'Envy, Malice and Pareto Efficiency: An Experimental Examination'. *Social Choice and Welfare,* 19: 349–367.

Benassy, J.-P. (1982). *The Economics of Market Disequilibrium.* New York: Academic Press.

Bentham, J. (1776). *A Fragment on Government.* T. Payne, London. Revised and edited by J. H. Burns and H. L. A. Hart. London: Athlone Press, 1977.

Bergson, A. (1938). 'A Reformulation of Certain Aspects of Welfare Economics'. *Quarterly Journal of Economics,* 52: 310–334. Reprinted in (1966): Essays in Normative Economics. Cambridge, Mass.: Belknap Press, Harvard University Press, 3–26.

—— (1948). 'Socialist Economics'. In H. S. Ellis (ed.), *A Survey of Contemporary Economics.* Reprinted in (1966): Essays in Normative Economics. Cambridge, Mass.: Belknap Press, Harvard University Press, 193–236.

—— (1976). 'Social Choice and Welfare Economics under Representative Government'. *Journal of Public Economics,* 6: 171–190.

Black, D. (1948). 'On the Rationale of Group Decision Making'. *The Journal of Political Economy,* 56: 23–34.

—— (1958). *The Theory of Committees and Elections.* Cambridge: Cambridge University Press.

Blackorby, Ch., Donaldson, D., and Weymark, J. A. (1984). 'Social Choice with Interpersonal Utility Comparisons: A Diagrammatic Introduction'. *International Economic Review,* 25: 327–356.

Blau, J. H. (1957). 'The Existence of Social Welfare Functions'. *Econometrica,* 25: 302–313.

Blin, J.-M. and Satterthwaite, M. A. (1976). 'Strategy-Proofness and Single-Peakedness'. *Public Choice*, 26: 51–58.

Borda, J. C. de (1781). 'Mémoire sur les élections au scrutin'. *Histoire de l'Académie Royale des Sciences*, 657–665.

Braithwaite, R. B. (1955). *Theory of Games as a Tool for the Moral Philosopher*. Cambridge: Cambridge University Press.

Chichilnisky, G. (1980). 'Social Choice and the Topology of Spaces of Preferences'. *Advances in Mathematics*, 37: 165–176.

—— (1982). 'Social Aggregation Rules and Continuity'. *Quarterly Journal of Economics*, 97: 337–352.

—— and Heal, G. (1983). 'Necessary and Sufficient Conditions for a Resolution of the Social Choice Paradox'. *Journal of Economic Theory*, 31: 68–87.

Ching, St. (1992). 'A Simple Characterization of the Uniform Rule'. *Economics Letters*, 40: 57–60.

Clarke, E. H. (1971). 'Multipart Pricing of Public Goods'. *Public Choice*, 11: 17–33.

Condorcet, Marquis de (1785). *Essai sur l'application de l'analyse à la probabilité des décisions rendues à la pluralité des voix*. Paris.

Cusanus, N. (1434). 'De concordantia catholica'. In G. Kallen (ed.), *Nicolai de Cusa Opera Omnia*, vol. XIV. Hamburg: Felix Meiner, 1964.

D'Aspremont, C. and Gevers, L. (1977). 'Equity and the Informational Basis of Collective Choice'. *Review of Economic Studies*, 44: 199–209.

Deb, R., Pattanaik, P. K., and Razzolini, L. (1997). 'Game Forms, Rights, and the Efficiency of Social Outcomes'. *Journal of Economic Theory*, 72: 74–95.

Dodgson, C. L. [Lewis Carroll] (1876). *A Method of Taking Votes on More than Two Issues*. Oxford: Clarendon Press.

Dummett, M. and Farquharson, R. (1961). 'Stability in Voting'. *Econometrica*, 29: 33–43.

Dutta, B. (1977). 'Existence of Stable Situations, Restricted Preferences and Strategic Manipulation under Democratic Group Decision Rules'. *Journal of Economic Theory*, 15: 99–111.

Farquharson, R. (1969). *Theory of Voting*. New Haven: Yale University Press.

Fishburn, P. (1973). *The Theory of Social Choice*. Princeton: Princeton University Press.

Fleurbaey, M. and Gaertner, W. (1996). 'Admissibility and Feasibility in Game Forms'. *Analyse & Kritik*, 18: 54–66.

Foley, D. (1967). 'Resource Allocation and the Public Sector'. *Yale Economic Essays*, 7: 45–98.

Gärdenfors, P. (1973). 'Positionalist Voting Functions'. *Theory and Decision*, 4: 1–24.

Gaertner, W. (1983). 'Equity- and Inequity-Type Borda Rules'. *Mathematical Social Sciences*, 4: 137–154.

—— (1986). 'Pareto, Interdependent Rights Exercising and Strategic Behaviour'. *Journal of Economics*, Suppl.: 5, 79–98.

—— (1992). 'Distributive Judgments'. chapter 2 in W. Gaertner and M. Klemisch-Ahlert (eds.), *Social Choice and Bargaining Perspectives on Distributive Justice*. Berlin, Heidelberg, New York: Springer-Verlag.

—— (1993). 'Rights and Game Forms, Types of Preference Orderings and Pareto Inefficiency'. In W. E. Diewert, K. Spremann, and F. Stehling (eds.), *Mathematical Modelling in Economics. Essays in Honor of Wolfgang Eichhorn*. Berlin, Heidelberg, New York: Springer-Verlag.

—— (1994). 'Distributive Justice: Theoretical Foundations and Empirical Findings'. *European Economic Review*, 38: 711–720.

—— (2001). *Domain Conditions in Social Choice Theory*. Cambridge: Cambridge University Press.

—— (2005). 'De Jure Naturae et Gentium: Samuel von Pufendorf's Contribution to Social Choice Theory and Economics'. *Social Choice and Welfare*, 25: 231–241.

—— and Heinecke, A. (1977). 'On Two Sufficient Conditions for Transitivity of the Social Preference Relation'. *Zeitschrift für Nationalökonomie*, 37: 61–66.

—— and Jungeilges, J. (2002). 'Evaluation via Extended Orderings: Empirical Findings from Western and Eastern Europe'. *Social Choice and Welfare*, 19: 29–55.

——, Jungeilges, J., and Neck, R. (2001). 'Cross-Cultural Equity Evaluations: A Questionnaire–Experimental Approach'. *European Economic Review*, 45: 953–963.

—— and Krüger, L. (1981). 'Self-Supporting Preferences and Individual Rights: The Possibility of Paretian Libertarianism'. *Economica*, 48: 17–28.

Gaertner, W., Pattanaik, P. K., and Suzumura, K. (1992). 'Individual Rights Revisited'. *Economica*, 59: 161–177.

Gans, J. S. and Smart, M. (1996). 'Majority Voting with Single-Crossing Preferences'. *Journal of Public Economics*, 59: 219–237.

Gauthier, D. (1978). 'Social Choice and Distributive Justice'. *Philosophia*, 7: 239–253.

—— (1985). 'Bargaining and Justice'. In E. Frankel Paul, J. Paul, and F. D. Miller Jr. (eds.), *Ethics and Economics*. Oxford: Blackwell.

—— (1986). *Morals by Agreement*. Oxford: Clarendon Press.

Geanakoplos, J. (1996). *Three Brief Proofs of Arrow's Impossibility Theorem, mimeo*. Cowles Foundation, Yale University.

Gibbard, A. (1973). 'Manipulation of Voting Schemes: A General Result'. *Econometrica*, 41: 587–602.

—— (1974). 'A Pareto-Consistent Libertarian Claim'. *Journal of Economic Theory*, 7: 388–410.

Groves, T. (1973). 'Incentives in Teams'. *Econometrica*, 41: 617–631.

Hammond, P. J. (1976). 'Equity, Arrow's Conditions, and Rawls' Difference Principle'. *Econometrica*, 44: 793-804.

Harsanyi, J. C. (1953). 'Cardinal Utility in Welfare Economics and in the Theory of Risk-Taking'. *Journal of Political Economy*, 61: 434–435.

—— (1955). 'Cardinal Welfare, Individualistic Ethics, and Interpersonal Comparisons of Utility'. *Journal of Political Economy*, 63: 309–321.

—— (1975). 'Can the Maximin Principle Serve as a Basis for Morality? A Critique of John Rawls's Theory'. *The American Political Science Review*, 69: 594–606.

—— (1977). *Rational Behavior and Bargaining Equilibrium in Games and Social Situations*. Cambridge: Cambridge University Press.

—— (1978). 'Bayesian Decision Theory and Utilitarian Ethics'. *American Economic Review, Papers and Proceedings*, 68: 223–228.

Helvétius, C. A. (1758). 'De l'esprit'. Discours I, IV in *Oeuvres Complètes*, Tome I-XIV. Paris 1795. Reprint by Georg Olms Verlagsbuchhandlung. Hildesheim 1969.

Hurwicz, L. (1972). 'On Informationally Decentralized Systems'. In C. B. McGuire and R. Radner, *Decision and Organization. A Volume in Honor of Jacob Marschak*. Amsterdam: North-Holland.

Hutcheson, F. (1725). *An Inquiry into the Original of Our Ideas of Beauty and Virtue*. London.

Imai, H. (1983). 'Individual Monotonicity and Lexicographic Maxmin Solution'. *Econometrica*, 51: 389–401. Erratum in Econometrica 51, 1603.

Inada, K. (1969). 'The Simple Majority Decision Rule'. *Econometrica*, 37: 490–506.

Jackson, M. O. (2001). 'A Crash Course in Implementation Theory'. *Social Choice and Welfare*, 18: 655–708.

Jehle, G. A. and Reny, Ph. J. (2001). *Advanced Microeconomic Theory*, 2nd edn. Boston: Addison Wesley.

Kalai, E. (1977). 'Proportional Solutions to Bargaining Situations: Interpersonal Utility Comparisons'. *Econometrica*, 45: 1623–1630.

—— (1985). 'Solutions to the Bargaining Problem'. In L. Hurwicz, D. Schmeidler, and H. Sonnenschein (eds.), *Social Goals and Social Organization. Essays in Memory of Elisha Pazner*. Cambridge: Cambridge University Press.

—— and Smorodinsky, M. (1975). 'Other Solutions to Nash's Bargaining Problem'. *Econometrica*, 43: 513–518.

Kelly, J. S. (1988). *Social Choice Theory. An Introduction*. Berlin, Heidelberg, New York: Springer-Verlag.

—— (1993). 'Almost All Social Choice Rules are Highly Manipulable, But a Few Aren't'. *Social Choice and Welfare*, 10: 161–175.

Kemeny, J. (1959). 'Mathematics without Numbers'. *Daedalus*, 88: 571–591.

Klemisch-Ahlert, M. (1992). 'Axiomatic Characterizations of Gauthier's Bargaining Solution'. Chapter 4 in W. Gaertner and M. Klemisch-Ahlert (eds.), *Social Choice and Bargaining Perspectives on Distributive Justice*. Berlin, Heidelberg, New York: Springer-Verlag.

Kolm, S.-Ch. (1971). *Justice et équité*. CEPREMAP. Paris.

Konow, J. (2001). 'Fair and Square: The Four Sides of Distributive Justice'. *Journal of Economic Behavior & Organization*, 46: 137–164.

—— (2003). 'Which Is the Fairest One of All? A Positive Analysis of Justice Theories'. *Journal of Economic Literature*, 41: 1188–1239.

Kreps, D. M. (1979). 'A Representation Theorem for Preference for Flexibility'. *Econometrica*, 47: 565–577.

Lagerspetz, E. (1986). 'Pufendorf on Collective Decisions'. *Public Choice*, 49: 179–182.

Lancaster, K. J. (1966). 'A New Approach to Consumer Theory'. *Journal of Political Economy*, 74: 132–157.

Leininger, W. (1993). 'The Fatal Vote: Berlin versus Bonn'. *Finanzarchiv N.F.*, 50: 1–20.

Luce, R. D. and Raiffa, H. (1957). *Games and Decisions*. New York: John Wiley.

McLean, I. and London, J. (1990). 'The Borda and Condorcet Principles: Three Medieval Applications'. *Social Choice and Welfare*, 7: 99–108.

Mas-Colell, A. and Sonnenschein, H. (1972). 'General Possibility Theorems for Group Decisions'. *Review of Economic Studies*, 39: 185–192.

Maskin, E. (1995). 'Majority Rule, Social Welfare Functions, and Game Forms'. In K. Basu, P. K. Pattanaik, and K. Suzumura (eds.), *Choice, Welfare and Development. Festschrift for Amartya Sen*. Oxford: Clarendon Press.

May, K. O. (1952). 'A Set of Independent Necessary and Sufficient Conditions for Simple Majority Decision'. *Econometrica*, 20: 680–684.

Michaud, P. (1985). *Hommage Condorcet (version intégrale pour le bicentenaire de l'essai de Condorcet)*. Centre Scientifique IBM France, Report No. F-094.

Mishan, E. J. (1960). 'A Survey of Welfare Economics, 1939–1959'. *The Economic Journal*, 70: 197–265.

Mongin, Ph. (2001). 'The Impartial Observer Theorem of Social Ethics'. *Economics and Philosophy*, 17: 147–179.

Moulin, H. (1980). 'On Strategy-Proofness and Single-Peakedness'. *Public Choice*, 35: 437–455.

—— (1988). *Axioms of Cooperative Decision Making*. Cambridge: Cambridge University Press.

Muller, E. and Satterthwaite, M. A. (1977). 'The Equivalence of Strong Positive Association and Strategy-Proofness'. *Journal of Economic Theory*, 14: 412–418.

Nash, J. F. (1950). 'The Bargaining Problem'. *Econometrica*, 18: 155–162.

—— (1953). 'Two-Person Cooperative Games'. *Econometrica*, 21: 128–140.

Ng, Y.-K. (1979). *Welfare Economics. Introduction and Development of Basic Concepts*. London and Basingstoke: Macmillan.

Nitzan, S. (1981). 'Some Measures of Closeness to Unanimity and Their Implications'. *Theory and Decision*, 13: 129–138.

Nozick, R. (1974). *Anarchy, State and Utopia*. New York: Basic Books.

Nurmi, H. (2002). *Voting Procedures under Uncertainty*. Berlin, Heidelberg, New York: Springer-Verlag.

Pattanaik, P. K. (1976). 'Collective Rationality and Strategy-Proofness of Group Decision Rules'. *Theory and Decision*, 7: 191–203.

—— (1978). *Strategy and Group Choice*. Amsterdam: North-Holland Publishing Company.

Pattanaik, P. K. and Xu, Y. (1990). 'On Ranking Opportunity Sets in Terms of Freedom of Choice'. *Recherches Economiques de Louvain*, 56: 383–390.

—— and —— (1998). 'On Preference and Freedom'. *Theory and Decision*, 44: 173–198.

Peleg, B. (1998). 'Effectivity Functions, Game Forms, Games, and Rights'. *Social Choice and Welfare*, 15: 67–80.

Puppe, C. (1996). 'An Axiomatic Approach to "Preference for Freedom of Choice"'. *Journal of Economic Theory*, 68: 174–199.

Ratliff, T. C. (2001). 'A Comparison of Dodgson's Method and Kemeny's Rule'. *Social Choice and Welfare*, 18: 79–89.

Rawls, J. (1971). *A Theory of Justice*. Cambridge, Mass.: Harvard University Press.

Reny, Ph. J. (2001). 'Arrow's Theorem and the Gibbard–Satterthwaite Theorem: A Unified Approach'. *Economics Letters*, 70: 99–105.

Roberts, K. W. S. (1977). 'Voting over Income Tax Schedules'. *Journal of Public Economics*, 8: 329–340.

Roemer, J. E. (1996). *Theories of Distributive Justice*. Cambridge, Mass.: Harvard University Press.

Roth, A. E. (1979). 'An Impossibility Result Concerning *n*-Person Bargaining Games'. *International Journal of Game Theory*, 8: 129–132.

Rubinstein, A., Safra, Z., and Thomson, W. (1992). 'On the Interpretation of the Nash Bargaining Solution and Its Extension to Non-Expected Utility Preferences'. *Econometrica*, 60: 1171–1186.

Saari, D. G. (1995). *Basic Geometry of Voting*. Berlin, Heidelberg, New York: Springer-Verlag.

—— (1997). 'Informational Geometry of Social Choice'. *Social Choice and Welfare*, 14: 211–232.

Saari, D. G. and Merlin, V. R. (2000). 'A Geometric Examination of Kemeny's Rule'. *Social Choice and Welfare*, 17: 403–438.

Samuelson, P. A. (1947). *Foundations of Economic Analysis*. Cambridge, Mass.: Harvard University Press.

—— (1967). 'Arrow's Mathematical Politics'. In S. Hook (ed.), *Human Values and Economic Policy*, 41–51. New York: New York University Press.

Saporiti, A. and Tohmé, F. (2004). 'Strategy-Proofness and Single-Crossing'. *Discussion Paper*, Queen Mary College, London, Department of Economics.

Saposnik, R. (1975). 'On Transitivity of the Social Preference Relation under Simple Majority Rule'. *Journal of Economic Theory*, 10: 1–7.

Satterthwaite, M. A. (1975). 'Strategy-Proofness and Arrow's Conditions: Existence and Correspondence Theorems for Voting Procedures and Social Welfare Functions'. *Journal of Economic Theory*, 10: 187–217.

Schokkaert, E. (1999). 'Tout-le-monde est "post-welfariste". Opinions sur la justice redistributive'. *Revue économique*, 50: 811–831. Available in English as: 'Mr. Fairmind Is Post-Welfarist. Opinions on Distributive Justice'. *Discussion Paper DPS 98.09*. Catholic University of Leuven, Department of Economics.

Scitovsky, T. (1942). 'A Reconsideration of the Theory of Tariffs'. *Review of Economic Studies*, 9: 89–110.

Sen, A. K. (1966). 'A Possibility Theorem on Majority Decisions'. *Econometrica*, 34: 491–499.

—— (1969). 'Quasi-Transitivity, Rational Choice and Collective Decisions'. *Review of Economic Studies*, 36: 381–394.

—— (1970a). 'The Impossibility of a Paretian Liberal'. *The Journal of Political Economy*, 78: 152–157.

—— (1970b). *Collective Choice and Social Welfare*. San Francisco, Cambridge: Holden-Day.

—— (1973). *On Economic Inequality*. Oxford: Clarendon Press.

—— (1977a). 'Social Choice Theory: A Re-Examination'. *Econometrica*, 45: 53–89.

—— (1977b). 'On Weights and Measures: Informational Constraints in Social Welfare Analysis'. *Econometrica*, 45: 1539–1572.

—— (1985). *Commodities and Capabilities*. Amsterdam: North-Holland.

—— (1986). 'Social Choice Theory'. In K. J. Arrow and M. D. Intriligator (eds.), *Handbook of Mathematical Economics*, Vol. III. Amsterdam: North-Holland.

—— (1987). 'Social Choice'. In J. Eatwell, M. Milgate, and P. Newman (eds.), *The New Palgrave*. London and Basingstoke: Macmillan.

—— (1988). 'Freedom of Choice. Concept and Content'. *European Economic Review*, 32: 269–294.

—— (1993). 'Markets and Freedoms: Achievements and Limitations of the Market Mechanism in Promoting Individual Freedoms'. *Oxford Economic Papers*, 45: 519–541.

—— (1995). 'Rationality and Social Choice'. *American Economic Review*, 85: 1–24.

—— and Pattanaik, P. K. (1969). 'Necessary and Sufficient Conditions for Rational Choice under Majority Decision'. *Journal of Economic Theory*, 1: 178–202.

Sengupta, M. and Dutta, B. (1979). 'A Condition for Nash-Stability under Binary and Democratic Group Decision Functions'. *Theory and Decision*, 10: 293–309.

Sprumont, Y. (1991). 'The Division Problem with Single-Peaked Preferences: A Characterization of the Uniform Allocation Rule'. *Econometrica*, 59: 509–519.

Strasnick, S. (1976). 'Social Choice Theory and the Derivation of Rawls' Difference Principle'. *Journal of Philosophy*, 73: 85–99.

Suzumura, K. (1999). 'Paretian Welfare Judgements and Bergsonian Social Choice'. *Economic Journal*, 109: 204–220.

Thomson, W. (1994a). 'Resource-Monotonic Solutions to the Problem of Fair Division When Preferences Are Single-Peaked'. *Social Choice and Welfare*, 11: 205–223.

—— (1994b). 'Consistent Solutions to the Problem of Fair Division When Preferences Are Single-Peaked'. *Journal of Economic Theory*, 63: 219–245.

—— (1994c). 'Cooperative Models of Bargaining'. In R. J. Aumann and S. Hart (eds.), *Handbook of Game Theory*, Vol. 2. Amsterdam: North-Holland.

—— and Lensberg, T. (1989). *Axiomatic Theory of Bargaining with a Variable Number of Agents*. Cambridge: Cambridge University Press.

von Neumann, J. and Morgenstern, O. (1944). *Theory of Games and Economic Behavior*. Princeton: Princeton University Press.

von Pufendorf, S. (1672). *De jure naturae et gentium, libri octo*. Translated into English (using the edition of 1688) by C. H. and W. A. Oldfather, 2 vols. (1934). Oxford: Clarendon Press.

Weymark, J. (1991). 'A Reconsideration of the Harsanyi–Sen Debate on Utilitarianism'. In J. Elster and J. E. Roemer (eds), *Interpersonal Comparisons of Well-Being*, 255–320. Cambridge: Cambridge University Press.

Yaari, M. E. and Bar-Hillel, M. (1984). 'On Dividing Justly'. *Social Choice and Welfare*, 1: 1–24.

Young, H. P. (1974). 'An Axiomatization of Borda's Rule'. *Journal of Economic Theory*, 9: 43–52.

—— (1975). 'Social Choice Scoring Functions'. *SIAM Journal of Applied Mathematics*, 28: 824–838.

—— (1988). 'Condorcet's Theory of Voting'. *American Political Science Review*, 82: 1231–1244.

Zeckhauser, R. (1973). 'Voting Systems, Honest Preferences and Pareto Optimality'. *The American Political Science Review*, 67: 934–946.

Zeuthen, F. (1930). *Problems of Monopoly and Economic Warfare*. London: Routledge & Kegan Paul.

# ☐ AUTHOR INDEX

# ☐ SUBJECT INDEX